T0019340

Sister Ignatia

"Not to know Sister Ignatia is not to fully understand Dr. Bob and Bill W. She was their early and persevering catalyst."

—Father John Baptist D. McCarthy, S.T.

"The life of Sister Ignatia is extremely relevant to today's alcohol and drug issues. Her emphasis on faith *in the ability of the person to recover, the* hope *she instilled in the individual that recovery was possible, and her* love *for the human being afflicted with alcoholism is timeless—especially when we see the re-stigmatization of the alcoholic and the covert denial of the right to effective treatment taking place in our field today."*

—Professor Glenn H. Snyder, M.Ed.
Addiction Studies, University of Akron
Akron, Ohio

Sister Ignatia

Angel of Alcoholics Anonymous

Second Edition

Mary C. Darrah

Hazelden Publishing

Hazelden Publishing
Center City, Minnesota 55012-0176
hazelden.org/bookstore

©1992, 2001 by Mary C. Darrah
All rights reserved
Originally published by Loyola University Press 1991
Second edition published by Hazelden 2001
Printed in the United States of America
No portion of this publication may be reproduced in any manner
without the written permission of the publisher

Library of Congress Cataloging-in-Publication Data

Darrah, Mary C.
    Sister Ignatia : angel of Alcoholics Anonymous / Mary C. Darrah—2nd ed.
        p.   cm.
    Includes bibliographical references and index.
    ISBN 978-1-56838-746-8 (paperback)
    1. Gavin, Mary Ignatia. 2. Alcoholics Anonymous—Biography. 3. Volunteer
workers in rehabilitation—United States—Biography. 4. Alcoholics—
Rehabilitation. I. Title.

HV5293.G35 D37 2001
362.29'286'092—dc21
[B]

                                                              2001039194

Editor's note
The Twelve Steps and Twelve Traditions are reprinted with permission of Alcoholics Anonymous World Services, Inc. (AAWS). Permission to reprint the Twelve Steps and Twelve Traditions does not mean that AAWS has reviewed or approved the contents of this publication, or that AAWS necessarily agrees with the views expressed herein. AA is a program of recovery from alcoholism *only*—use of the Twelve Steps and Twelve Traditions in connection with programs and activities which are patterned after AA, but which address other problems, does not imply otherwise.

Cover design by David Spohn
Interior design by Rachel Holscher
Typesetting by Stanton Publication Services, Inc.

To my mother,
Eleanore Van de Motter Darrah,

first to sing me a lullaby of angels,
first to bathe me in Ignatia's light

M.C.D.
September 14, 1991

Contents

Foreword to the Second Edition

To overlook the life and good works of Sister Mary Ignatia, born Della Mary Gavin, would be to miss one of the most important stories in alcoholism treatment and Alcoholics Anonymous (AA) history. The significant contributions of Sister Ignatia, with the help and guidance of AA cofounder Dr. Robert Holbrook Smith, are interwoven with the growth of hospital care for the alcoholic and the acceptance and growth of AA. The foundation for these facts could only have happened in one place: Akron, Ohio, the birthplace of AA.

By learning of Sister Ignatia's work at St. Thomas Hospital in Akron, we follow the story of alcoholics treated with respect and dignity. In 1947, AA cofounder Bill Wilson wrote an article entitled "Adequate Hospitalization . . . Our Great Need" in *The AA Grapevine* magazine. He began the article: "Despite the general effectiveness of the AA program we often need the help of friendly agencies outside AA. Nowhere is this more strikingly true than in the field of hospitalization." The work of Sister Ignatia and Dr. Bob makes Bill Wilson's statement as important today as in 1947.

The clients who come to Hazelden in Center City, Minnesota, for treatment are first admitted to Ignatia Hall. In this facility, all clients are evaluated for detoxification procedures to prevent withdrawal complications. Once medically cleared in Ignatia, the clients are sent to one of the treatment units where they begin a recovery program. Tens of thousands of individuals have begun their recovery journey in Ignatia Hall. This Hazelden connection is another of the many legacies of Sister Ignatia.

This biography was the first and most thoroughly documented account of Sister Ignatia and Akron AA history. We are proud to bring this book to its second edition. Mary Darrah's continuing dedication in telling the story of Sister Ignatia and the significance of Akron is commendable. She was the first to bring a woman's perspective to AA history. That alone deserves tremendous thanks and gratitude from us all.

BILL PITTMAN
Director of Historical Information
Hazelden Publishing and Educational Services

Foreword to the First Edition

In my long life, spent largely in the company of Alcoholics Anonymous's friends, a most fortunate encounter was an unexpected meeting in 1985 with a Clevelander named Mary Darrah. She introduced herself, by telephone, as a former alcoholism counselor who was engaged in writing the biography of Sister Mary Ignatia Gavin, C.S.A., who was known to me and to many thousands of other recovering people as "the Angel of Alcoholics Anonymous." Mary hoped to visit me in Boston with a view to learning more about the early days of AA in Ohio, where I had visited Sister Ignatia and Dr. Bob Smith shortly before his death in 1950. At the time, I was a practicing moral theologian and, as a sideline, an instructor at the Yale School of Alcohol Studies. My other acquaintances included AA's cofounder Bill Wilson; Mrs. Marty Mann, founder of the National Council on Alcoholism (NCA); Dr. E. M. Jellinek, scholar of alcoholism's disease concept; and many others of modern alcoholism's pioneers. I initially discouraged Mary's plan to interview me in Boston, but something powerful intervened. I startled even myself when, over the telephone, I told Mary of my own alcoholism and recovery from it some forty years earlier under the care of Dr. William Silkworth at New York's Towns Hospital. The miracle of AA made this conversation possible. The strong spiritual link that exists between witnessing members was brought to bear once more through the honest sharing of two strangers' personal experiences, through the story of Sister Ignatia, and through the early history of Alcoholics Anonymous.

The spiritual nature of Sister Ignatia's work is recalled in this book. Alcoholics Anonymous has Twelve Steps that make up a program of moral and spiritual regeneration. They mention drinking once. These Steps are essentially spiritual exercises, and somehow or other, they work in rehabilitating alcoholics. If a program of moral and spiritual regeneration is the thing that helps alcoholics most and arrests their sickness, then that sickness must be at least partly of a moral and spiritual nature. If it is a spiritual medicine that works a cure, it looks as though this sickness is at least partly a spiritual sickness. With the author, I recalled the early 1950s, when I taught at the Yale School of Alcohol Studies, edited *Twelve Steps and Twelve Traditions* and *A.A. Comes of Age* for Bill Wilson, and met Sister Ignatia and Dr. Bob Smith. Today I see that Sister Ignatia's great spirit silently unified all of our pioneering efforts. Soon, like Ignatia, I too encouraged the Catholic Hospital Association to treat alcoholism and face the greatest spiritual and social dilemma of our times. As a moral theologian, I often wondered: Is alcoholism a sickness? a mental or emotional problem? a moral problem? I think the answer is: It is all three. That is why Sister Ignatia's biography is a crucial instruction to our modern, more sophisticated treatment of alcoholism and other drug dependencies.

The basic ingredient of quality sobriety is one of spiritual surrender to this spiritual illness and recovery through the spiritual values so exemplified in Sister Ignatia's life. To recall her life is to recall her work, and her work was the spiritual conquest of addiction. Since the spiritual quality of her mission transcends time, her message is now preserved for all future generations of recovering people.

JOHN CUTHBERT FORD, S.J.
Campion Center
Weston, Massachusetts
July 31, 1988
Feast of St. Ignatius of Loyola

John Ford died in January 1989. He will long be remembered and honored for his great contributions to the field of alcoholism and to Alcoholics Anonymous.

Preface to the Second Edition

Yesterday, Today, and Tomorrow

Why would anyone take the time to update a book that has already received ten years of her undivided attention? That is a question I am often asked. To me, the answer is simple: There remains much to know, learn, and share about alcoholism's history.

Sister Ignatia has acted as a mentor to me in my search for knowledge and in my struggle to lead a good life. She is like a burr underneath my skin, always pushing and prodding me to say more, sometimes seeming to irritate me or rub me the wrong way. Other times I think I hear her frequently spoken words "Time is running out and I must work while I can."

As she was in the beginning of AA, Ignatia remains today. AA's angel is a tough reminder of who we can be and what we can do if we apply ourselves to the problems we see at hand.

Ignatia warned us in 1954 that the twentieth century would one day be known as the age of sedation. In 2001 her words have made her a prophet.

It is left to each of us who care about victims of alcoholism and drug addiction to follow her timeless example and find our answers in the pages of her game book.

AA's angel will always guide us.

Preface to the First Edition*

The Messenger and the Message

My primary motive for writing Sister Ignatia's biography is simple. I view this work as a tribute to the angel whose message saved my life.

When I was a small child, Sister Ignatia used to visit my home. I was five years old when she came to Cleveland and opened Rosary Hall at St. Vincent Charity Hospital and Health Center. My father, Donald C. Darrah, was a physician, surgeon, and vice president of the medical staff. My mother, Eleanore, had graduated from its nursing school. My parents' marriage grew out of their professional work at Charity. Often, my sisters, Ann and Jane, and I made Sunday morning hospital rounds with our father and visited our mother's aunt, Sister Germaine Dworning, C.S.A., who lived at Charity Hospital.

I grew up hearing about the miracles of Sister Ignatia's work with alcoholics. I watched her carefully when she came to our home, because my mother often told me that Sister Ignatia was a living saint—a curious, mesmerizing idea to a five-year-old! I remember her as a kind lady who often winked and smiled at me. When my father suddenly died ten years later, her abundant compassion at his wake collided with my frozen grief. I could not look at her then, because she saw too easily the sorrow that I could not bear.

Many years later, I found myself a patient in an alcoholism treatment center far away from home. It was the Christmas season. I was overwhelmed with loneliness, fear, and shame. If ever I had needed an angel, it was then. At that time, I had been a sober member of an

---

* Formerly the epilogue.

anonymous organization for seven years and was a professional working in the field of alcoholism treatment when I relapsed. I was certain I would never get well again. In fact, I despaired of sobriety.

A few days after arriving for treatment, I prayed with the greatest anguish I had ever known, "God, if I could only see someone from home; I feel so alone."

Later that morning, a stranger introduced himself to me at a self-help group. When he learned I was from Ohio, he said, "Let me give you a small gift from our group. It's a new book about people from your area. Maybe if you read about folks from home, you won't feel so alone here."

He handed me a book called *Dr. Bob and the Good Oldtimers.* It smelled new and it was stiff. I cracked the binding and the book fell open.

There she was—smiling at me with outstretched arms—welcoming me, beckoning me, offering me her heart—AA's angel, Sister Ignatia, rescuer of alcoholics. Just the sight of her picture took me back to the warmth and safety of childhood, to fond memories of my home and family, to my loved ones, to Christmases past when Sister Ignatia came to my home for lunch. Something broke inside me. I was never the same again.

When I met Ignatia's eyes on the glossy pages of an AA history book, an immediate and powerful spirit consumed me. My life became very clear. I knew for the first time that there was a God who loved me, and I was *not* alone. I could hear Sister Ignatia's soft voice telling me to trust God, surrender, and do whatever they told me to do. I knew I would be all right, and I knew that I had been healed.

I cried, unashamed, for the first time in many years. The pain I had held inside all the while left. Faith and Hope reached out to me. Gratitude overwhelmed me. A deep, unexplainable Love embraced me; an unfamiliar spiritual peace filled me.

I knew then that Sister Ignatia's power was real and still very much within the reach of those of us who need miracles. I sensed that she still wanted to help the addicted people of this world, that she wanted to come back to us. I felt so certain of my recovery that I vowed to tell her story and bring her magic to any and all who would listen. That is what first prompted me to write this book.

As I gathered up the fragments of her life, I found a woman whose immense spirit, talent, and enormous contributions to Alcoholics Anonymous and the twentieth-century recovery movement had been almost entirely obliterated in the chronicles of our century. I could not let a woman of her greatness, world stature, love, and example be forgotten, particularly as she related to Alcoholics Anonymous's history. She was the person who breathed life into the hearts of AA's two cofounders, William G. Wilson and Dr. Robert H. Smith, just as she has done to me.

I learned that Sister Ignatia was the only person in AA's long and colorful history to be the lifelong friend and spiritual advisor to *both* male cofounders. This fact—or coincidence—made her indispensable to the great success and spiritual formation of the Alcoholics Anonymous program. God's greatest messages to humankind are always carried by angels. Alcoholics Anonymous is no exception. Once Bill and Bob surrendered their addiction to their Higher Power, AA's angel was fast upon the scene.

Ignatia had thus emerged at the exact moment in AA's history (1939) when Smith and Wilson realized that AA could not grow without sympathetic hospitals where they could treat their new members. Wilson wrote, "Meanwhile we found we needed services we could not perform ourselves. Chief among these was hospitalization. Doctoring and physically caring for the very sick was not and could not be AA's business."[1]

Providing reliable hospital services was the part of AA's growth problem that Sister Ignatia solved. However, the deep compassion that she had for the alcoholic was an unforeseen bonus. The huge growth of AA's numbers began when Sister Ignatia gave AA its first hospital. Her 1939 program and vision were then repeated in the early 1940s at Cleveland's St. Vincent Charity Hospital by Sister Victorine Keller, C.S.A., and then in New York by Dr. William D. Silkworth and a nurse named Teddy.

Since that time, hospital treatment for addiction, as pioneered by Sister Ignatia and combined with the Alcoholics Anonymous program, has been the benchmark for successful recovery from addictive diseases. More than fifty years later, the microcosm of Ignatia's work is found in all credible treatment programs around the world.

Now it is time to retap the heart of AA's own history by recognizing the woman—the angel—in Ohio who was most responsible for AA's hospitals and thus its vast growth. In addition, however, her own religious bearing personified AA's struggling spirit to "trust God, clean house, and help others."

Today we realize that it is no sentimental coincidence that Sister Ignatia became "the Angel of Alcoholics Anonymous." As West Virginian Charlie B. articulately stated, "Her title reflects two spiritual words: angel and AA—the messenger and the message. And her life gave the spiritual message of AA its wings."

Recovering alcoholics, who represent most of the world's religions, acclaimed this Catholic churchwoman to be their angel of deliverance from the powerful army of addiction's powerless souls. Her weapon was compassion, her strategy love. These transcended false religiosity and the moral judgment that drove searching souls from God to the bottle. The mosaic of faiths comprising Alcoholics Anonymous's nonsectarian membership responded not to her old-fashioned religious garb or her prominence in the world community but to the message she gave them. As the "God is dead" chant riddled the 1960s culture, those who knew Ignatia found that God in the form of a universal spirituality and enduring love—the God of Recovery had emerged.

When I began writing this book in the early 1980s, alcoholism treatment in the United States had reached its high point. New treatment centers opened every day. "Why look back?" one treatment provider asked me. "The field of alcoholism has progressed way beyond Ignatia and the old-timers."

Soon, however, the tide changed as insurance carriers and managed care providers stopped paying for treatment. A health care crisis existed. Those who had questioned the need for this book now asked impatiently, "When will Sister Ignatia's story be published? The field needs her help."

Try as I would, I could not finish this book quickly. I became resigned to the fact that one day I would finish it, and that it would happen in God's time, not my own—another lesson I have learned from Sister Ignatia.

Now I understand why this work took nine years. Messages are not heard until they are needed. And today the professional field of addiction needs Sister Ignatia's spirit, values, direction, and philosophy as desperately as AA's cofounders needed her hospital beds.

At this point in the short history of alcoholism treatment and recovery, many of the same problems that the AA pioneers met and answered have subtly resurfaced. Alcohol's stigma, its moral condemnation, and society's denial that alcoholism is indeed a disease (the number-one health problem in the world) have all resurfaced. Misinformation and denial regarding the illness and the recovery abound once more.

As the twenty-first century dawns, the age of sedation identified by Sister Ignatia in 1954 takes on new meaning, because it threatens to stunt the growth of modern civilization. Alcoholism is not laughable. It is deadly. And it is epidemic.

As AA's angel warned, the twentieth century has indeed achieved identity as the age of sedation. Alcoholism and other drug addictions have waged a holocaust of unimaginable proportions on all of humanity, their spiritual plague subtly destroying families, nations, values, religions, and youth.

Today's war on drugs does not even address the deadly alcoholism that underlies most other drug addictions. Most of the government funding available for this problem goes not to the treatment of the disease—which *can* be arrested—but to the costs of incarcerating addiction's victims.

Alcoholism underlies most chronic health problems; untreated, it inflates all health care costs. It costs the U.S. economy $30 billion per year in lost productivity. It imprisons the poor and the homeless in helplessness, crowds our jails, imperils our highways, leaves lifetime scars on fetal alcohol syndrome (FAS) babies, impairs church and government leaders, and increases the incidence of all violent crimes of passion.

That is why alcoholism today needs its angel. Sister Ignatia, the

Angel of Alcoholics Anonymous, began a whole new chapter in medical and spiritual rehabilitation. Her message in 1939 brought alcoholics to treatment, but today we are challenged to bring her treatment to alcoholics.

With a present global epidemic of addiction, there is greater need of an angel's message than ever before. As AA's angel, as the pioneer of alcoholism treatment, as the archetype of all alcoholism professionals, this contemporary saint's life and work offer enduring, universal guidelines for all people who are in some way affiliated with or affected by the care and treatment of addictive diseases. Thus Sister Ignatia remains a vessel of outreach to a troubled world. As a woman of love and action, she would want to be part of the solution.

Acknowledgments

I wish to thank the many people who patiently assisted me throughout the research, writing, and editing of this work. These include family members, friends, co-workers, AA and Al-Anon members, groups, organizations, foundations, and even strangers. They are too numerous to recount but too special ever to forget.

Most of all, I thank the dear people in my life who let go of me so that I could write but who never abandoned me so that I could not. I was never alone during this work because the prayers, notes, and good wishes of many people sustained me.

Perhaps chief among those are the faithful trustees of the Sister Mary Ignatia Gavin Foundation, whose mission it was to commence this work. These were a loyal group of men and women who provided much of their time, financial resources, and moral support for the research and preparation of the initial manuscript. On this same note, special thanks must go to Coleman A. Foster; his mother, Lyla (Mrs. Clyde T.) Foster; and the Clyde T. and Lyla C. Foster Foundation. They were the first to agree with the need for Sister Ignatia's biography.

Other trustees of the Sister Mary Ignatia Gavin Foundation were Martha (Mrs. Richard) Baker; Henry Birkenhauer, S.J.; Sally (Mrs. Robert F.) Black; Edward B. Brandon; Frank H. Bretz; Jack Burry; Robert B. Cummings; John J. Dunlavey; Joan Gallagher, C.S.A.; Franklin Milgrim; Charles L. Nagle; Ellen (Mrs. Kevin) O'Donnell; the Hon. Francine Panehal; James V. Patton; the Most Rev. Anthony M. Pilla; David A. Simpson; Robert R. Smith; Bridget (Mrs. Joseph A.) Thiel; Susie Timken; Ned (Edward P.) Whelan; and the Rev. Msgr. Robert C. Wolff.

In addition, John F. Finnegan assisted me with much of the early research and supported me with his courage and enthusiasm.

The Sisters of Charity of Saint Augustine, especially Sister Joan Gallagher, major superior, and Sister Cheryl Keehner, archivist, provided needed assistance, documentation, and insight for this work. Many of the other sisters participated in individual and group interviews and were invaluable sources of information and kind support. Among them were the late Sisters Victorine Keller and Beatrice Brennan, Sisters Ruth Kerrigan, Adele Hart, Marie Estelle Kosick, M. George Paytas, David Hopkins, Mary John Halter, Coletta McNamee, Clement Beargie, Maura Hannan, and many others.

Cleveland Bishop Anthony M. Pilla provided assistance through the diocesan archives, especially through the help of diocesan archivist Chris Krosel.

The Rev. James Flood offered his special talents and skills in photography by assembling and providing many of the photographs for this work.

Alcoholics Anonymous World Services, Inc., permitted my access to their archives in New York, and many people there answered endless questions. Special thanks go to Frank Mauser, archivist, and Nell Wing, his predecessor.

Many special friends were also there when I needed readers and moral support. They are Sonya Obert; Helen (Mrs. Carl F.) Mayer; John and Ruth Kuhn; Ernie Kurtz; Mary Beirne Bole; James Egan, S.J.; Brother Terry, S.J.; Alfred T. Hennelly, S.J.; Father Sam Ciccolini; Kathleen Whelan Fitzgerald; Barbara Summers Brant; Sister Ruth Kerrigan, C.S.A.; Mary Ellen Stanton; (H. Margaret) Peggy Lawrence; and Father John McCarthy, S.T.

Regina Miller, Bob, and Rose edited, typed, advised, and encouraged me through the last difficult months of this book. Also publisher George Lane, S.J., and editors at Loyola Press (Chicago), who patiently sustained me until the last *t* was crossed and the last *i* was dotted. Their talent is so reflected in the final product.

My sisters and brother-in-law, Jane Darrah and Ann and Fred Ritty, agonized with me and kept me going when the going got tough.

And led by the God of Recovery, the anonymous members of Twelve Step groups everywhere prompted the inspiration and determination needed to raise Sister Ignatia to her rightful place in history.

As the second edition of this book goes to press, I must wholeheart-edly thank the thousands of people who read and corresponded with me over the ten-year life span of the first edition of *Sister Ignatia*. Your letters and reviews touched me deeply. My gratitude to my readers is inestimable.

Also I am indebted to George Lane, S.J., publisher at Loyola Press (Chicago), for giving this book its official birth. He and his staff worked arduously to bring *Sister Ignatia* to the public. The Rev. Msgr. Robert C. Wolff has been an early and unwavering supporter of Sister Ignatia's story.

In addition, I extend special thanks to Bill Pittman, Becky Post, Kate Kjorlien, and all the unseen employees of Hazelden for their hard work, enthusiasm, and talent in bringing forth a new edition of this book.

Thank you all for teaching me how to make a good book better.

Photo Acknowledgments

The photographs in the center section between chapters 4 and 5 are courtesy of the following:

Mary C. Darrah (photos 1, 15)

Sisters of Charity of Saint Augustine, Mount Augustine Archives (photos 2, 3, 4, 7, 8, 9, 10, 11, 17, 19, 20)

Sister Marie Estelle, C.S.A. (photo 5)

Mrs. Claire Stancik and Mrs. Carl F. Mayer (photo 6)

John Seiberling (photo 12)

Akron Beacon Journal (photo 13)

Rev. Peter Woll (photo 14)

Rev. James F. Flood. ©1991 (photos 16, 21, 22, 23)

Father John McCarthy, S.T. (photo 18)

One

Legend and Lore of Sister Ignatia

Birth named her Della Mary Gavin. Religious life renamed her Sister Mary Ignatia. History titled her "the Angel of Alcoholics Anonymous." Eternity may honor her as the saint for alcoholism and other addictions. There is no way of knowing what the late vicar for religious of the Cleveland Catholic Diocese sensed her lasting identity to be. But in a letter to the Sisters of Charity of Saint Augustine (C.S.A.), written one day after her funeral, it is clear that he meant Sister Ignatia to be remembered:

April 6, 1966

Mother M. Roberta, C.S.A.
Mount Augustine
5232 Broadview Road
West Richfield, Ohio

Dear Mother Roberta:
    The memory and work of Sister Ignatia will live for many years to come. To help preserve this for future generations, I would urge that you keep all papers, however unimportant, concerning Sister Ignatia's life. I know that someone will go through Sister's personal belongings, and I hope that it is a historian who can exercise good judgment in retaining things of value.
    It would also be in the best interests of your Community to have your historian begin collecting anecdotes of the life of Sister Ignatia. All of your Sisters should be asked to submit accounts of their experience with Sister Ignatia to enrich her memoirs.

A project could also be started with the surviving relatives of Sister Ignatia. They should be asked to record everything they can remember from the early life of Sister. The information that is gathered should be kept in a separate file. I know that this will make an interesting project for some historian. In fact, one of your own Sisters could make this her project for a dissertation.

The loss of Sister Ignatia has been keenly felt by the entire community, and I hope that we will do something to preserve her memory before it is too late.

With kind best wishes at this Holy Season, I am,

Sincerely yours in Christ,
Rt. Rev. Msgr. Francis A. Karwoski
Vicar for Religious[1]

Sister Ignatia's death captured Cleveland's attention in the early spring of 1966. During that memorable first weekend in April, downtown hotel rooms sold at a premium when movie celebrities and mournful travelers, most recovering from alcoholism, swarmed to northern Ohio to pay her their last respects. Ignatia had amassed so many friends during almost three decades of AA work that the Sisters of Charity graciously opened their motherhouse to the public. Some visitors estimated that the nuns poured more than six thousand cups of coffee for the dignitaries, strangers, family, and friends who visited the convent on the Sunday afternoon of Sister Ignatia's wake.

Mother Roberta and Bishop Clarence J. Issenman determined that the crowds were too enormous for the sisters at Mount Augustine to manage. If this many people attended her wake, how many could they expect at her funeral? Accordingly, they relocated the funeral site from the convent's rural chapel to Cleveland's urban cathedral twenty miles away.

The next morning, hundreds of people overflowed the church entrances, crowding the steps and streets outside. The famous grieved alongside the not-so-famous. Bing Crosby mingled with the congregation, undisturbed by his fans—a memorable testament to both the reverence of the moment and Ignatia's wide array of friends. Outside, mourners shared grateful tributes to Sister Ignatia, while television crews hurried to splice the scenes for the evening news.

Ed Fisher, a popular Cleveland radio personality, wrote and broadcast a poignant message for his listeners on April 4, the morning of the funeral:

> This morning a requiem Mass will be said in the Cathedral for one of God's most dedicated servants. Many will gather to pay last homage to Sister Ignatia. I'm sure they will come from all walks of life: truck drivers, clerks, businessmen, factory workers, secretaries, entertainment personalities, professional men. The one thing most have in common: they're alcoholics. They have come to say goodbye to a little slip of a nun to whom most of them owe a debt that can't be measured. For Sister Ignatia is known the world over as the nun of Rosary Hall, an alcoholic's first step back into society.
>
> Surely on this earth she was blessed. It's been estimated that she helped over ten thousand drunks first in Akron, then in Cleveland. Yet she was the most humble of persons. When asked for her autograph she would write, "Please pray for me. Sister Ignatia." It's long been a saying among Alcoholics Anonymous that if the Catholic Church doesn't canonize her, the Protestants will make her a saint.[2]

The Wider World

Anticipating that a future cry for Ignatia's canonization might require exhuming her remains, Mother Roberta chose a Calvary Cemetery gravesite for future accessibility should it need to be reopened. There, amidst murmurings of her sainthood, Sister Mary Ignatia Gavin was laid to rest.[3]

After the funeral, Bill Wilson, Alcoholics Anonymous's remaining cofounder, feared that oral tradition alone would distort Ignatia's future worth to the AA program. Borrowing heavily from the funeral eulogy written and delivered by Jesuit Father Thomas Coonan, Wilson published a biographical tribute to Ignatia in the August edition of AA's world publication, *The AA Grapevine*. Cleveland area writers followed suit and circulated their own articles to local AA groups.

In response to the vicar's letter, the Sisters of Charity collected vignettes, photos, newsprint, and historic memorabilia. They selected Father Coonan, friend and homilist at her funeral, to write Sister Ignatia's biography. However, some months later while working on the manuscript in New York City, Father Coonan relapsed into alcoholic drinking. Not long after, he was found dead in his parked car. With him were all the materials he had recently amassed on Sister Ignatia's life. In the wrenching days that followed, much of Sister Ignatia's collected history disappeared, never to be recovered. Coonan's brother later found fragments of a manuscript and its related notes among the Jesuit's possessions and returned them to the convent.

Meanwhile, condolences from around the world flooded the motherhouse. Tributes to Ignatia mounted. Those who were unaware of her impact on AA wondered why everyone loved this tiny, unremarkable nun so fiercely. But alcoholics from all over the world knew and responded, "She saved my life. I found God and sobriety through her. She loved me when there was nothing about me to love. She was AA's angel."

Indeed, to those who had suffered from the despair of alcoholism, Ignatia represented salvation from addiction's madness. She quite literally guided deadened, demoralized alcoholics back to the fullness of life. Ignatia administered lessons of elementary spiritual hygiene to crippled, helpless souls. First, she aroused an awareness of the God of their understanding. Then she taught them to care for one another. In the process of bonding to a Higher Power and in the act of reaching out to alcoholics still in pain, the miracles of recovery happened.

Astonishingly, the self-centeredness that mired alcoholics in their own pleasures and pain lifted. Denial, which protected the option to drink, again faded. Feelings of guilt and worthlessness diminished. Self-knowledge replaced self-loathing. Gratitude melted away resentment. Honesty opened the way to truth. By healing their relationships to God and others, alcoholics discovered that they inadvertently healed themselves too. All they had needed was one loving friend, Sister Ignatia, to teach them the simple way.

Ignatia did not extend her compassion only to alcoholics, however. In the interest of preserving the family unit, she counseled thousands of coalcoholic spouses and children. Employers who knew nothing of alcoholism, or recovery from it, learned the value of her assistance to their alcoholic employees. Catholic bishops recovered the services of alcoholic priests who, in sobriety, became some of the Church's most effective guides.

The alcoholic's world changed because the Sisters of Charity of Saint Augustine permitted Sister Ignatia's pioneering work with addiction to develop within their Akron and Cleveland hospitals. Largely because of the early vision of Sister Ignatia and her religious community of sisters, recovering alcoholics today can become useful members of society rather than useless statistics of morgues, prisons, and mental institutions.

Ignatia's treatment model offers important reminders for modern rehabilitation centers: Blend basic science with simple spirituality to effect lasting recovery. Do not overprofessionalize treatment with psychological method and interpretation, or the alcoholic will be distracted from the goal of sobriety. Thus, the essential ingredients contained in Ignatia's treatment strategy included

1. total abstinence from alcohol and other drugs
2. dependence on a Higher Power
3. commitment to the Alcoholics Anonymous program
4. frequent outreach to those still suffering

Ignatia's willingness to welcome alcoholics into medical treatment for their illness reminds health care workers today that recovery depends on more than merely addressing addiction's physical and emotional ills. Staff and sponsors need also extend acceptance, respect, and compassion to alcoholic patients. Administrators and trustees must not allow profit to be their predominant motive for opening treatment facilities. Thus, the rapid evolution of Ignatia's ministry to alcoholics once again showed the world that when unpopular problems plague humanity (such as alcoholism, violence, AIDS, and homelessness), caring people find solutions.

Not surprisingly, the key to understanding Sister Ignatia's life and her contribution to Alcoholics Anonymous lies not in rediscovering lengthy writings and transcripts of her speeches, which are few. Rather, it lies in the values she projected into her work and shared with AA's cofounders.

Thus, Ignatia is best remembered by the long record of lives she restored. Fifteen thousand alcoholics overcame their addiction under her direct care. An additional sixty thousand coalcoholic family members are estimated to have benefited from her healing. As these recovering people reached out and saved others, the numbers of lives affected by Sister Ignatia's work soon rose to millions. Not to be forgotten is the fact that these numbers reflect recoveries that occurred prior to the growth of the treatment industry, during the time when Ignatia's alcoholic wards were the *only* treatment wards.

1928: Akron Beginnings

Sister Ignatia's first record of achievement is found in Akron, Ohio, during the days of Prohibition and the Great Depression. The American economy had reached rock bottom and so had American drinking practices. Sister Ignatia's history and her second career began on September 28, 1928, when St. Thomas Hospital opened.[4]

Fragile in health and anxious about her recent transfer from Cleveland by the mother superior, Sister Ignatia emerged at this time as the registration clerk in the new hospital's comfortable admitting office. Assuredly, she felt far from comfortable herself when she turned on the light and entered her office for the first time. Then thirty-nine, she was recovering from a nervous breakdown that two years earlier had abruptly ended her twenty-year-long career in music.

Because she had never before worked in health care, Ignatia felt insecure in hospital work. What did a music teacher know about illness? Nonetheless, she exchanged her traditional gray gown and black veil for the white nursing habit of her community. At first glance, the change in dress color from dark to light exaggerated her frailty. But instantly, the stark white hospital clothing injected an unforgettable blue into Ignatia's Irish eyes. Framed by a starched, sweeping headdress, her compelling eyes acquired surprising depth and vigor. A knowing intensity of expression all at once overcame her otherwise fragile features.

Ignatia became discouraged when she reviewed her qualifications for hospital work. Only a brief period of occupational therapy she received earlier that year at St. John's Hospital in Cleveland served as both her introductory course and graduate training in health care. While recuperating there, at her physician's urging she audited some nursing courses and familiarized herself with medical terminology. With the working vocabulary this provided, she typed records for the outpatient clinic and filed claims for the hospital's industrial commission cases.[5]

Sister Mary John Halter, a co-worker, remembered Ignatia's anxiety over the radical change in her career:

> I think it was around 1928. The hospital was just opened. I was one of the first ones [nuns] there. Just out of the novitiate, I was the nurse anesthetist, and she was brand new. She'd just left music. Because of her nervous condition, they were advised not to put her back in music, but to let her take music just as she found it in people, ordinary people. She was a noted musician.
>
> In Akron, she was to be the admitting clerk. When we went down, she said, "Oh, Sister, will you please help me? I don't know anything about hospital work."[6]

Ignatia had good reason to be tense. In the late 1920s there were no written guidelines that taught prospective administrators about the complex changes that had turned simple patient-care methods into post-World War I organizational networks called "hospital administration." Music had not prepared Ignatia to nurture the delicate relationships required between administration and the medical staff. Or had it? Such a harmony had to be reached if hospitals hoped to maintain a steady occupancy rate, offset rising costs, and still generate enough income to cover the expense of charity work.[7]

During these days of administrative infancy, one of the most important staff members serving the hospital was the sister administrator in charge of admissions and bed assignments. Her special task was to convince physicians that St. Thomas was the best hospital in Akron. Her rapport with the doctors guaranteed a steady flow of paying patients to underwrite hospital costs.[8]

This was an important function because, in the first half of the twentieth century, very little medical insurance existed to pay for hospital care. Inevitably, hospitalization forced individuals to pay expenses out of their own pockets. In the former days, wealthier patients had frequently added a generous contribution to their payment, thus offsetting the cost of health care for the poor.[9] For this reason, the paying patient, the popular physician, and a friendly admitting registrar comprised a hospital's three most valued assets.[10]

As the registrar of St. Thomas Hospital, Ignatia presented a positive, outgoing image for the hospital. Her musical ways and Irish charm exuded friendliness and warmed the sterile, medicinal atmosphere. She welcomed doctors, visitors, and patients, then accommodated their various hospital needs. She became adept at human relations and soon attracted a following of favorite patients and physicians.

The Quiet Years

The years between 1928 and 1939 proved to be formative ones for Sister Ignatia. While making the change from musical artist to health care provider, she endured many moments of bewilderment and self-doubt. Nonetheless, Ignatia utilized her time of midlife transition to redirect her talents. Recovery slowly transformed creative energy, previously directed to music, into character strengths that permitted her to emerge from her time of darkness as a pioneer in alcoholism treatment. Learning patience, humor, and unremitting surrender to the will of God rejuvenated her energy and spirit. A confident, competent woman emerged, dominated only by a driving need to help others.

Well advanced on the road to recovery herself, she had a natural sympathy for Dr. Robert Smith's effort to reestablish his professional reputation after a bout with alcoholism had eliminated him from the physician service rosters of Akron's better hospitals. It was easy to recall her own experiences of struggling back from personal adversity, of earning back respectability.

Perhaps that is why Ignatia had only fond recollections of Dr. Bob. In all references, she reported him to be both a quality physician and person:

> Dr. Bob operated occasionally at St. Thomas after its opening, and was appointed to the staff in 1934. Dr. Bob was the essence of professional dignity. He had a fine sense of humor and an exceptional vocabulary. He rarely came into the hospital without visiting the Admitting Office.[11]

In truth, Sister Ignatia met Dr. Bob for the first time in 1928, shortly after St. Thomas Hospital opened. Sister Mary John observed that, from their first meeting, Sister Ignatia and Dr. Bob had an immediate mutual affinity. That very day Ignatia came to Sister Mary John and said, "There's a doctor, a lovely gentleman. He wants to see about getting on staff here."[12]

Their friendship evolved as Smith wound down his drinking years and Ignatia mastered her new career. Childhood experiences had sensitized her to alcoholism, and hospital work had confirmed the frequency of alcoholism as a presenting problem in emergency room patients. Much earlier, however, during Ignatia's impressionable girlhood in Ireland, her strict Catholic mother had taught her that drunkenness was a serious offense against the law of God. An account of Ignatia's early training shows that even as a child, she demonstrated a raw compassion for the problems of alcoholism, although the common judgment of moral failure tainted her perspective. Hardly evidenced now were the fragile personality and her rigid childhood beliefs about alcoholism. Years later she reflected:

> My beloved departed mother, God rest her dear soul, taught
> me as a child never to say that anyone was drunk, because
> drunkenness was such a grievous offense against the good
> God that no one should ever mention the word, much less ac-
> cuse anyone of being drunk. That impression was so deeply
> implanted in my mind that even to this day, I rarely use the
> word. Whenever I would see anyone under the influence of
> liquor, it actually made my heart sick. I would try to offer
> everlasting reparation to the Sacred Heart of Our Lord to
> make up for the offense against His Divine Majesty.[13]

From her earliest memories in Ireland to her assignment at
St. Thomas Hospital some thirty years later, Ignatia saw the misery of
alcoholism and resolved to remedy it. In essence, childhood sympathy had matured into midlife empathy and, finally, action.

Unwilling to accept the day's prevalent notion that nothing could
be done medically for alcoholics, in 1934 Ignatia befriended a young
emergency room intern named Thomas P. Scuderi. Before long, she
convinced the new doctor that alcoholics were sick, accident-prone
victims of the drink and persuaded him to let them "rest" in the hospital before he sent them, unaided, onto the streets. Late into the night,
Ignatia and Dr. Scuderi conspired together to hide dangerously ill alcoholics in a tiny anteroom directly across from the hospital chapel.
While Scuderi doctored them, Ignatia prayed.[14]

Their earliest efforts to treat alcoholics were primitive, at best.
Since there was no textbook treatment plan for alcoholics, Dr. Scuderi
controlled their unpredictable behavior by administering large doses
of morphine. As the drug took effect, Ignatia placed her calming
hands on the patients, offered them to God's care, and retired to the
chapel where she prayed until Dr. Scuderi sent word that they were
out of danger.[15]

Thereafter, Sister Ignatia's private crusade to care for alcoholics
acquired a strong medical ally, at least during the emergency room's
graveyard shift. These are the doctor's recollections of the beginning
years of their work with alcoholics, predating the founding of
Alcoholics Anonymous:

One of the first cases we admitted was hurried into a room across from the chapel. This fellow started to curse and the profanity was unbearable. Sister Ignatia came to me and said, "Doctor, it was a mistake putting him so close to the chapel. I don't know what to do." I administered four grains of morphine to him, and he went out like a light, and the profanity stopped. Then Sister Ignatia said to me, "I want him less sedated." She sat there with us and she was thinking hard. . . . She looked worried. So next, I gave him a shot to wake him up. She sat right along with us, praying. She was always praying and touching people. She held the man's hand and talked to him in a soothing sort of manner.

She was severely criticized by some of the nuns, and most of the doctors were bastards to her. She always had a lot of criticism from others, and it would hurt her terribly. I'd try to cheer her up. I'd say, "You're doing all right, Sister. You got two men better this week. There's no need of you crying." She was doing such a wonderful job, but she never thought she was doing enough. My brother was going through medical school at that time, and I didn't have the finances to help pay his tuition. It was during the Depression, and my dad was poor.

My brother was going to have to leave medical school. During one of our long vigils together, I shared my heartache with Sister Ignatia. Not long after, my brother wrote me a letter. He said, "Tom, my tuition was paid somehow. Where did *you* get the money? Did you steal it? How did you do it?" Later I learned through my pastor that Sister Ignatia got it taken care of by a friend. She never said a thing about it.

She was a great influence on my life as a physician. She taught me about loving people.[16]

Recollecting these times, Dr. Scuderi said he could not estimate how many alcoholics he and Ignatia treated between 1934 and 1939, before AA and hospital treatment officially began. What he remembered was his and Ignatia's discovery that alcoholism was not choosy in selecting its victims. More to the point, Scuderi quickly learned that skid row derelicts, the stereotypical caricatures of alcoholism, were by far the exception. More often, he and Sister Ignatia treated professional and working-class people who were unable to control the outcome of their drinking episodes.

Gradually, as their experience in treating alcoholism increased, Dr. Scuderi lightened the doses of morphine, and Sister increased her prayers. After the immediate crisis passed, Sister Ignatia then nursed the patient with large quantities of black coffee and fruit juices laced with vitamin B-enriched dark Karo syrup—then thought to quiet the nerves.[17] A lawyer whom they secretly treated in 1934 was Bill D., the man now known in AA history as "AA number three." Bill V., another of the original AA members from Akron, reviewed these early days, explaining how he met Sister Ignatia in 1936:

> We made a change of hospitals and went over to St. Thomas, starting from a four-bed room. We eventually would end up with our own ward. Sister Ignatia was a little angel who helped us in this angle of the work. I might say that I was familiar with Sister Ignatia and the second floor long before the opening of the alcoholic ward [1939]. This alcoholic ward at St. Thomas was opposite the chapel. During my later years when I was at my bottom, I was picked up along skid row in Akron; and, instead of being taken to jail, I was taken to the emergency room at St. Thomas because I recognized the "brass" riding in the cruiser. The officer told the driver to take us bums to the emergency at St. Thomas. We were laid on cots in the hallway, opposite the chapel and the present alcoholic ward. This was probably 1936. That night it took five shots to quiet me. My pal, and I don't know who he was, died before the night was over. After a couple of days there, I got acquainted with Sister Ignatia.[18]

The Admitting Office

Perhaps as part of a design of Providence, Sister Ignatia's opportunity to pioneer the first alcoholism ward utilizing the Alcoholics Anonymous philosophy arose from a convergence of people, circumstances, and events in Akron in 1939. Pragmatically, Ignatia's function as the admitting officer provided the key to her success in extending medical assistance to new Alcoholics Anonymous members.[19] Her professional duties within the admitting office offered the direct linkage needed to foster a working relationship between AA and the hospital. Thus, an inside view of the office and its resident administrator reveals how and why AA gained a foothold at St. Thomas Hospital but not at any others.

Admitting offices of the 1930s were small meccas of administrative power and control. Though census management defined the ostensible function of admissions, its central location in the hospital's main corridor invited requests for solutions to a variety of hospital problems. Ignatia's assignment to this particular area of the hospital automatically granted her a strong base of operation. Additionally, rumors had long confirmed that when faced with resistant problems, the tiny nun in admissions found magnanimous, although not always orthodox, solutions.

For example, besides providing a gathering place for physicians, chaplains, and restless visitors, Ignatia's workstation also sheltered her unauthorized but highly effective "gray market" adoption service.[20] Not surprisingly, her concern for the orphaned had been a deep personal commitment from her earliest days in the convent. Doctors, knowing this to be the case, sought her skills in the placement of unwanted infants and children.

Her resources for finding homes seemed almost unlimited, but it was really her hard work that brought the desired results. Ignatia spent many hours conversing with patients and visitors, supporting them through personal trials, and listening to their most intimate hopes and dreams. In this compassionate way, she acquired confidential information and, from this, an uncanny aptitude for making one person's problem another person's solution. Eventually, the hardship of an illegitimate child birthed at the hospital became a source of joy to a childless couple who had confided their anguish to Sister Ignatia.

Legal adoptions between consenting parties posed no difficulties, either. Ignatia knew many attorneys who gladly gave their time and professional services to her to ameliorate a troubled domestic situation. In the end, unwed mothers, adoptive parents, and pro bono attorneys gained self-worth for having helped Sister Ignatia solve a problem.

The more practical aspects of her job required ingenuity too. As part of her official duties, Ignatia made hospital rounds several times daily, counting and balancing filled and unfilled beds against a constantly changing roster of admissions, discharges, and transfers. Like most hospitals at this time, St. Thomas was overcrowded. Because Ignatia was the first to know the whereabouts of available beds, increasing demands for them added to her growing power.

Her method of operation was relatively simple. When patients were discharged, the floor supervisor reported bed vacancies to the admitting office, thereby keeping Ignatia advised of the hospital's available beds. She also maintained a tally of offices and hallways that could accommodate a bed or two when all the usual rooms were filled. Likewise, Ignatia had the authority to transfer patients from ward to ward in the interests of efficiently clearing and utilizing hospital space.

The only person who might have challenged her decisions was the nursing supervisor. Because of her nursing expertise, the supervisor was held responsible for assigning patients to areas of the hospital where their conditions could best be medically monitored. Aware of this arrangement, Ignatia made her own bed transfers between shift changes while the nursing supervisor was occupied in report and record keeping. In this way, Ignatia created and controlled bed space as she or her favorite doctors needed it. A former supervisor explained:

> Sister Ignatia had all the beds, and the one in the admitting office could give the beds to any doctor she liked. Basically and fundamentally, she controlled all the beds. It [admitting] was one of the key positions of power to have in the hospital, and she had it.[21]

To an experienced registered nurse, the situation sometimes seemed preposterous. The fact that Ignatia had no formal nursing education or medical training sometimes triggered strong reactions from the nursing department:

> And what was Ignatia? She was a *musician!* She wasn't even a nurse! And if you dogged with her . . . well, she had all the characteristics of an artist, plus she was Irish. She was "dumb like an Irishman"![22]

And so it happened that the very tactics that so frustrated the nursing supervisor also made it possible for Ignatia to reserve a few experimental beds for alcoholics. Thus, her administrative style elicited the tacit comment that "she was a shrewd operator."[23]

Census control was a key issue that Ignatia mastered when, much later, she acquired space in the hospital to use for the first alcoholic ward. Because alcoholics needed detoxification far more rapidly than they recovered, there were never enough beds to meet their demands. So, when the alcoholism ward was filled and she needed another AA bed, Ignatia's authority as admitting officer permitted her to transfer the detoxified patient to another floor, thus freeing up the needed AA bed. While such heroics thoroughly enamored her to the alcoholic population, championing their cause in this unorthodox way infuriated and insulted many of the other supervisors.

The First AA Admission: 1939

Indeed, her shrewdness met the challenge of the new procedure she initiated on August 16, 1939.* On that day Dr. Bob persuaded Ignatia to admit Walter B., a notorious alcoholic and a regular consumer of paregoric, an over-the-counter opiate then easily available to the general

---

*Two dates are consistently found in both AA's and Sister Ignatia's records regarding the exact date of the first official AA admission to St. Thomas Hospital. Both August 16 and August 18 are consistently interchanged and recorded in the archives of AA, Mount Augustine, and Rosary Hall. St. Thomas Hospital was unable to research or provide an answer to the discrepancy. The date of August 16, 1939, is most often referenced by Sister Ignatia and has thus been selected by the author as the most appropriate date to be documented in this book.

public. Without much discussion, Ignatia labeled his problem acute gastritis to gain him admission into the crowded hospital.

Skeptical about accepting the man largely because of a recent disastrous experience with an alcoholic, she responded more to Dr. Bob's personal anguish and frustration than to a momentary inspiration. Finally, the doctor's honest sharing of his own drinking problem and subsequent spiritual recovery aroused her admiration and her compassion.

She admired the kindly physician who had been as controlled by drinking as the man he was now trying to help. Dr. Bob's quiet dignity gave way to desperate pleading. He humbled himself and thus won his plea for one bed, and one chance, to hospitalize Walter. Many years later, Ignatia recalled her reaction on this memorable day:

> . . . a few of the Akron hospitals admitted these patients for a time under various diagnoses but soon gave up the venture in favor of what they considered more serious illness. Dr. Bob was told in no uncertain terms to seek refuge for his jittering patients elsewhere. I had never seen Doctor in a depressed mood before that memorable day. I thought he was ill, but I soon learned the cause of his discouragement.
>
> As he explained, these thoughts were running through my mind: during the eleven years prior to the inauguration of this program, 1928 to 1939, had we not admitted many alcoholics under varied circumstances? I recalled very distinctly coming to the Chapel for prayer shortly after five one morning, only to be met by the night supervisor who told me in unmistakable terms that the next time I admitted a D.T. to the hospital, I had better stay up all night and run around the corridors after him. It didn't end there, either! Therefore, Doctor's plea struck a resonant chord. Prompted by the grace of God, a tentative plan was formulated.[24]

Sister Ignatia knew through experience that Walter B. might well cause trouble. Familiar with the behavior of intoxicated patients, she surmised that a private room would best suit the new admission.

However, no private rooms were available that day. As Walter's physical distress visibly increased, Ignatia hurriedly said that this patient is suffering from acute gastritis. She recommended getting him to bed immediately. He was moved to a double room that was available.[25] Not long after settling the patient in a two-bed ward, Dr. Bob returned to the admitting office. Rather sheepishly he explained to Ignatia that some men would be coming to talk to Walter about his drinking. He asked her to move his patient to a private room.

However, the hospital was filled to capacity. No more rooms were available that day, private or otherwise. Exasperated and pressured to act, Ignatia quickly reviewed her options. In past emergencies, she had temporarily hospitalized patients in some out-of-the-way places like isolated hallways, the supervisor's office on the pediatrics division, and even the tiny room at the end of each hallway where the sisters watered the patients' flowers. Since the Flower Room was also used as a temporary holding area for corpses awaiting transfer to the morgue, Ignatia knew that she could fit a bed through the small doorway. Besides offering an unusual degree of privacy for Walter, use of the Flower Room answered some of Ignatia's problems on the memorable day.[26]

Remembering her clashes with the night supervisor over previous alcohol-related admissions, Ignatia wanted time privately to assess the condition of the patient, calm him down, and find another room that would be isolated but still suitable to the needs of Dr. Bob, the alcoholic visitors, and the secret patient. Her clever use of the Flower Room suited everyone's needs, even Walter's. In a stupor, he slumbered peacefully beneath the acrid odor of flower bouquets and stale alcohol. Like the honored corpse at an Irish wake, Walter lay unconscious in the pungent fragrance while respectable visitors streamed in and out.

Meanwhile, Ignatia awaited the usual reports of trouble that accompanied the admission of a patient with DTs (delirium tremens). None came. Dr. Bob and several other men who he claimed were alcoholics like Walter and himself visited the patient. Fascinated, she observed the dress and demeanor of these reformed visitors. All said they were alcoholics, and yet they claimed recovery from their addiction. Even more peculiar, each made it his own responsibility to visit and care for the intoxicated man. On questioning them, Ignatia observed that they were sober, they were God-fearing, and they reached out in a firm but loving way to share their freedom from alcohol's obsession with a sick, irascible stranger named Walter B.[27]

To believe that the events of August 16, 1939, occurred exactly as Sister Ignatia later reported them stretches the limits of the imagination. For one thing, she and Bob Smith had frequently discussed alcoholism from their first meeting in 1928, so it may not be true that the August 16 admission happened entirely by chance. For another, she had been personally working on the problem of alcoholism for five years. There was also much hospital gossip that circulated around both Ignatia and Dr. Bob. Thus, to suppose that their clandestine activities in favor of alcoholics had escaped each other's notice would seem quite unlikely.

Ignatia and Dr. Bob Share Problems

Ignatia and Smith shared much; both were mending broken lives, both knew the personal importance of recovery, and both had grasped the necessity of invoking a Higher Power to effect and maintain wellness. Humility kept them from committing their daily successes to journal keeping during Bob Smith's lifetime. Besides, Ignatia felt that record keeping was God's job.[28]

Unfortunately, Dr. Bob died in 1950, several years before Bill Wilson saw the value in preserving the history of AA's early years. Only one talk, delivered and recorded in Detroit (1948) gives Smith's account of the pioneering days in Akron. Years later, when Ignatia searched for it in AA's New York archives, she found that the recording was first mislabeled, then lost and recovered, next damaged, and finally destroyed.[29] After Wilson began collecting AA's history in 1954, Ignatia was the sole surviving hospital pioneer from the early Akron days. Only then, because of the need for securing Dr. Bob's proper place in AA's chronicles, did she consent to record her memories with Wilson.

Fortunately, Bill realized the importance of writing down historical material while it was fresh in the fellowship's memory. Witnesses were needed to record the pioneering of hospital treatment in the context of AA's larger development, so he called upon Ignatia to help AA set the hospital record straight.

Among other things, Ignatia checked the accuracy of the Flower Room story; she shared the legendary material in Dr. Bob's admission of his alcoholism to her and his plea for help. With laudable humility, she downplayed much of her own earlier role in caring for alcoholics as she finalized the story of AA's beginnings in Akron.

Nonetheless, this legendary story must be added for the sake of history. Having requested a bed for Walter B., Smith immediately revealed his association with a Manhattan stockbroker named Bill Wilson. The doctor explained to Ignatia that only four years earlier, in 1935, Wilson had volunteered his aid when the doctor was grappling with his own alcohol obsession. In sharing this experience, the two had stumbled upon the discovery that one sober man could relate his drinking miseries to a man still drinking, and both could gain victory over the uncontrollable compulsion. Reaching out to another human being's suffering strengthened Wilson's own resolve to stay sober. That first meeting between Smith and Wilson had occurred at the Akron residence of Henrietta Seiberling on Mother's Day, May 12, 1935.[30]

However, several weeks before Bill had come to Akron, Bob had confessed his drinking problem at a regular Wednesday night meeting of the Oxford Group. He said, "Well, you good people have all shared things that I am sure were very costly to you, and I am going to tell you something which may cost me my profession. I am a silent drinker."[31]

As was customary in the Oxford Group, Henrietta began praying that Bob would be open to guidance. The next day she told him, "Bob, you must not touch one drop of alcohol." Bob reluctantly tried to follow her spiritual advice. But at that point his compulsion for alcohol still outweighed his desire for sobriety. Deeply chagrined and unable to stop drinking, he returned often for the benefit of Henrietta's wise and caring counsel. Bob recalled one of his painful discussions with her:

> I would go to my good friend Henri and say, "Henri, do you think that I want to stop drinking?" Henri, being a very

charitable soul, said, "Yes, Bob. I'm sure you want to stop."
And I would say, "Well, I can't conceive of any living human
being who really wanted to do something as badly as I
thought I wanted to do it, who could be so total a failure." I
said, "Henri, I think I'm just one of those 'want-to-want-to'
guys."

She said, "No, Bob. I think you want to. We just haven't
found the way to work it yet."[32]

Before Bill Wilson arrived in Akron, Dr. Bob had already learned
to identify certain aids to sobriety through the Oxford Group. He
much later told a group of recovering alcoholics:

1. I had done an immense amount of reading, which they
   recommended.
2. I had refreshed my memory on the Good Book, and I'd
   had an excellent training on that as a youngster.
3. They told me that I should go to their [Oxford] meetings regularly, and I did, every week.
4. They said I should affiliate myself with some church,
   and we [I] did that.
5. They also said that I should cultivate the habit of
   prayer, and I did that . . . at least to quite a considerable
   extent for me.

But I got tight every night, and I mean that. It wasn't once
in a while, it was practically every night, and I couldn't understand what was wrong. I had done all the things that these
good people had told me to do, every one of them, but I still
continued to overindulge.[33]

Providentially, Bill Wilson came to town at this critical moment
and helped turn Dr. Bob's life around. Henrietta Seiberling told her
version of the momentous events that transpired that May:

Bill, when he was in a hotel in Akron and down to a few dollars and owed his bill after his business venture fell through,

looked at the cocktail room and was tempted and thought, "Well, I'll just go in there and get drunk and forget it all, and that will be the end of it." Instead, having been sober for five months in the Oxford Group, he said a prayer. He got the guidance to look in a minister's directory, and a strange thing happened. He just looked in there and he put his finger on one name: Tunks. And that was no coincidence, because Dr. [Walter] Tunks was Mr. Harvey Firestone's minister and Mr. Firestone had brought 60 of the Oxford Group people down there for 10 days out of gratitude for helping his son, who drank too much. His son had quit for a year and a half or so. Out of the act of gratitude of this one father, this whole chain started.

So Bill called Dr. Tunks, and Dr. Tunks gave him a list of names. One of them was Norman Sheppard, who was a close friend of mine and knew what I was trying to do for Bob. Norman said, "I have to go to New York tonight but you call Henrietta Seiberling." When he told the story, Bill shortened it by just saying that he called Dr. Tunks, but I did not know Dr. Tunks. Bill said that he had his last nickel, and he thought, "Well, I'll call her." So I, who was desperate to help Bob in something I didn't know much about, was ready. Bill called, and I will never forget what he said: "I'm from the Oxford Group and I'm a rum hound." Those were his words. I thought, "This is really manna from heaven." And I said, "You come right out here." And my thought was to put those two men together.

Bill, looking back, thought he was out to help someone else. Actually, he was out to get help for himself, no thought of helping anyone else, because he was desperate. But that is the way that God helps us if we let God direct our lives. And I told him to come to church with me next morning and I would get Bob, which I did.[34]

Dr. Bob cooperated with Bill and stopped drinking that very day. However, his recovery was not yet complete. By early June, a medical convention lured the compliant doctor to Atlantic City. The holiday atmosphere tempted him. Rationalization, denial, and half-hearted surrender rapidly deteriorated his resolve to stay sober. Within a week he was poured off a train in Akron and redelivered to Wilson.

Bill took him home to Annie Smith, Dr. Bob's wife. They doctored him with Bill's personal remedy of sauerkraut, stewed tomatoes, supportive conversation, and Annie's spiritual readings. Then, on June 10, Wilson claimed the honor of pouring Smith his last known drink. A jigger of spirits, served to the doctor for medicinal purposes, calmed his tremulous hands long enough for him to perform surgery. Within the hour, Wilson and Anne Smith chauffeured the quaking physician to the hospital where his surgical skill, bolstered by the chaser of alcohol, eased him through a tricky operation. So concluded Dr. Robert Holbrook Smith's drinking career. That afternoon, his resolve to stay sober directed him to make amends to all the innocent people he had harmed by his drinking. With his conscience cleared and his ego thus humbled, Bob had eliminated all the excuses he might conjure up to rationalize any future self-indulgence. The next day he said, "Bill, don't you think that working on other alcoholics is terribly important? We'd be much safer if we got active, wouldn't we?"[35]

So Bill and Bob began applying their newfound knowledge and recovery principles to others paralyzed by alcohol. To do so, they canvassed jailhouses and hospitals, rest homes and churches, in search of practicing alcoholics.

They experimented with methods and jargon, then sought novel approaches that would persuade other alcoholics to join them. At night, back at Smith's home, they conversed about their own drinking patterns and endlessly analyzed their recoveries, still awed by the seeming miracle of sobriety. They philosophized. They prayed. They thanked God for their new-won freedom. After a few determined weeks they recruited Bill D., AA number three, and convinced him to join their ranks.

Within four short years, their numbers rose to about one hundred, and Dr. Bob became convinced that "if his prospective patient could be taken from his environment and drinking companions and placed in a hospital under professional care, the individual would have a much better chance of being properly treated and indoctrinated with the philosophy of the Alcoholics Anonymous program."[36] At exactly this point in AA's history, Sister Ignatia's quest to restore alcoholics to useful, sober lifestyles converged with AA's dire need for hospital beds.

Influence of the Big Book

Meanwhile, Ignatia read AA's message in the newly published book *Alcoholics Anonymous,* also called the Big Book. The recovery testimonials that Bill and Bob described paralleled her own. Though not an alcoholic, she had walked a similar path and been healed of a broken spirit the same as they had. Their written words gave credence to a universal journey:

> The great fact is this, and nothing less: that we have had deep and effective spiritual experiences which have revolutionized our whole attitude toward life, toward our fellows, and toward God's universe. The central fact of our lives today is the absolute certainty that our Creator has entered into our hearts and lives in a way which is indeed miraculous. He has commenced to accomplish those things for us which we could never do for ourselves.[37]

Ignatia agreed with the cofounders' statements that identified the importance of life-changing spiritual experiences for healing. She saw that Wilson and Smith's alliance synthesized those spiritual forces that conquered, then replaced, the grip of alcoholism. Their writings in *Alcoholics Anonymous* explained:

> As soon as we admitted the possible existence of a Creative Intelligence, a Spirit of the Universe underlying the totality of things, we began to be possessed of a new sense of power and direction, provided we took other simple steps. We found that God does not make too hard terms with those who seek Him. To us, the Realm of Spirit is broad, roomy, all inclusive; never

exclusive or forbidding to those who earnestly seek. It is open, we believe, to all men.[38]

Ignatia wholly identified with the spirit that bound the cofounders. What rose between them was a simple charity evolved from their own willingness to share their beliefs and hopes with others trapped in the spiritual blindness that characterizes problem drinkers. Both Bill and Bob called the unaccounted-for power in their lives "God," for independently each had come to the realization and the acceptance that he could not conquer alcoholism through human means alone. Ignatia embraced the rationale of their approach, as described in the Big Book, *Alcoholics Anonymous.*

> If a mere code of morals or a better philosophy of life were sufficient to overcome alcoholism, many of us would have recovered long ago. But we found that such codes and philosophies did not save us, no matter how much we tried. We could wish to be moral, we could wish to be philosophically comforted, in fact, we could will these things with all our might, but the needed power wasn't there. Our human resources, as marshaled by the will were not sufficient; they failed utterly. Lack of power, that was our dilemma. We had to find a power by which we could live, and it had to be Power greater than ourselves. Well, that's exactly what this book is about. Its main object is to enable you to find a Power greater than yourself which will solve your problem. That means we have written a book which we believe to be spiritual as well as moral. And it means, of course, that we are going to talk about God.[39]

Fortunately, a measure of religious balance guided the cofounders during the manuscript's preparation. They made brilliant use of the diverse stories and accounts of drinking contributed by AA's pioneering members. From others who were not directly involved in the AA membership—like Henrietta Seiberling, Anne Smith, and Sister Ignatia—spiritual values rather than spiritual writings marbled the text, adding soul to the varied stories of human frailty.

Wisely, however, the cofounders recognized that the sobriety movement's growth could be permanently stunted if its members became known as religious banner wavers for a miraculous new cult of reformed alcoholics. Already steeped in religious overtones, the collective consciousness of the first one hundred members was challenged to define the spiritual basis of their "cure" in terms acceptable to deists and nondeists alike. The early timers redefined *God* to mean "a Power greater than ourselves."[40] In a plea for spiritual openness, they even reached out to nonbelievers by writing:

> We who have traveled this dubious path, beg you to lay aside prejudice, even against organized religion. We have learned that whatever the human frailties of various faiths may be, those faiths have given purpose and direction to millions. People of faith have a logical idea of what life is all about. Actually we [alcoholics] used to have no reasonable conception whatsoever. We used to amuse ourselves by cynically dissecting spiritual beliefs and practices when we might have observed that many spiritually-minded persons of all races, colors, and creeds were demonstrating a degree of stability, happiness and usefulness which we should have sought ourselves. Instead, we looked at the human defects of these people, and sometimes used their shortcomings as a basis of wholesale condemnation. We talked of intolerance, while we were intolerant ourselves. We missed the reality and the beauty of the forest because we were diverted by the ugliness of some of its trees. We never gave the spiritual side of life a fair hearing.[41]

Preparation of the Manuscript

These earliest of AA writings were first circulated in April 1939. The men and women who contributed took good advantage of time and hindsight to reflect on drinking, Prohibition, and the Great Depression decade. They read, pondered, examined, and discussed the philosophical works of their own time.

As it happened, the 1930s were a decade enriched by scientific and philosophical commentaries of God, humanity, the world, and the universe. Economic depression had prepared the ground for the seeding of old truths re-dressed in the contemporary style of AA's Big Book. Many writers of the day faced the problems of human survival that resurfaced in Depression-time questions heavy with God and religion. Philosophers and ordinary laypeople around the world engaged in the timeless reexploration of spiritual truths. The founders of AA joined in the attempt to make spiritual teachings more understandable and palatable.

Before Wilson, Smith, and Ignatia joined forces, each had sought ways to meet the crises of life through their studies of God and the universe. For example, Wilson studied *The Varieties of Religious Experience* by William James; Smith repeatedly devoured the Holy Bible and the writings of Emmet Fox; Sister Ignatia immersed herself in Thomas à Kempis's *The Imitation of Christ* and in *The Spiritual Exercises* of St. Ignatius of Loyola, the fifteenth-century Spanish mystic who founded the Society of Jesus, or Jesuits.

In 1930, while Wilson and Smith were still drinking, American realist philosopher William Pepperell Montague wrote and published a ninety-eight-page treatise on God and religion called *Prometheus Bound.* A professor of philosophy at New York's Columbia University, Montague presented the soul as humankind's answer to the psychophysical dimension of life, with God as the driving power. He concluded:

> The Promethean God, unlike the old God of evil tradition, would be life-affirming, not life-negating; he would not pull us back from our interests and recall us from the world. We should be lifted up and carried forward, as by a wave, further into the world and its life than before, our interests broadened and deepened and our souls miraculously quickened.[42]

Montague was well established in New York's philosophical circles. Though no conclusive proof exists that he had a relationship with Wilson and the New York AAs, there are, however, a proximity of time and place and a shared terminology that call for consideration. Montague may have unwittingly provided the solution to the alcoholics' dilemma of what to call God when he began the third chapter of *Prometheus Bound* with these words and idea in 1930: ". . . we defined religion as the belief in *a power greater than ourselves* that makes for good."[43]

This concept that *a power greater than self* could reflect God became a fundamental plank of the AA program, without offending atheists and agnostics. The founders needed just such an abstract formula of spiritual power to teach sobriety.

That Bill Wilson or another astute New Yorker made contact with or read Montague while writing *Alcoholics Anonymous* in 1939 is, indeed, possible. If so, the inspiration was never deemed important enough to be given credit in AA's history. A more plausible explanation of that uncanny coincidence of words repeated in AA's Big Book is traced to Wilson's avid readings in contemporary history and philosophy and to his keen ability to retain key ideas.

Whatever the reason, there obviously exists in the Second of the Twelve Steps of Alcoholics Anonymous Montague's formulation—"a power greater than ourselves"—which became Wilson's maxim for recovery. Wilson, too, wrote: "Came to believe that a Power greater than ourselves could restore us to sanity."[44]

Of the general period during which the book was written, Wilson later revealed, "I soon found I was no author, I was only an umpire. I shipped the chapters to Akron, they shipped them to New York where we discussed them in the New York meetings. And the brawls over what was to go into that book were something terrific."[45]

Akron's Hidden Influences

It is no wonder, then, that back on the Akron front, another spiritual influence in the person of Sister Ignatia slowly inspired the cofounding duo. Though previous histories of this period in Ohio cite 1939 as the beginning of the working relationship between AA's doctor and the "sickly nun,"[46] in actual fact 1939 was the turning point for all the actions and ideas that had challenged the two from the membership's earliest years. For more than ten years, 1928–39, Ignatia had worked on alcoholics and doctors. One of them was Dr. Bob himself.

Part of the sway she exerted on Dr. Bob emanated from her own spiritual training, her own rebirth, her inner peace, and her charitable example. Thus, in subtle ways of the spirit, Ignatia surely influenced the thought, development, and spiritual content of Dr. Bob's contributions to the book *Alcoholics Anonymous* and to the Twelve Steps contained therein.

Suggestions of other spiritual influences affecting AA's development follow closely at this time. For example, moving ahead of the story to the spring of 1940, a Jesuit priest by the name of Edward "Puggy" Dowling happened to visit Cincinnati, Ohio, and to read a copy of the Big Book. So familiar were the spiritual nuances embraced by the Twelve Steps that he became convinced that Jesuit spirituality was at the base of the nonsectarian AA writings. So he made his way to Akron, where he located Dr. Bob and the members of the "Alcoholic Squadron" of the Oxford Group.[47] However, in Akron his spiritual inquiries yielded no results. Most of the early AAs there were Protestant and had never heard of St. Ignatius or his *Spiritual Exercises.* Unable to satisfy the priest's curiosity, the Akronites referred him to Bill Wilson in New York. While flattered when Dowling compared his writings to one of the Catholic world's great spiritual guides, Wilson flatly declared that he had no firsthand knowledge of Jesuitry and claimed authorship of the Steps by inspiration. In the end, Dowling had perhaps been closer to discovering the source of the Ignatian link and influence during his earlier trip to Akron, when he met Dr. Bob Smith.

Had he also been introduced to Sister Ignatia at that time, her relationship with Dr. Bob as well as her Jesuit spirit of "love through action" would have been apparent. No one in Akron would have disputed that Sister Ignatia and Dr. Bob had become "soul friends" during Smith's early recovery period. Newly sober, Smith eagerly embraced spiritual knowledge and spiritual people. Ignatia attracted him because she personified both. Of equal importance, Bob Smith found in Ignatia a compassionate listener—a wise friend who understood his every problem and contributed to each solution.

When Smith was not doctoring people himself, however, he acted as spokesperson for Akron's contributors to the Big Book. As bearer of the final word on what was sent to the New York writing head-quarters, Bob had to assimilate thoughts, beliefs, and practices of the sober Akronites and their caregivers. Not a writer himself, he filtered the information through an Akron-area writer, Jim Scott, before for-warding his edited copy to Bill.[48] He prepared for this by talking to his close friends and confidants. Over coffee, he reviewed his thoughts with Sister Ignatia. Her nearness to his professional life illuminated many of the spiritual principles that Smith embraced and then passed on to Wilson, who only then summarized them in writing.

Several years later, Dr. Bob publicly explained his view of the ori-gins and the authorship of the Twelve Steps. At the time, he claimed responsibility for his own participation and provided an explanation for the Steps' early formation. Speaking in Detroit during 1948, Smith stressed to his audience the important part that outside influence and lengthy discussion with others had played in the development of the Twelve Steps and in the mind of Wilson, the writer.[49] Only Smith's candid remarks explain how the dynamics worked between him and Wilson much earlier:

> It wasn't until 1939 that the teachings and efforts and studies that had been going on were crystallized in the form of the Twelve Steps. I didn't write the Twelve Steps. I had nothing to do with the *writing* of them. I think probably I had something to do with them *indirectly* because after this June 10th epi-sode, Bill came to live at our house and stayed for about three months. [And] there was hardly a night in that three months that we didn't sit up until two or three o'clock discussing these things. [And] it would be hard for me to conceive that some-thing wasn't said during those nightly discussions around our kitchen table that influenced the actual writing of the Twelve Steps.[50]

Since Dr. Bob rarely had time for public speaking, it is fortu-nate that his 1948 speech appropriately emphasized his own strong influence on AA's formation. Smith and Wilson together had verbalized most of AA's precepts during the earliest years of the program, before the formalized Twelve Steps appeared on Wilson's legal pad. However, it is also possible that Smith delivered this clarifying speech for other reasons too.

Smith often served as a balancing agent for Wilson's enthusiastic ego and historical accuracy. Coincidentally, around the time that Smith spoke in Detroit, Wilson was battling a recurrence of manic-depressive illness; at this juncture, his episodes of grandiosity were interrupted by lengthy bouts of melancholic depression. Having conquered alcoholism, Wilson then struggled to confront and master his emotional instability. Deeply chagrined at the setback in his own progress, he wrote to friends in Cleveland that he "needed a long rest," and was "thinking of resigning from A.A."[51] Under the circumstances, it is conceivable that Smith's speech served his own need both to clear the historical record and to jolt Wilson back to reality.

Although the recorded history of 1938 does not overtly reflect it to be the case, Ignatia and Smith's ten-year relationship was already cemented before they admitted their first patient. The two pioneers were not as casually acquainted as Ignatia's brief accounting of their first official hospital admission implies:

> A reputable doctor who had recovered from alcoholism asked admission for a patient. A room was available. The patient was admitted. It was as simple as that.[52]

Too off-handed a remark to be taken seriously, Ignatia's concise report of her introduction to Dr. Bob and Alcoholics Anonymous is not in keeping with its historical significance. Nonetheless, her statement reveals a splendid sample of the humility through which she and Dr. Bob viewed their own roles during the "flying blind"[53] period of AA's history.

More realistically, because Sister Ignatia was the hospital's admitting officer, Dr. Bob relied heavily on her to solve obstacles he encountered as a medical doctor who was attempting to treat alcoholics. Whether talking with her in the admitting office or engaging her sympathies over a cup of coffee,[54] Smith seemed deeply affected by her sensitivity to the puzzle of addiction and by the subtle humor she so deftly offered its victims.

Closer to the truth, both he and the newly formed abstinence program needed Sister Ignatia's strong and willing spirit in order to survive and push their efforts forward. For organizational upheaval and disunity, 1939 was AA's banner year. All was in a state of flux when Ignatia joined the scene. The year 1939 was also the height of AA's struggle to be birthed and baptized with a lasting identity. In the midst of such implosive turmoil, AA's angel stepped forth from the wings.

AA's Early Association with the Oxford Group

Ignatia's rising importance emerged from AA's stormy origins. The earliest years of its formation, 1935–39, were fragmented, complex, and submerged within a popular spiritual movement of the 1930s called the Oxford Group. Alcoholics Anonymous, as it is known today, did not suddenly surface intact but, more accurately, gradually evolved from the teachings of the Oxford Group. One old-timer from Akron explained succinctly, "I've been sober since March 1, 1939. I came into the Oxford Group. There was no AA then."[55]

Also known as "Moral Rearmament," the Oxford Group was founded in 1908 by a disillusioned Lutheran preacher named Frank Buchman. Following a disagreement with the trustees of a young men's hospice that he had founded earlier, Buchman abruptly left the United States and settled in England. There, in a small village, he heard a simple sermon delivered by a laywoman on the meaning of the cross. The experience of the woman's testimony was life changing for Buchman. Shortly thereafter, he organized "house parties" for small bands of Christians who wished to bear witness to their reborn faith. The most notable of the house parties occurred at Oxford University, and thus the group acquired its name. The house parties combined fellowship with faith, open confession of sin, and the public sharing of joy, gained through freeing the conscience of guilt. Buchman's mission taught partygoers that "the key to social reformation lies in personal transformation."[56]

The Oxford Group's primary tenet encouraged the practice and renewal of first-century Christianity, which was viewed as applicable in the modern world. Because the Oxford Group was not a formal sect, its members held no theological positions and remained active within their respective religions, using the group to augment their existing beliefs and practices. Following a six-point plan that fostered group confession and group guidance, members shared testimonies, prayers, and spiritual evangelization.

In 1932, when Bob and Anne Smith could find no relief for the doctor's compulsive drinking, they began attending Oxford Group meetings in Akron. Likewise, before Bill Wilson had his last drink near the end of 1934, a former drinking companion named Ebby Thacher visited him. Ebby told Bill he had found the answer to his own drinking compulsion through religion. The "religion" that Ebby discovered and introduced Bill to was called Buchmanism, another name for the Oxford Group.

Thus the Oxford Group strongly influenced both AA cofounders and their wives. Subsequently, before the idea to have group meetings for alcoholics occurred to them, they encouraged all newly sober people to attend Oxford Group meetings together. So it was that the earliest New York and Akron alcoholics took their first steps to sobriety under this movement's influence.[57] Nevertheless, by 1937, problems began to surface from the alcoholics' association with the Oxford Groupers. Recalling these days in Akron, Dr. Bob's son, Smitty, explained:

> I went over to some of the Oxford Group meetings then. In the Oxford Group, you worked the other guy's program for him. You got divine guidance for somebody else, and they got it for you. Well, you can imagine how that went over with the drunks! Of course, the wives were ready to give this guidance to their husbands at any time, but the drunks sure didn't want any part of it. That was one of the things that made the Oxford Group totally unacceptable to the alcoholics. They got some strange guidance from other people.[58]

Both New Yorkers and Akronites ultimately severed ties with the Oxford Group, but their respective memberships did so for different reasons. The "four absolutes" of the Oxford Group—honesty, purity, unselfishness, and love—seemed unattainable, even self-defeating goals to New York alcoholics. Moreover, Oxford Group practices of team guidance and aggressive evangelization alienated and frightened newly sobered AA members. But of greater historical significance to AA, the Oxford Groupers sought expansion of their upper-middle-class membership through publicity and prestige at exactly the time when AA was forging a fundamental principle of anonymity as its spiritual cornerstone.[59]

Literature about AA had not yet been written, so there was no sure way to convince incoming alcoholics that the Oxford Group was not a new religion or a Protestant sect.[60] This posed a critical problem for the alcoholic pioneers, who still easily confused religion with the nonsectarian spirituality that only later characterized Alcoholics Anonymous. Left unresolved, the situation held serious religious consequences for Catholics who needed the sobriety support available from the Oxford Group but whose faith did not permit active participation in religious denominations outside the Catholic tradition. Irish Roman Catholics, who heavily populated the New York and Cleveland membership bases, thus faced a trying choice between newfound sobriety through the Oxford Group or strict conformity with the rules of Catholic practice, which to date had not kept them sober.[61]

In Akron, similar stresses surfaced but not as early. Only 20 percent of Akron's population claimed Roman Catholicism as their religion. Early confusion of the Oxford Group with Protestantism caused no major rifts within the Akron membership until alcoholics from Cleveland joined their ranks. Though less than fifty miles north of Akron, Cleveland's Catholics comprised nearly 60 percent of the city's total population.[62] Accordingly, religious complications arose in 1937, when large numbers of Clevelanders, most of whom were Catholics, sought help for their alcoholism through Akron's Alcoholic Squadron of the Oxford Group.

Once sober, Clevelanders joined Dr. Bob and the other sober Akronites for the Wednesday night meeting of the Oxford Group. A nonalcoholic friend of Dr. Bob's, T. Henry Williams, had opened his home weekly to the Alcoholic Squadron. Clevelanders grew very excited about a "cure" for alcoholism that got results. They returned home and told their parish priest that, at a meeting in Akron, they had finally found the answer to their drinking problems. But when the priest learned of the Alcoholic Squadron's alignment with the Oxford Group, he forbade the men to return because of the group's suspected Protestant overtones.

Thus, alcoholic Clevelanders faced the dilemma of choosing between their newly found sobriety or their religion. But sobriety had been hard won. Their faith, too, had recovered slowly. Cleveland alcoholics resolutely refused to relinquish either gift. Instead, they exerted pressure on Dr. Bob to abandon the Alcoholic Squadron's association with the Oxford Group and to establish a separate fellowship free of perceived religious affiliation.[63]

A time of anguish followed for Dr. Bob. Reason told him that T. Henry Williams had stood by him through the worst of his drinking days. Had not T. Henry and his wife, Clarace, been among the first nonalcoholics to extend themselves and the weekly use of their living room to Smith and his band of friends? They had never once complained when teeming ashtrays and half-filled coffee cups burned or marred the mahogany credenza or when newer members, not quite sober, trampled through the daffodils.

For several months, try as he would, Smith could not understand the Clevelanders' vehement refusal to continue meeting at T. Henry's home. According to Smith's daughter, Sue Windows, "Dad was very upset with the break of the Oxford Group. He actually got physically ill and went to bed. But he was pressured by the group to make a decision."[64] Unable to resolve his own turmoil, Smith avoided a final decision until November 1939. But before he gave in to the Clevelanders' demands, a number of momentous events intervened and forced his hand.

No Religious Affiliation

In May 1939, the book *Alcoholics Anonymous* was finally published. At the same time, debate in Akron over allegiance to the Oxford Group escalated into open hostility. With the newly published book for a base, the angry Clevelanders left T. Henry's home and organized their own group in Cleveland, far removed from the influences of the Buchmanites.

Led by Clarence S., they called themselves "Alcoholics Anonymous," taking their name from the title of the newly published book. They held their first meeting of the newly named Alcoholics Anonymous group on May 18, 1939, at the Cleveland Heights home of Abby G. When attendance was recorded, sixteen members were officially present. Thus, the first group to officially call itself Alcoholics Anonymous convened in Cleveland, Ohio.[65]

During that spring in Akron, Bob Smith's problems with the fellowship reached monumental proportions. Not only was he losing the use of sympathetic hospitals for the alcoholics, he was also losing the Clevelanders' strong impact on the Akron program. With new groups quickly forming in Cleveland, Smith finally realized that even the merest hint of religious connection to the Oxford Group would exclude needy alcoholics from participation in a program for sobriety that brought results. The religious question, no longer restricted to Catholics, now struck close to home. Bob and his family had been ostracized from their local church because of their Oxford Group affiliation.[66] Finally Smith acknowledged that although religion was often the by-product of surrendered alcoholism, it could not be the primary inducement to AA membership. *Sobriety,* not religion, was the Alcoholic Squadron's long-term goal.

Therefore, by late November, Smith followed the lead of the New Yorkers and the Clevelanders and left the shelter of the Oxford Group for the overall preservation of the AA movement. Most of the Akron members joined him. For a few weeks they held their meetings at Smith's home and, for the sake of unity, also attended the Cleveland meetings. By January 1940, they selected a permanent Akron meeting site at King's School. AA's split from the Oxford Group was thus complete.

Nonetheless, the question of AA's relationship to the Oxford Group remained a source of interest to members and scholars alike. In 1960, John C. Ford, S.J., an instructor at the Yale School of Alcohol Studies, offered an incisive explanation:

> The differences between the fundamental attitudes of the early AA's and the Oxford Groupers were so pronounced that there never was a real ideological integration of AA into that movement. There was initial inspiration and association rather than integration. AA sprang from the Oxford Groups but almost immediately sprang away from them.[67]

The Hospital Question

The timing of Smith's resolution of the Oxford Group association can now be seen as providential. Had not the question of Protestant affiliation been resolved, Sister Ignatia could not have promoted Alcoholics Anonymous at a Catholic institution. And St. Thomas Hospital was Dr. Bob's last hope for refuge in Akron.

With publication of the Big Book, development of the Twelve Steps, growth in Cleveland, and the break from the Oxford Group accomplished, AA emerged in late 1939 with a name, an identity, a new independence, and an effective program for sobriety. Still needed, however, was a sympathetic hospital that would tend to the alcoholics' medical needs while allowing the spiritual medicine of Alcoholics Anonymous to take hold.

In these earliest days, alcoholics usually hit very low "bottoms"[*]

---

*The meaning of "high bottoms" and "low bottoms" has changed over the years in accepted interpretation. Originally, these terms were used to describe the times when an alcoholic characteristically drank to excess. A person who drank when feeling emotionally low was considered to be a "low bottom" drunk or while emotionally high, a "high bottom" drunk. Over the years, usage has come to be more associated with the consequences of an alcoholic's drinking. Example: One who has lost family, home, job, etc., is considered to be "low bottom" whereas one who ceases to drink before consequences are severe is now considered to be "high bottom."

before they sought help. Most had lost homes, jobs, health, family, and financial resources. Critical medical complications accompanied alcoholism, such as DTs, malnutrition, diabetes, and heart, lung, and liver disease. The need for good medical care at the beginning of sobriety was not just an emergency measure, but a realistic concern for the cofounders. Thus, hospitalization had come to be an important first step in recovery.

For a time, Wilson and Smith entertained grandiose plans for providing AA with paid missionaries, hospital workers, and special AA hospitals. The support they received from trustees and friends of the John D. Rockefeller, Jr., Foundation in 1938 fueled their hopes. A longtime Rockefeller friend, Frank Amos, volunteered to visit Akron and conduct a feasibility study that might produce a Rockefeller donation to the struggling society. After all, Rockefeller had his family roots in Ohio. More important, Dr. Bob and the Akron AAs had the first and strongest group effort to demonstrate. With Smith's medical expertise in the picture, Akron was AA's logical location to build a philanthropic medical mecca for alcoholics. But despite Amos's recommendation that a $50,000 contribution be granted to Smith and Wilson, Rockefeller declined financial involvement, stressing that large amounts of money might inadvertently ruin the spirit of AA's endeavors.[68]

Rockefeller's decision quickly dashed hopes for an AA hospital. Dejected and approaching financial ruin, Smith continued to operate discreetly from Akron City Hospital, Just-A-Mere-Home, and other rest homes in the area. Still, the need for dependable hospital resources became more urgent as AA's numbers increased. Wilson wrote of the dilemma that he and Dr. Bob faced:

> Meanwhile we found that we needed services that we could not perform ourselves. Chief among these was the right kind of hospitalization. Doctoring and physically caring for the very sick was not and could not be AA's business. Here great friends like Dr. Silkworth and Sister Ignatia came to our aid.[69]

Providing reliable hospital services for alcoholics was precisely the work of AA's angel. Sister Ignatia's arrival on AA's horizon was timed to perfection, occurring halfway through the most tumultuous year in AA's history. Added to all the other AA 1939 beginnings was an AA-affiliated hospital in Akron, befriended and led by a woman possessed of spiritual stature, understanding, and an unparalleled compassion for suffering alcoholics.

By early 1941, little more than one year after Ignatia made hospitalization available to alcoholics, AA's membership soared from four hundred active members to over two thousand recovering men and women. This rapid increase in numbers was generally attributed to AA's first successful publicity campaign and the zealous evangelization of AA's Cleveland membership. Not considered, however, is the impact that the hospital treatment pioneered in Akron had on the membership at that time. Of great significance to AA's history, the bulk of the sixteen hundred new members lived in and around Ohio, where part of the offering to newcomers that was not available in other areas of the country included hospital care.

That alcoholics could get sober with a combination of quality medical care and AA indoctrination comprised Sister Ignatia's treatment philosophy. Recognition that AA, not the hospital, held the road map to alcoholic recovery demonstrated her humility and wisdom. That God could and would help alcoholics if asked defined her unyielding belief.

Therefore, without relying on psychiatrists to identify character types prone to addiction or personality tests that warned of impending alcoholism, Ignatia used good judgment to detect the illness and good sense to address its victims' physical and spiritual needs. Using equal measures of toughness and tenderness to offset the emotional highs and lows that often precipitated her patients' potential drinking episodes, she drove home the message of long-term sobriety. That is why many AA members today consider Sister Ignatia to have been a spiritual cofounder of AA and the grass roots catalyst for AA's huge success.

Put briefly, AA's angel was a strong, empathetic woman who extracted goodness from every situation that she faced and resolved each day to leave the world a little better than she had found it. Ignatia had all the charisma of an Irish *anmchara,* or soul friend, so she easily folded the troubled into her heart. She was also an artist able to transform her creative impulses into actions, and an unremitting idealist whose faith in her God made all things possible. With such gifts and traits defining her character, she confronted the daily challenges of life and participated in all the solutions.

"The Incomparable Sister Ignatia"[70] was truly AA's insider in pioneering the hospital treatment of alcoholics and a willing accomplice in the early work of caring for its suffering ones. Abandoned by society and having abandoned their God, they needed an advocate who believed in them. In fact, they needed a healing far beyond what people and medicine could provide.

Devising a hospital plan that applied the guidelines for recovery offered in AA's Twelve Steps challenged Ignatia's spiritual abilities. Of equal importance, the discovery of a sympathetic admitting clerk who understood their recovery program and was willing to jeopardize her job for the alcoholic's best interests was an opportunity that AA dared not pass by.

In part, Ignatia's religious vocation prepared her for this work. Having been named for St. Ignatius Loyola (the author of *The Spiritual Exercises*) provided her with an ideal role model whose spiritual teachings were more than compatible with AA's own. Soon after working with Dr. Bob's patients, she discovered that her Ignatian spirituality indeed reflected AA's Twelve Steps. Consequently, she was no stranger to the meaning of the Steps, nor was she spiritually ignorant about their application to life. Ignatia embraced the universal spiritual philosophy later expressed in Alcoholics Anonymous that became a common ground for recovery.[71]

Thus, like the AAs, she made good use of retreats and quiet times to study the writing of her Catholic spiritual masters: Ignatius Loyola, Augustine, Teresa of Avila, John of the Cross, Francis of Assisi, Therese of Lisieux, and Thomas à Kempis were her favorites. The topics of spiritual interest that she recorded in her journal and wove into her talks for alcoholics centered on her readings on faith, hope, and charity, love of neighbor, the angels, prayer, humility, obedience, modesty, and silence.[72]

In her pocket she carried two well-worn prayer books that provided her with daily inspiration. Kempis's *The Imitation of Christ* was pencil-marked with special passages and dates during the early 1930s. The other small book she carried was called *A Thought from Saint Ignatius for Each Day of the Year,* published in 1887.[73] *Twenty-Four Hours a Day,* so popular with AAs, is similar in thought, format, and size to Sister Ignatia's book. In the early days of the AA ward, she began the practice of giving the patients a copy of one or the other book before they left the ward. On the inside cover, she would write their name, their date of discharge, and a short message like this:

> May God bless you and yours always. May he keep you ever close to His Sacred Heart.
>
> Sister M. Ignatia
> Please say a little prayer for me.[74]

As she nursed the alcoholics, she paused throughout the day and offered her prayers in the tiny hospital chapel. The lovely stained-glass windows threw prisms of light into the darkened sanctuary. The rich red carpet bled into rainbows. Above the altar, embedded in a colorful splash of mosaic tiles was written the command from the parable of the Good Samaritan, "'Go and do thou in like manner.'"[75]

Day after day, Ignatia knelt in prayer and meditation inside the hospital chapel. The words above inspired her. In August 1939, her life became summarized by the altar's inscription: "Go and Do."

"Do what?" she undoubtedly asked.

As she glanced about the chapel at the luminously inscribed stained-glass windows, reflected light in each of the six panes told AA's angel:

> Feed the Hungry
> Give Drink to the Thirsty
> Clothe the Naked
> Visit the Sick
> Visit the Imprisoned
> Bury the Dead.[76]

Two

Beginnings of History

*Like a lighted candle she gave light to darkened souls, and
at the same time, the giving consumed her.*

—Sister Therese Marie, C.S.A.
May 14, 1966

It was a bleak, rainy evening in April 1838 when the first Irish temperance movement of any great significance began. A huge crowd had gathered at Blackamoor Lane School in County Cork and was anxiously awaiting the response of Father Theobald Mathew, their beloved parish priest, to William Martin, a teetotaling Quaker merchant who had challenged Father Mathew to join his crusade against the careless drinking habits of Irish society. The night air hung heavy with anticipation that a momentous event was about to occur. When Father Mathew stepped to the podium, not a sound could be heard from the crowd. He cleared his throat, signed himself with the cross, and began:

> I feel I am bound as a minister of the gospel to throw all personal considerations aside and give a helping hand to gentlemen like Mr. Martin, who have afforded me so excellent an example . . . After much reflection on the subject, I have come to the conclusion that there is no necessity of intoxicating drinks for anyone in good health. I will be the first to sign my name in the book which is on the table, and I hope we shall soon have it full.[1]

Martin had made a wise choice of message carriers in Father Mathew. Catholics and Protestants alike flocked to Holy Trinity

Church to hear Theobald Mathew's earthy sermons. With their strong traditions of total abstinence from smoking and drinking, Protestants were more receptive to Martin's efforts to abolish alcohol than the rank and file membership of the Catholic Church and its hierarchy. William Martin knew that his informal temperance movement would not become an effective tool of Catholic persuasion without the leadership of an influential Catholic priest.

Most Catholic clergymen ignored the problem of alcohol consumption among their priests and people. Martin knew that their apathy granted silent permission for Catholics to continue deadly drinking practices, condoned by most priests as "human weakness." However, such clerical silence often spelled death for alcohol's victims.

As a Capuchin monk, Father Mathew served the very poor of Blackamoor Lane. He had witnessed the destruction of families, the forfeiture of homes, and violent crimes and debts—all rooted in alcoholism. He was a simple, gentle, and well-loved priest. William Martin knew Corkonians, and Catholics would rally around Father Mathew if he could convince the priest to advance the cause of temperance.

On that April evening, then, after considering the disdain his actions would elicit from his fellow Catholic priests, Father Mathew courageously told his gathered people:

> I promise, with the Divine Assistance, to abstain from all intoxicating liquors and to prevent as much as possible, by advice and example, intemperance in others.[2]

He signed the book, took the "pledge," and at that moment initiated his own movement for total abstinence by saying, "Here goes in the Name of God."[3] Within three months, twenty-five thousand Irish had joined him in a lifelong vow of temperance.

Influence of the Irish Temperance Movements

Father Mathew's total abstinence movement attracted Catholics and Protestants alike, creating the hope for an ecumenical solution to alcoholism through the practice of sobriety. He held abstinence meetings three times each week and distributed holy medals and badges to his followers as gentle reminders of their commitment to temperance.

Soon known as "the Apostle of Temperance," Father Mathew cautiously removed partisan politics from the cause of temperance, stating often, "There is nothing political amongst us; whoever wants politics must go elsewhere."[4]

Father Mathew's abstinence movement spread from Ireland to Scotland and England, where another seventy thousand took the pledge and signed the book. However, by 1845 financial problems and the Great Famine brought the abstinence movement to an end. Only one year later, three hundred thousand Irish were dead of typhoid and starvation. Those who survived were desperate for relief from the famine's physical and emotional ravages. They abandoned Father Mathew, the pledge, and the total abstinence movement and returned to the practice of drinking.

Relieved of the great burden of Father Mathew's popular influence, politicians and Catholic clergy scorned and abandoned the movement too. With his crusade in shambles, Father Mathew left Ireland in 1848 for a trip to the United States.

For the next two-and-one-half years, the weary priest carried the temperance movement to the Irish in America, firmly spreading his ideals in their New World parishes. Traveling to twenty-three U.S. states, he administered the pledge to six hundred thousand immigrants before returning to his native country in 1851.

Though the movement in Ireland ceased with his death in 1856, Father Mathew had managed to "banish forever the image of the drunkard as a jolly companion."[5] Later, he was credited with being the inspiration for the Pioneers Total Abstinence Association of the Sacred Heart (1898) by its Irish Jesuit founder, Father James A. Cullen.

Gavin Family Roots in Ireland

Three decades after the Great Famine had depleted Ireland's land and population, another famine overtook the western coast in 1873. The second wave hit the residents of County Mayo, where Della Gavin's parents had been born and raised.

Patrick Gavin and Barbara Neary married in the early 1880s when the harshness of the land dictated Ireland's living conditions. Only Pat Gavin's willingness to work long months of the year in England on the bountiful British farms guaranteed the family a livelihood. Barbara remained in Ballyhane, where she planted and harvested crops to feed the family. There were no frills in the cobblestoned countryside where the Gavins lived. A pair of cloth sandals called *tohleens* protected her feet from the rocky earth as Barbara struggled against the barren land.

The birth of children made living conditions crowded and uncomfortable in the Gavin home. As was the custom, Barbara Gavin covered the dirt floor of their cottage with mounds of loose straw for comfort and warmth. The family's diet was sparse, consisting mostly of buttermilk and boiled potatoes. On Sundays, the parish church of the Holy Rosary offered them temporary hope and relief from their impoverished existence. Soon Barbara Gavin bore three children, two of whom—Patrick and Della—survived. Though the town of Shanvilly near Castlebar offered schooling, farm children could not spare the time to book learn. Farm chores claimed all the daytime hours for Della and her brother, Pat.

In the villages of western Ireland men *and* women had alcohol problems. Drinkers masked life's harshness in alcohol-induced euphoria, remembering the days when standards of living were higher and America had not beckoned all of their breadwinners.

By the time Bridget Della Mary Gavin—Ignatia's full baptismal name—was born on January 2, 1889, a generation of renewed intemperance had separated the Irish in her Ballyhane birthplace from Father Mathew's ideals. Many of her neighbors and relatives had succumbed to the temptations of drink or had suffered otherwise from its effects.

As a child growing up in this atmosphere, Della became physically fragile and emotionally sensitive to poverty and drunkenness. The unpredictable behavior of the intoxicated villagers she met in Ballyhane's streets often frightened her. Their drunkenness disquieted Barbara too. To temper her child's fear of alcoholics and allay her anxieties, she taught Della to pray for them. From her mother,

Della learned an early compassion for those who hid themselves in the "drink."

Gavins Embark for America

By the fall of 1895, Barbara Gavin's deteriorating health prompted her husband to resettle his family in America. There, it was said, Barbara could receive good medical care, and their children could go to school. Stating that it was "a wonderful Providence that God inspired my dear parents to come to this country," Sister Ignatia later elaborated:

> Mother needed surgery and my father felt the surgeons in the States were more skilled than those over there. I think that was the one thing that prompted him to come [here].[6]

The Gavins were joined in their immigration plans by Pat's sister, Mary Dunn, her husband, and their seven children. In January 1896, the two families memorized the familiar sights of the gentle hills, the silvered lakes, and the purple-heathered moors of their birthplace. They boarded ship with seven-year-old Della, turned their gaze toward America, and left Ireland.

In those days, how immigrants traveled to America reflected their economic status. Most made the journey on one ship and disembarked at one of several American harbor cities along the East Coast. But a more frugal way to sail divided the trip into two stages, the first one ending in Newfoundland, Canada. A stopover there afforded immigrants the option to end the crossing and take on temporary labor or book a less expensive vessel for the final journey to the United States. Like the Gavins, those who chose the cheaper way were condescendingly referred to as *two-boaters* by Irish Americans already living in the large port cities of New York, Boston, Philadelphia, and Baltimore.[7]

The fourteen-day passage to Newfoundland aboard the White Star Shipping Line sharpened the Gavins' hope for a new life in America. Young Della's excitement peaked just before reaching port; the captain ceremoniously rewarded her for being the first to sight land.[8]

Thus the first glimmer of her visionary nature and pioneering spirit found natural expression on the journey to America.

Arrival in America

In April 1896, three months after leaving Ireland, the Gavins arrived in Cleveland, Ohio. They made their first home at 29 Mason Street, just east of the Cuyahoga River, in Immaculate Conception parish. At the time, Robert E. McKisson was the city mayor; a future U.S. president, William Howard Taft, was northern Ohio's circuit judge. Cleveland thrived with industry and throbbed with activity. Thirty-three churches comprised the Cleveland Catholic Diocese, which stretched from Cleveland to Toledo. Numerous benevolent societies addressed the social issues of the day, one being the problem of alcoholism among Irish immigrant families and workers.

Aware that their parishioners tended to overindulge in liquor, the Irish pastors at St. Augustine, St. Bridget, St. Malachi, and St. Patrick had established abstinence societies for the men that offered concurrent but separate meetings for the women.[9] Most popular of these was the well-known Father Mathew's Total Abstinence and Benevolent Society, which met the first Sunday of each month in the Newburgh section of Cleveland. From this group, additional chapters, called the Knights of Father Mathew, sprang up throughout the city.

These influential organizations squarely faced the overwhelming problems and the devastating ramifications of intemperance in a city flooded with hard-drinking dockworkers, steelworkers, salt miners, and longshoremen. New immigrants registered at churches and simultaneously took the pledge—the clergy's well-meaning antidote for neutralizing alcoholism among immigrant laborers. Sermons reciting the evils of "demon rum" often dominated Sunday pulpit messages. In addition to Catholic Church efforts, local chapters of the Women's Christian Temperance Union (WCTU) labored to halt the drinking excesses of Cleveland's growing population.

Sister Ignatia remembered from her youth that clergy and community leaders were often on the lookout for budding drinking problems, especially among the young. She often retold the story about Father

J. J. Quinn, a beloved pastor at her own parish, Immaculate Conception Church:

> He [Father Quinn] was on a trip somewhere, and he was coming [back] home. It was a wet, slippery night and he had a bag in each hand. Two of the young men from his parish met him and said, "Father, can't we help you?" So each one took a bag and went on ahead. They finally got to the front steps of the house, put the bags down, and Father said, "That's fine boys, that's fine." While he was unlocking the front door he said, "Do you boys drink?" They said, "Oh, once in a while." [He replied,] "Come in right now, and I'll give you the Pledge."[10]

Clearly, to be Irish and Catholic in Cleveland guaranteed exposure to the potential dangers of alcohol. That is why Cleveland's religious and secular organizations seized every opportunity to impress the value of abstinence on the young. Leaders knew that once drinking began, Irish youths—hurrying to become Irish men—consumed alcohol with little thought of moderation. Sobriety as a virtue was preached from the pulpit and respectfully praised from the pews but rarely, if ever, practiced.

School and Church in America

Drinking was only one issue that the Gavins faced in Cleveland. The schooling of their children was another. In Ireland, learning was not a priority. Basic survival and limited career opportunities canceled the need for formal schooling. But in their new country, the Gavins discovered that education provided the way to future success. Though it was nearly the end of the term when the Gavins arrived in Cleveland, they enrolled the children in school at once:

> Some of the relatives advised Mother and Dad to send me to the public school two streets down. I was dying to go to the Catholic school, but it was across the railroad tracks. Being strangers (we didn't have the trains running down the open

highways in Ireland), they were afraid we'd get run over by a train. So they said, "Well, it's the end of the school year, only another month, why not let them go to the public school?" So that's what they did. We started to the public school.[11]

The Gavins' newness to urban life and their lack of sophistication to city ways showed. After the first morning at Waring Public School, Della returned home confused. "At noon I came home and said to Mother, 'They have a German and [an] English first grade. Which one do you think I should go into?' She said, 'Well, you're late in getting started so you might as well learn all you can. Go into the German first grade.'"[12]

Not long afterward, the classroom issue resolved itself when Patrick Gavin encountered the infamous Father Quinn in the confessional. Enraged that a good Irish father would knowingly permit his children to attend a public school, the garrulous priest refused to give Pat absolution for his sins unless he agreed to transfer his children to the parish school at once. So, despite the nearness of Waring Public School to the Gavins' home, on Monday morning the children crossed the dangerous railroad tracks and took their new seats in Immaculate Conception's Catholic classrooms. The next Saturday, Father Quinn smugly absolved Patrick Gavin and, for a penance, recruited him as a Sunday usher. With their integration into the parish fold accomplished, the Gavins began adapting to life in America.

The Gavins soon found that minor problems and adjustments constantly challenged immigrant life. After all, everything in America was new to them. In contrast to their depleted but picturesque homeland, they now lived in a large and cluttered city. Urban living was a radical change from their simple rural existence. Thus their melancholic Irish hearts sought familiarity and safety in the local parish community, which quickly became their primary source of spiritual and economic hope. There the musical rituals and the drone of familiar Latin prayers momentarily masked the chaotic din of Cleveland's industrial settlements. For an added benefit, parish churches and the Catholic religion provided immigrants with a sense of identity in an otherwise unfamiliar and often unwelcoming society.

The Gavins' church in Cleveland, known affectionately by the Irish as "the Mac," remains largely unchanged from the day of Della's girlhood. The forms of saints she prayed to still adorn the windows and the walls. At the turn of the twentieth century, Immaculate Conception Church furnished thousands of Irish immigrants—and the Gavins—with a spiritual home in Cleveland.

Careers and Choices

Of all the members of the Gavin family, Della's father most found city life to be difficult. Consistent with the experience of many newcomers, he changed jobs annually and uprooted the family residence almost as often. Between 1896 and 1906, the City of Cleveland Directory recorded six different addresses for the Gavins. Also, on the list of head-of-household occupations, Patrick was most often identified simply as "laborer." During these years, he moonlighted as a night watchman and an elevator operator. Much later, he dabbled in the insurance business and, for a brief time, he and his son struggled to operate a small grocery store. City employment always proved elusive and unsatisfying for an uneducated, middle-aged man accustomed to earning his living from the land.

Meanwhile, Della finished high school, studied music, and worked at the Jewell Ice Cream Parlor next to St. John's Cathedral. She later described this period of her life with great fondness:

> I went to the high school of the Sisters of St. Joseph, and followed the music, and felt God's wonderful providence . . . how He makes *us* His instruments to carry out His designs.[13]

As Della physically matured, her mother grew anxious over her beautiful daughter's future. Like other Irish women of her day, Barbara knew that marriage would not necessarily guarantee a secure life. Her thoughts on wedlock reflected the Irish experience. Lamentably, lack of skills and education often eroded the self-esteem of Irish males in America, so they were not always considered to be reliable partners in marriage. A subtle disdain for members of the opposite sex had worked its way into Irish American society. As a result, good Irish mothers warned their eligible daughters to beware the pitfalls of marriage, especially *early* marriage to a "Johnny-come-lately-ne'er-do-well."[14]

Consequently, Barbara Gavin wanted her only daughter prepared for a career that would guarantee her a future of self-sufficiency, dignity, and financial security. Aware of her child's affinity for music, Barbara persuaded her to study and teach piano, voice, organ, and violin. With this goal in mind, the entire Gavin family worked and pooled its resources so that Della could be educated for a career in music. Until they could afford to buy her a piano, she practiced her lessons at the home of her music instructor, Miss Clegg. Later Della mused:

> I wonder how my poor mother and father could even get a piano in those days. It was quite a luxury [because] Dad was just a laborer. He didn't have any fancy job in those days. But Mother was rather persuasive and [she] figured it would be the only way she could keep me always close to her.[15]

Piano lessons were only the beginning, however, for Miss Clegg soon discovered in Della a wealth of musical talent. At the strong urgings of both teacher and mother, Della enrolled at the Wolfram College of Music Theory and Practice in downtown Cleveland. For the next few years she studied advanced musical theory and composition and learned the rudiments of teaching.

As a student teacher, she taught piano lessons at home to the neighborhood youngsters. When she graduated from Wolfram's at age nineteen, she weekly earned a dollar per lesson from each of her fifty students.

With the added income derived from Della's teaching now minimizing financial worries, the Gavins began to enjoy life in America. Barbara Gavin's well-executed plans for her daughter's career had unfolded on course.

Five years passed by with Della wholly immersed in music teaching and conventional but satisfying goals. Her accomplishments and excellence advanced the Gavins to a hard-earned middle-class status.

On the surface, Della's lifestyle befitted a properly raised young woman and spoke well of the virtues of education and hard work. An air of respectability attended her interests and activities; fierce parental pride, mostly maternal, directed her decisions and behavior. Soon enough, despite Barbara's strict control, Della's growing independence sought expression. A clash of wills resulted when Della's personal longings surfaced and conflicted with her mother's plans.

As a child, Della had often gone to pray at the nearby Shrine of St. Paul, where Franciscan nuns (Poor Clares) lived cloistered, contemplative lives. Della was attracted to the hidden choir of voices—heard but not seen—that arose from behind the massive main altar. Something of their mystery always lingered with her; secretly, she longed to join them.

Della confided her yearnings to her confessor, Father Burke. However, instinct warned him that the life of a contemplative nun was the wrong vocational choice for Della Gavin. Yet he could not deny that the young woman kneeling before him heard and felt something spiritual luring her. Having no clear sense of direction to offer, he advised her to pray and wait for signs of God's will.

When Della broached the subject of religious life with her mother, Barbara was stunned. Her own plans and sacrifices for Della's future had gone exceedingly well, surpassing even her own expectations. That Della might have different goals from her own was a possibility she had never entertained. The thought of her only daughter leaving home and career for the life of a nun chilled her heart. Accordingly, she took clever advantage of Father Burke's advice. In seeming deference to the priest's counsel, she instructed her troubled daughter to concentrate on her career, adding the assurance that "a true call from God would withstand the test of time."[16]

Barbara's attitude toward religious life was understandable, taken in the context of her own life. After all, she had carefully groomed Della for a profession that could be practiced from within the safe confines of the family parlor. There, Della worked under Barbara's watchful eye, safe from harm and insulated from the world around her. Unresolved grief over the earlier loss of a child had left Barbara with an obsessive need to protect and control her remaining daughter.

Settled into the orderly routine of her work, in 1909 Della took out a listing in the Cleveland directory as one of 560 music instructors in the area. Teaching consumed her professional life, and a limited but pleasant social life filled out her leisure hours. To pass the time, she frequented ice cream socials, attended Sunday vespers and church meetings, and took long strolls along the city's tree-lined streets. During the summer, outdoor operas and brass band concerts added pleasant diversion to her regimented activities.[17] Acquaintances from those days remembered that Della was much admired by her friends and peers. A Sister of Charity reminisced:

> It was during her early teens that we became acquainted. My sister and I became members of the Sodality, where Della was an active member. Frequent meetings at Church affairs brought us close together. When Della entered the convent no one was surprised, as she had always been a model young lady. She had been giving private lessons in music in her home for several years before becoming a religious.[18]

Vocation Crisis

Initially Della followed her mother's advice and made no decision about entering the convent. Life went on as usual. Her passion for music wholly consumed her. She worked hard for the sheer pleasure of working, developing little regard for the money she earned. Many times she labored long hours with her students and then forgot to collect her fees. Della was as dispassionate about money as she was impassioned about music. After a long day, Barbara often found dollars and coins absentmindedly tucked beneath tablecloths and lace doilies, forgotten as quickly as they had changed hands.

When piano lessons were finished, Della usually invited her young pupils into the family quarters for freshly baked cookies and steaming Irish tea. In the warm and fragrant kitchen, easy conversation and Irish laughter lifted the hearts of the neighborhood children. They shared their secret hopes and dreams freely with the gentle Gavin women. One student remembered young Miss Gavin the piano teacher as being "very beautiful, with a peaches-and-cream complexion and a beautiful smile." She was "a wonderful teacher, very exacting and efficient. You toed the mark with her."[19]

Just that hint of delicate Irish beauty brought Della to the attention of Cleveland's eligible young men. For a time, it seemed that music had indeed stifled her desire to be a nun. Talk of spiritual longings faded into the background of her busy, prosperous life. For her part, Barbara silently hoped that the matter of religious life would remain buried. Time passed, and life moved forward on an even course until, unexpectedly, the attentions of a male admirer brought new urgency into Della's world.

Little is known about the young man who courted her, aside from the fact that he was a successful Irish businessman who desperately wanted Della Gavin to be his wife. They kept company and even agreed to marry. Before a wedding could be planned, however, Della abruptly changed her mind and broke off the relationship. Apparently, when she faced the prospect of marriage, her unresolved calling to religious life resurfaced. Though she had sought answers from family, friends, faith, and religion while she struggled to determine a vocational direction, romance, oddly, was the catalyst that finally resolved her spiritual conflict and solidified her decision to become a nun.

Not surprisingly, many obstacles still tested her sincerity before she entered religious life. In a desperate effort to force her to reverse her decision, her wounded fiancé sent his brother, a Catholic priest, to intervene on his behalf. The priest ridiculed the young musician's choice of convent life and accused her of destroying his brother's life. The next obstacle surfaced when her brother, Pat, announced his betrothal to a neighbor girl, Anna McCarthy. With her only brother marrying and leaving home, the burden of care for the older Gavins fell squarely on Della, but the most trying problem facing Della was her mother. Barbara Gavin was inconsolable over her daughter's decision, having come to believe that Della's interest in a religious vocation had long ago vanished.

Della empathized with the strong feelings of her loved ones, knowing the hardships her choice would cause them. Nonetheless, it was time for her to mature, to determine her own needs and commitments, and to resolve the lingering conflict created by her indecision.

During her teaching years, her attempts to put convent thoughts aside and to content herself with life as it was unfolding yielded only temporary comfort. She had even considered the marriage proposal in an effort to conform to parental and societal expectations. Always, though, the yearning for commitment to a deeper love returned. It forced examination of the nagging question that would not leave her soul: Is God calling?

She returned to Father Burke for spiritual direction. She convinced him that her fervor for religious life was time tested and valid. Father Burke then offered serious concrete advice. This time her plan for entering the convent crystallized.

Della's sincerity and fidelity convinced the priest that her calling to religious life was, in fact, a true one. Still he remained opposed to her choice of a contemplative convent. He offered her a compromise instead that would permit her to answer her call yet remain accessible to both the growing needs of the Church and her elderly parents. Finally, Father Burke suggested that Della apply for admittance to the Sisters of Charity of Saint Augustine, an active religious order of women who cared for the sick and orphaned.

Della surrendered her goal of entering the cloister and accepted Father Burke's advice. On her next visit with him, they completed her formal application to enter the convent of the Sisters of Charity of Saint Augustine.

March 25, 1914, was the date appointed for Della's entrance to the order. She was then twenty-five years old and an accomplished musician. On the eve of her entrance, her family and friends gathered to say farewell:

> The night before she entered the convent many of her friends went to her home to say goodbye. It was impossible to get inside the door of her apartment because of the immense crowd that had come. Della stood at the door, dressed in a pretty blue summer dress, her cheeks like roses, and her brown curly hair framing her face. She greeted the newcomers and

said goodbye to those leaving, but the stream of people seemed endless. Many of the girls she knew in that parish followed her into the convent. Not that she tried to advise them: her example was enough.[20]

The next morning Della packed two black dresses, a cap and veil, a warm cape, and her bed linens into a small dark satchel.[21] Accompanied by her saddened but resigned parents, she left home at long last to become a nun.

While the transition to religious life required few material goods of the potential "bride of Christ," the ritual of leaving home and beginning a new life in some ways resembled traditional marriage customs. At the appointed hour, like parents of brides-to-be, Barbara and Patrick Gavin solemnly gave the sisters their daughter, replete with her dowry and the satchel containing all of her earthly goods. When they returned home that day, the sight of the huge piano in their front parlor reminded them of the space in their lives that Della had always filled.

Early Convent Life

Once in the convent, Della began a short-term probationary period called postulancy—a trial time in which she experienced and evaluated convent life. New postulants also learned community history and customs along with the apostolic opportunities that would become available to them as professed sisters. When she completed her postulancy in June, Della petitioned the community for permission to wear their official habit, enter noviceship, and receive a new name.

Her clothing ceremony began on June 16 with a procession of postulants carefully clothed in exquisite wedding gowns and veils sewn of handmade ivory lace. Amidst the chapel's plentiful flowers and soft candleglow, the setting created a stunning illusion of the material beauty Della relinquished for her symbolic betrothal to Jesus Christ. Rejoicing followed her solemn exchange of wedding gown for religious attire and the donning of a new name. The mother superior chose to call her Sister Ignatia, after a community pioneer named Sister Ignatius who had died in 1912.

As a new novice, Ignatia began a serious study of religious life. To guide her, the 1909 *Rule of Saint Augustine* outlined her rigorous daily schedule:

Chapter XXV

Daily Order of Hours and Exercises

1. The Sisters shall rise at 5:00 A.M. and twenty minutes after 5:00 all will assemble in the chapel for morning prayer and meditation, which will continue until 6:00. Little hours will then be said.

At 6:30 all will assist at the Holy Sacrifice of the Mass. Twenty minutes after Mass, breakfast.

At 11:45 the examination of conscience will be made.

At 12:00 dinner followed by recreation until 1:30 P.M.

At 1:30 recite Vespers and Compline.

At 5:00 Matins and Lauds will be said.

At 5:30 Meditation will be made until 6:00.

At 6:00 Supper.

At 7:15 recreation will begin and continue until 8:20 when all will assemble in the Chapel for night prayers and the points of meditation for the morning. Then all will retire so as to be in bed at 9:00, unless there be a real necessity, and a special permission obtained beforehand from the Mother Superior.[22]

Lastly, the evening observance of Grand Silence dropped a blanket of stillness over all community activities until after breakfast the following day.

The Rule of Saint Augustine governed the community and provided the monastic guidelines for daily living. A community code, the *Rule* unified members' attitudes, prayers, and behaviors while advancing the Great Commandment. The first page of Ignatia's *Rule* book said:

Chapter I
The Love of God and Neighbor

My Dear Sisters: Before all things love God and then your neighbour, for these are the principal Commandments which have been given to us.[23]

This was the theme that would develop Sister Ignatia's spirit as a nun. It also expressed the intended charisma of her community. The message espoused heroic charity that, on the one hand, fostered community spirit and, on the other, individualized the path to spiritual growth.

Like the other novices in her class, Ignatia memorized the *Rule* and meditated on its contents. In the novitiate years she struggled to master the practice of charity while harnessed to a rigid schedule. Before she took First Vows in June 1916, she was practiced in the rule of obedience to her superiors, she was versed in community prayers and worship, she carried her full share of the daily workload, and she suppressed her individuality to blend better with her sisters. However, Ignatia's assimilation into the group was a trying one. After all, Ignatia was a musician who had joined a community of nurses. Only her strong determination and deep desire to be a religious overcame the petty jealousies, irritations, and misunderstandings that commonly occurred within community life.

Not surprisingly, the sisters who lived with Ignatia in her early convent years described her as being like "a china doll,"[24] too flighty and fragile to master many of the regular convent chores. Nonetheless, in an effort to obey and conform, she scrubbed floors, washed, starched, and ironed cumbersome religious habits, and mastered bread baking in old-fashioned woodburning stoves. Ignatia struggled less to obey than to belong. Even her physical stature was visibly frail in contrast to that of most of the other women.

Nevertheless, those who knew Ignatia in the novitiate held her in high regard for the kind of woman religious that Sister Ignatia was becoming:

Sister Ignatia was a senior novice when I was a postulant and junior novice. She was always an example and inspiration. In those days, there was much manual labor, and although she had never done that kind of work, she did her full share always cheerfully, if not efficiently, and her genuine goodness always shined through. She could laugh at herself—a great grace! Later, I lived with her when she was beginning her apostolate with the A.A.s, and what has been said of her in the novitiate was true of her in later years. She was a great and holy nun, and must have been very dear to God. My loving thanks to her![25]

Her contemporaries' reflections reveal the fondness and admiration they felt for Ignatia. Deep respect is vivid in Sister J. Frances's thoughts too:

As I recall the life of Sister Ignatia I am always mindful of how prayerful, how charitable she always was to all who came in contact with her. As a novice she was so virtuous and always an example to the new ones entering the novitiate. [She was] not physically strong, yet she was always at her post of duty. Even the extra work, such as helping in the laundry on wash-days, Sister worked untiringly. Sister had charge of the altar bread room as a novice. When I was a postulant, she taught me how to bake. This was hard at first for me to learn with the type of stoves we had in those days. It was a problem to get the right heat to bake. Then Sister would call on our Blessed Mother to help. She was always so patient and kind; never did we hear a complaint or a murmur. Her memory is a benediction.[26]

Ignatia had a lifelong ability to win her companions' hearts. While this characteristic was inherently hers, religious life refined it.

Along the way many Jesuit spiritual directors made use of her unusual insights into the human personality and sought her help in their own conversion work. Sister Marie Estelle Kosick met Ignatia through

Jesuit Father Frederick Seidenburg, himself a pioneer of social work in the United States. Recalling their first meeting, she emphasized the deep impression Ignatia made on her:

> It was in Chicago, Illinois, where I lived in 1917 and 1918 that I first learned about the wonderful Sisters of Charity and Sister Ignatia. After Mass one morning, the Rev. Frederick Seidenburg, S.J., stopped to talk to me, and he wondered if I would be interested in becoming a nun.
>
> Eventually, he wrote a letter of introduction to Sister Ignatia, telling her that I was on my way to New York and would be stopping in Cleveland to see her. I did stop at the Saint Augustine Convent for two days. This was in 1918. Sister Irene, then assistant superior, introduced me to Sister Ignatia. She was a very busy music teacher but always most gracious and sweet. Perseveringly, Sister Ignatia sent letters to me in the following years. Finally, I made my decision to enter the convent in 1920.
>
> As a postulant, I was given violin lessons by Sister Ignatia. Later, she was my organ teacher, which made it possible for me to be the first organist at Parmadale when we moved there in 1925.
>
> Throughout the years, Sister Ignatia was always interested in my welfare. She had a great deal of confidence in me. She counseled and encouraged me.[27]

These were the years when Jesuits guided the spiritual life of the community, said Mass in the chapel, and conducted the sisters' annual retreats. Thus the basis of the community's spiritual development was rooted in *The Spiritual Exercises* of St. Ignatius of Loyola.

The *Exercises* taught Ignatia orderly methods of prayerfully integrating the body, mind, and spirit. Mastering them deepened the experience of prayer and enhanced the ability to discern God's will. Along with disciplines of prayer, meditation, fasting, and self-denial, a daily examination of conscience cleansed the spirit of guilt and opened the way for personal transformation. Thus, the soul, purged of self-will, was reborn for God's use. The hoped-for spiritual conversion inspired a life of action, motivated by love. Mottoes like "Love through action" helped transform spiritual qualities into charitable works. Ignatia took the *Exercises* to heart and attempted to grow according to the development they fostered. However, growth could be elusive in a convent regimented by time constraints and inflexible schedules. Consequently, to deepen her own spirituality, Ignatia sacrificed personal time to increase her devotional reading and meditation periods, often arising at three or four o'clock in the morning to pray.[28]

Work with the Orphaned

In the novitiate Ignatia also prepared for the work she would do as a professed sister. Life fell into routine until one day in early 1916 when the superior at St. Vincent Orphanage needed a musician for the children's annual St. Patrick's Day play. Eager to work with children again, Ignatia volunteered for the job.

A few months later, on June 28, Ignatia pronounced her first vows. Afterward, the community assigned Ignatia to teach music to the youngest boys at the orphanage, but the needy and unruly preschoolers soon got the better of her nerves. Bouts of insomnia troubled her, so the superior reassigned her to teach a fourth-grade class. The older boys were lively, energetic, and also unmanageable. She soon found that disciplining homeless youngsters was a more difficult task than she had first imagined. She would have to find a solution if she hoped to remain at the orphanage.

Luckily, she soon discovered that the bars and scales of music seemed to be the perfect antidote to calm aggressive childhood behavior. However, the orphanage had no piano and thus no means of implementing Ignatia's plan. Still, convinced of music's power to redirect the boys' interest from mischief to music, Ignatia sought the donation of a piano through friends and musicians she had known before entering the convent.

Her scheme worked. Chopin polonaises and Sousa marches restored classroom order and provided healthy outlets for youthful, pent-up energy. Sister Ignatia mesmerized the children by teaching them marching games set to music. By now, music was Ignatia's mode of expression; teaching it was her own creative way of relating the human condition to the divine. To Ignatia, an artist-nun, music assisted humankind's effort to find God.

The following March, with a trio of orphans at the piano and another trio playing violins, Ignatia orchestrated her first musical for the chaplain's feast day celebration on Saint Patrick's Day. Ignatia's pied-piper effect on the children attracted considerable notice. Soon, the mother superior summoned her back to the motherhouse and asked her to pioneer a private music school at St. Augustine's Convent in Lakewood, the first of its kind in Cleveland.[29]

The Music School's Growth

Within a few years of the music school's opening, Ignatia's popularity as a music teacher peaked as it had before she entered the convent. Forty to fifty students again filled her workdays every week. Because an academy of music pioneered by a Catholic sister was an institutional novelty, parents from all over Cleveland enrolled their children for instructions.

For example, Ted and Gerry Van de Motter traveled across town every Saturday for their music lessons. The children's aunt, Sister Germaine Dworning, had often told their mother, Anna, of Sister Ignatia's music school. Germaine's own knowledge of Ignatia's skillful teaching was firsthand. The two nuns had become good friends while working together at St. Vincent Orphanage, where Sister Germaine taught art to many of Sister Ignatia's music students.

Recalling their music lessons with Sister Ignatia, Ted spoke fondly of the days when he and his older sister, Gerry, "hopped the streetcar" on Saturday mornings en route to the West Side music studio:

> Those were the days! Sister Ignatia was a tough teacher, and there were no shenanigans during our lessons. I had to practice my violin, or I'd really get in trouble. I remember one time she compared me to Gerry and said, "Ted, your sister had a wonderful lesson because *she practiced!*" I was mad because

I'd practiced every day that week, and Gerry hadn't practiced
once. So I winked at my sister, and we both burst out laugh-
ing. All of a sudden, Sister Ignatia's book hit the floor, hard.
We could never put anything over on Sister Ignatia. And if
we tried, we always got caught. But the really funny thing
was this: Gerry always had better lessons when she didn't
practice.[30]

Children like the Van de Motters spread the school's reputation
across the Greater Cleveland area. Meanwhile, Ignatia's schedule
swelled to meet her growing fame.

The Troubled Twenties

The initial joy in teaching music during Ignatia's early years of convent life soon turned sour as changes in her professional and personal
life left Ignatia feeling overwhelmed and distressed.

The 1920s proved to be a turbulent decade for her. Up until that
time, music and religious life had nourished her spirit and sustained
her fundamental needs. With seeming ease and abundant energy,
Ignatia had accomplished two major goals by the age of thirty-two:
She pronounced her final vows, becoming a professed nun, and pioneered an innovative, thriving music school for children.

With these achievements securely behind her, Ignatia fast approached a time of critical testing that would challenge the fiber of
her faith and nearly deplete her physical, mental, and spiritual sta-
mina. By early 1927, the self-assured musician would be admitted to
St. John's Hospital—near death—suffering from bleeding ulcers, paralyzed arms, and total exhaustion.

At the time, God no doubt seemed heavy-handed when testing
her with trials. But Ignatia could not then know that divine goals for
her life encompassed far more than she could accomplish through
music. Only years later would she realize that God interrupted the
course of her life, ever so slowly drawing her back to himself. However, in 1921 the struggling nun had no inkling of a greater destiny.
Confused and bewildered, she accepted her suffering. Crisis after

crisis drove her to the outer limits of human endurance. As God tinkered with her heart, Ignatia slipped into the unknown depths of powerlessness and isolation.

Along the paths to her breakdown many warnings surfaced. Ignatia once alluded to this time of darkness in her life—"I entered the order in March 1914. It was wonderful for about seven years"[31] and thereby pointed to 1921 as the beginning of her hardships. Thus 1921 marks a turning point, a year that offers clues to her coming crisis, and a year that changed the outcome of her life—and history too. What had prompted so much upheaval?

Conflict Arises from Diocesan Changes

One obvious source of Ignatia's troubles grew from the naming of Joseph Schrembs as Cleveland's bishop in 1921. In general, his episcopacy created problems for many of the Sisters of Charity of Saint Augustine. In particular, because Sister Ignatia functioned as the community's musician, he focused much of his irascible temper on her interpretation of liturgical music, which differed from his own. A number of historically based reasons support their mutual antagonisms.

Early in the twentieth century, Pope St. Pius X issued new guidelines for the Church's ceremonial use of Gregorian chant. Translations of the papal decree from Latin to English were slow to reach the United States. Adaptations for common use in Church rituals were complicated arrangements for liturgists to learn, much less teach to others.

Cleveland's new German bishop considered himself a musical scholar, even a connoisseur of the new chants. However, unlike diocesan musicians, Schrembs favored an unpopular interpretation of the new music, one not commonly accepted or implemented by American Church musicians—among them, Sister Ignatia. As a result of their differing opinions, she encountered severe criticism of her musical abilities for the first time in her career. Anxiety built as obedience to the bishop chafed against her freedom of artistic expression and professional expertise.

The reason for Ignatia's discomfort was obvious enough. Before

Schrembs became bishop, she had mastered the American Church's widely accepted chants and rubrics. Also behind her were the tedious, grueling hours spent in teaching the new directives to the community:

> In 1920, Sister Ignatia taught the postulants and novices church music according to the directives of Pope Pius X. Sister was dynamic in her teaching and spared not herself to communicate the "new" Gregorian Chant. She was not impatient with us, as she realized that this was different and she repeated the same phrases over and over until it really registered. Then she taught piano up until 8:00 P.M., earning money for the community.[32]

Serious difficulties arose when the bishop voiced his displeasure with the French school's use of a *quilisme,* a timing pause favored by Ignatia and most American liturgists.[33] Differing with the bishop was a risky prospect, because he was perceived by many Clevelanders as a booming-voiced, relentless prelate who demanded absolute perfection from everyone. The new bishop—German and autocratic—was outspoken, stubborn, and difficult to please.

Whenever he visited the convent, the atmosphere grew tense and strained. Often, Ignatia, because she was the musician, bore the brunt of his wrath. One Sister of Charity recalled a typical episode:

> I believe it was 1922. I was a novice and there was a Clothing at St. Vincent Orphanage [postulants appeared as brides and left wearing the habit of the community]. To my way of thinking, the singing was beautiful. After the ceremony, the novitiate and Sister Ignatia were summoned to the professed community room where we all met the late Archbishop Joseph Schrembs.
>
> There must have been two schools of Gregorian Chant. Evidently, Sister Ignatia's choice did not please the Archbishop, who raised his voice (as only he could) and lashed into the group. Silence reigned supreme. Then Sister Jane

Frances (Lord rest her soul) came in all smiles and greeted the bishop.

"I suppose you were one of the singers," he asked.

"Yes, Bishop, wasn't it beautiful?" she said.

Oh, you can appreciate his reaction! Poor Sister Jane Frances filled Lake Erie with her copious tears, which fell the rest of the day.[34]

Chant, however, was not the only source of stress surfacing in Ignatia's life. That same year the Sisters of Charity of Saint Augustine resurrected a twice-abandoned plan to open a small boarding school on the grounds of the Lakewood motherhouse to instruct and house young women who intended to join their community.[35] The timing of this project strangely coincided with another urgent diocesan problem that Schrembs had inherited from his predecessor, Bishop James Farrelly.

During the last two years of Farrelly's episcopacy, diocesan officials had puzzled over the spiritual problems of an adolescent named Sarah who lived on Cleveland's East Side. After conducting endless studies and examinations of the girl, they reluctantly agreed that Sarah was obsessed (a lesser form of possession) by the devil. That is to say, the young woman was visibly tormented by an invisible source of power and evil—one capable of hurling heavy objects at priests who entered her room and boiling vials of holy water carried in their coat pockets.[36]

Devout Catholics, particularly those of Irish descent, feared the presence of this reported evil that thrashed about their diocese wherever Sarah went. Ignatia's parents belonged to Sarah's parish—St. Philomena's—and heard weekly recountings of diabolical events that were preached by the Irish pastor, Father Malloy. A mood of hysteria threatened to erupt as stories of Sarah's demon circulated in the diocese.

Local parish priests performed a simple rite of exorcism—a ritualistic driving out of demons—then celebrated a Mass in her home. However, Sarah's evil spirit demonstrated fierce strength and resistance to their prayers. In the course of events that followed, two attending priests suffered nervous breakdowns and had to be sent away for prolonged rest.[37]

The bishop ordered another exorcism. This time Anthony Wilwerding, a Jesuit priest, officiated. Wilwerding himself was an ascetic classical language teacher who assisted with weekend duties at St. Philomena's. He was also one of Cleveland's most highly respected spiritual directors. Teamed with Dr. John Merrick, the bishop's personal physician, Wilwerding conducted another exorcism, this time in the perceived safety of St. John's Hospital—a West Side facility that Ignatia's community owned and operated.[38]

Afterward, with the exorcism presumed successful, Wilwerding sent Sarah to live at the Sisters of St. Joseph's boarding school. As a safeguard against further attacks by the devil, Wilwerding gave Sarah his sacred stole, advising her to keep it with her always. However, despite his strongest efforts, Sarah's difficulties did not subside.

Records at St. Joseph's Academy indicate that Sarah resided there only briefly between September and December 1920. During that period she never left her bed. The Sisters of St. Joseph kept constant vigil at her bedside. Sister Agnes Therese, who often monitored Sarah, explained the tension-filled atmosphere:

> Everything was kept hushed. Sarah was in bed. We were talking, and she suddenly began to go into contortions. As a young sister, I knew stories of her background. I was terrified, and I prayed harder than I've ever prayed before. Afterwards, she had no recollection of anything that had happened.[39]

As more stories of Sarah circulated, hysteria threatened to disrupt the convent and boarding school's atmosphere. For the well-being of the nuns and students, Sarah had to leave, despite the fact that she was still suffering and, apparently, still obsessed.

Wilwerding held out hope that new surroundings would quell Sarah's demon. Next, he sent her to live with an aunt in Lakewood, but her condition still defied improvement. Perplexed, he sought the counsel of Father James J. Stewart, the pastor of St. Rose's Church. Like Wilwerding, Stewart was a spiritual man who was thought to have a saintly ability to heal the hopelessly sick.[40] For the next few months, as the two priests struggled to silence her obsessive and persistent demon, they alternated Sarah's residence between hospitals and the homes of willing relatives.[41]

It was during this period (1921) that Schrembs became bishop, and the Sisters of Charity of Saint Augustine opened a boarding school on the grounds of their Lakewood motherhouse for high school-aged girls who wanted to become nuns.[42] Sarah was among the first students enrolled, though it is unclear whether her admission was voluntary, arranged by Wilwerding, or declared mandatory by Schrembs. Whatever the case, the superiors met the controversial young woman's presence with a strong measure of caution. Unlike the other boarding students, Sarah was housed in a private suite of rooms, isolated from the other students and nuns.[43] A departure from community rules and customs, this was a condition seemingly set by the superior in advance of Sarah's enrollment.

Then, to forestall any possibility of further controversy, Bishop Schrembs imposed a decree of perpetual silence on the congregation regarding Sarah's presence at their convent and her rumored obsession with the devil.[44] Life proceeded normally enough that year for Sarah to complete high school and then immediately enter the Charity nun's convent. But whether she was then free of her obsession remains uncertain and clearly debatable.[45]

The truth is that Sarah was so well hidden by the bishop and so well protected by the community that little documentation of her case exists.[46] However, those still living who remember Sarah recall many conflicting scenarios. Most witnesses affirm that her obsessions were ongoing throughout the 1920s, occurring even after she entered the convent. Still others declare that Sarah's case was closed long before the convent accepted her as a candidate. But that her first vows were delayed and then repeated twice before she was professed suggests that some concern over her suitability for convent life did indeed exist. Whatever the case, knowledge of her difficulties with the devil trailed her throughout life, creating fear and stigmatizing her well beyond any known recurrences. Irrational fear of Sarah surfaced many years later when the pastor of a school where she taught refused to enter her classroom because she had previously been associated with the devil.[47]

Obviously, at the time of these events, there was reason to protect her privacy. As a result, only a few facts about Sarah can be agreed upon by most accounts, and they bear significant relationship to Sister Ignatia's deteriorating health. Sarah, too, was a musically gifted woman; her musical abilities brought her into direct contact with Ignatia's work; and Sarah was undeniably the subject of more than one diocesan-ordered exorcism—a fact that made many people shy away from her in fear.

Whether ill fated or ordained by God, circumstances forced a relationship between the two musicians. The music school had grown rapidly, soon creating a huge workload for Ignatia. To ease the strain, the superior ordered novices who had musical training to assist Ignatia with the beginning students—this despite a rule that did not permit novices and professed sisters to associate with one another.[48] Sarah was perhaps the most talented of the novices recruited to teach with Ignatia. Her presence, however, combined with Ignatia's personal turmoil, added to a growing tension experienced by some, but not all, who lived at Saint Augustine's convent.

Father John Brady, who functioned as the sisters' chaplain during these years, recalled the early 1920s as very trying days at Saint Augustine's. In 1922 Brady lived in a large brick residence that also housed the music school. His private suite of rooms was one floor above the studio where Ignatia and her helpers worked. As eyewitness to the times in question, Brady emphasized that the knowledge of Sarah's obsession with the devil had a rebound effect on her associates and "made us all very nervous."[49]

Brady described both women similarly, saying that they were Irish, sensitive, prayerful, and dedicated. However, the atmosphere became so tense that in 1925 Bishop James McFadden, then chancellor of the Cleveland diocese, went to live with Father Brady. Soon he himself experienced the loud nightly clamorings that surrounded the residence.[50]

One easily got the sense that wherever Sarah was, the devil was not far behind. Living and working amidst such tension frightened people, and someone like Ignatia was inordinately sensitive by nature and easily susceptible to the power of suggestion.

Ignatia's Personal Problems Escalate

The year 1922 brought no relief to Ignatia's increasing anxieties. In addition to referring Sarah to the Sisters of Charity of Saint Augustine that year, Schrembs unfolded new plans for the diocese that included a major expansion of the diocesan school system. However, to move his agenda forward, Schrembs needed teachers.

In a plucky move, he added primary and secondary teaching responsibilities to the community's existing mission to serve the sick and orphaned. Though the sisters agreed to cooperate with his order, their transition to teaching did not come about easily:

> In 1922, Bishop Schrembs formally proposed that the congregation take up teaching in the schools. It was decided that several sisters who had teaching experience be recalled to St. Vincent's Orphanage, where there was a well-organized school patterned after the diocesan school system and under the supervision of the diocesan superintendent of schools. Those preparing to teach were to be required to take courses at the various colleges and universities in the city and elsewhere. Many sacrifices were required of these sisters who added studies to an already full schedule of duties.[51]

Because Ignatia already had considerable teaching experience to her credit, the community recruited her for the new teaching mission. However, the new assignment added reeducation and retraining to her already burdened schedule. Before long she joined the other student teachers for classes at St. Vincent, all the while juggling her primary responsibilities back at the music studio with the training program at the orphanage. Merely to infer that these were busy times for Ignatia grossly understates the reality. Often, she spent the night at the orphanage, too exhausted to travel back to the Lakewood convent.

As if the busy teacher's nerves were not already strained beyond a

reasonable limit, late one night at the orphanage's convent, an intruder forced his way into the cloister where she slept. Perhaps sensing something out of the ordinary, or just because she was a light
sleeper, Ignatia awakened suddenly to find him poised above her,
clutching a towel-like cloth in his hands. Her terrified screams brought
help immediately, though not soon enough to apprehend the man.
Near her bed lay a chloroform-soaked rag, ominous evidence of the
seriousness of the intruder's intentions. With the evidence at hand,
authorities speculated that the assailant had indeed intended to attack
Ignatia physically or perhaps even abduct her.[52]

Word of the break-in sped through the convent's grapevine amidst
rumors that Ignatia had recognized her assailant and identified him
as her former suitor.[53] The rumors troubled and humiliated her, caus-
ing her gradually to withdraw from the view of her peers.

It takes neither a vivid imagination nor much knowledge of human
psychology to envision the atmosphere of a women's cloister defiled
by a male intruder in the early 1920s. The grave repercussions of
such an act can be measured by the Church's pronouncement of ex-
communication for any Catholic violating the private, sacred space of
women religious.[54] Unfortunately, the punitive focus concentrated almost entirely on doling out consequences for the transgressor. Little
attention was paid to the victims of violence or to their need for compassion and healing. Thus, victimized by the intruder, the pursuant
gossip, and the religious atmosphere in which she lived, Ignatia suffered needlessly as she struggled to dispel the frightening memory
from her mind and recover from the shock. For a long while afterward, two sisters accompanied Ignatia wherever she went. A community rule requiring a sister companion for all activities outside the
convent walls, which was rarely observed, was again strictly enforced.

When she worked in the music school, novices were sent to be
with her. When she traveled to the orphanage, two sisters rode on the
streetcar with her. It was an anguished, frightening time for Ignatia.
She kept her own counsel regarding her feelings and made no public
attempt to discuss the incident with her peers. She kept her deepest
feelings within herself, removed from the view and speculation of the
community. Besides the shock, the humiliation she endured was se-

vere, for it is said that some of the sisters secretly whispered that Ignatia, by virtue of her charm and beauty, had invited the attack herself. The pain of such judgments was almost more than she could endure. To survive, she prayed more than ever and abandoned herself to her work. But a pattern emerged whereby Ignatia slowly detached herself from community affairs and established herself as an individual who communed with God, her superior, her parents, and her work. For all intents and purposes, Ignatia coped with her emotional pain by increasing all of her other activities.

Sleeplessness again returned. Along with the usual insomnia came a loss of appetite and a near compulsion for severe fasting and self-mortification. Her harsh personal habits added a new burden of stress to reeducation, the growth of the music school, the worrisome problems of the troubled young boarding student (now a novice sent to help her), and the anxiety induced by the new bishop's criticism of her music.

Ignatia's life reached a dangerous crescendo. The more she attempted to contain it, the more frenetic her pace became. It was soon obvious to the other nuns that "Ignatia was never the same after the man broke into her quarters."[55]

In 1923 all of Ignatia's problems escalated in intensity. That year the Sisters of Charity of Saint Augustine, now trained for education, accepted teaching assignments at schools in Cleveland, Ashtabula, and Cuyahoga Falls—all great distances from one another. Although transportation methods were vastly improving by the early 1920s, travel remained a trying ordeal. Ignatia's anxiety level rose accordingly. Bone-tiring weariness consumed her as the constant demands of teaching, travel, and overnight journeys burned away her energy.

Final Days as a Musician

During the summer of 1924 the Sisters of Charity of Saint Augustine sent ten of their nuns, including Sister Ignatia, to summer school at the University of Notre Dame in South Bend, Indiana. At the end of the summer term, nine of the sisters returned to Cleveland.[56]

Though community records are sparse, it appears that Ignatia remained in South Bend after attending the university or, equally possible, she went to nearby Rome City, where a well-known sanitarium administered by old-world German nuns provided rest and recuperation to people suffering from nervous disorders.[57]

Whichever the case, by the summer of 1925, in June or August (community records cite both dates), the University of Notre Dame awarded Ignatia a bachelor of arts degree in music. At the same time, she also earned special certificates in piano, voice, organ, and violin. After graduating, she returned to Cleveland and again resided at the Lakewood motherhouse.

Nuns living with her at the time remembered thirty-six-year-old Ignatia as a visibly tense, high-strung woman. She often appeared to be distracted and preoccupied with personal matters that, for some reason, she was not inclined to discuss. Some of her peers observed that she worked even harder than before, prayed more intensely, and still took very little nourishment at meals:

> When I was at Saint Augustine's, Sister Ignatia would come into the infirmary, where I was working and wring her hands and ask for a cup of tea. I'd think, "If she would just be more natural and not wring her hands." But it was her nervous condition.[58]

Further signs of Ignatia's growing fragility became glaringly evident during rehearsals for the music school's annual recital that year. Once again she devoted many hours of her time to demanding practices, often projecting her own feelings of stress and anxiety onto everyone around her.

Sister Beatrice Brennan, then a novice, assisted Sister Ignatia at the music school that year. Her recollection of a long-ago rehearsal for the annual recital reveals elements of a quick temper, perfection, hypersensitivity, and loss of control surfacing in Ignatia's behavior:

> I think music's a terrible strain on a person. When you'd strike a note on the organ that was wrong, she'd nearly die. I mean, that was because she was so sensitive . . . oh yes, very

sensitive. I got to know her because she wasn't very well. I was a novice and she was professed. She'd been to Notre Dame, gotten her degree, and had given her recital when they decided she needed some help. She had a lot of beginners, so any of us who had had a bit of music were sent to help. Novices and professed sisters didn't mingle in those days. So the only time I saw her was when I taught for her. She was always in the studio when we helped out. The piano recitals were the worst. She demanded perfection, and the children weren't always well disciplined. She had a temper where music was concerned! If the practice wasn't going well, she'd stand on the stage, crack a book on the floor, and shout, "I want everyone to stop this minute."[59]

With another successful recital behind her, Ignatia resumed her regular teaching schedule, with one exception. A new assignment awaited her that momentarily at least renewed her vigor and enthusiasm. In September 1925 the community had closed St. Vincent Orphanage, moving all the children to Parmadale Children's Village, their new child care facility in southwest rural Cleveland. Ignatia spent her weekends there, again teaching music to the orphans. At Parmadale her strong pioneering spirit momentarily resurfaced. During the 1925–26 academic year, she created a musical legacy enjoyed by many future generations of Cleveland children when she organized the first children's orchestra in Ohio. Thereafter, schools across the state imitated the model band, adding another enduring accomplishment to Ignatia's musical legacy. For Ignatia and the Sisters of Charity, the band signaled a major achievement in the history of their developing education ministry that would long be remembered in Ohio.

With a portion of her former zest replenished by the children's orchestra, Ignatia mastered one more professional challenge before Providence recast her future. This time, the mother superior charged her with all of the musical and liturgical preparations for the community's diamond jubilee celebration in 1926. Her final musical assignment was made in response to Bishop Schrembs's command that the congregation celebrate their founding with a lavish, spectacular liturgy at St. John's Cathedral. The letter that the bishop issued to Mother Brigid Gribben read in part:

> It is my wish, therefore, that on Saturday morning, September 25th, at nine-thirty, the Diamond Jubilee of the coming of the Sisters of Charity of Saint Augustine to the Diocese of Cleveland be solemnly commemorated by a Pontifical High Mass of Thanksgiving at the Cathedral Church at which all your sisters will attend and to which you will invite the sister-communities of the Diocese to share the joy of your labors and your fruits in the spirit of sisterly love.[60]

Under ordinary circumstances, planning the music for a community anniversary would have elicited a sense of reverence for Ignatia—even a proud moment of personal and professional satisfaction. However, the wound of Schrembs's displeasure with her musical performance had been slow to heal. Its sting rankled and cut into the depths of her weary being, casting renewed self-doubt and insecurity over her professional capabilities. Combined with all the other pressures and recent crises in her life, the jubilee added one more source of conflict to the exhausted woman's life. Thus, with stoical resolve, Ignatia labored rather mercilessly over strenuous, repetitious choir practices, all the while ignoring the glaring signs of tension then building inside her. When the great day came that September, the sacred music flowed effortlessly, or so it seemed to those who had gathered for the celebration.

Ignatia's success at the jubilee Mass was not without its price, however. Summer had passed, and along with it went her opportunity for a much-needed rest from teaching. By October the seasonal planning for Advent and Christmas pageants at the convent, the schools, and Parmadale were under way but already behind schedule because of the jubilee preparations. Other worries added to her exhaustion too. In November, Father Wilwerding—the priest who had personally and spiritually supported Ignatia's troubled associate, Sarah (now a teacher at Parmadale)—passed away. His doctors attributed his death by stroke to years of harsh fasting and penance resulting from his work as Sarah's exorcist. With Wilwerding's death, an unspoken tension resurfaced as those who, like Ignatia, had been peripherally involved with Sarah's tragic problems feared their recurrence. Such suspicions may have been well founded, because some reports indicate that a few months after Wilwerding's death, Sarah indeed returned to St. John's Hospital victimized once more by her former problems. Ignatia riveted her attention on her work, prayer, and harsh fasting, becoming ever more exhausted in the process. Sister Beatrice Brennan recalled:

> She was a frail person, very frail. I can remember the superior saying, "That Sister Ignatia is just working too hard." Mother Mechtildes was very fond of her. Mother used to save a little steak or something nourishing for Ignatia, because she knew she was fasting, and she had a bad stomach. All of her life, Ignatia was somewhat frail.[61]

Ignatia's hold on life was weakening day by day. Then, shortly after the 1926 holiday season ended, the inevitable occurred. Like Wilwerding (and possibly Sarah) before her, Sister Ignatia collapsed. The functions of her body, mind, and spirit succumbed to many years of abuse and abruptly came to a standstill. Exhaustion voraciously consumed her.

Death Courts Ignatia

When the sisters finally rushed Ignatia to St. John's Hospital in early February 1927, her arms were paralyzed and her stomach festered with bleeding ulcers—critical symptoms for a woman of only thirty-eight. No mention was made regarding her mental condition; however, her physical symptoms were severe enough to warrant the speculation that she was mentally and emotionally depleted as well. Nuns at the Saint Augustine motherhouse believed that Ignatia was terminally ill:

> There's a lot to be told about . . . when she got sick that year. We expected her to die; she was so weak. So we disposed of her possessions—her veil, her habit, everything. When she

got well, she had nothing to wear. We decided to dispose of everything, quickly, because we felt certain that Ignatia wasn't ever coming back. There was a satchel of personal letters and mementos in the music studio, and we burned that. She was that ill.[62]

The only known record of Sister Ignatia's illness is her own testament, tape-recorded and transcribed by Bill Wilson and preserved in the New York archives of Alcoholics Anonymous. In 1954, she vaguely described her illness to AA's cofounder as "a sort of nervous breakdown; nerves of the stomach, and paralysis of the arms."[63]

Unyielding stress from 1921 onward, harsh fasting, and sleeplessness no doubt accounted for Ignatia's bleeding ulcers. However, no physiological conditions are known to explain her paralysis—a disconcerting symptom for a musician-pianist-organist whose ability to perform her art relied on the use of her arms.

Modern psychiatry can only attempt to interpret her symptoms and thereby impose a speculative clinical diagnosis on her grave illness. Thus, based on the few facts available for examination, Ignatia appears to have suffered from a classic conversion reaction, known in her times as hysteria. This illness can arise in obsessive-compulsive personality types following lengthy, unremitting periods of stress and anxiety.[64] Ignatia surely displayed such character traits and by then had endured long periods of nervous tension.

Inasmuch as Ignatia likely felt mired in helplessness and thus powerless to change her circumstances, a conversion reaction may have permitted her to exchange emotional paralysis for physical symptoms that would stop her problems for her. Emotional immobilization easily led to physical immobilization too. Interestingly, blindness, loss of sensation, and paralysis represent the common physical symptoms that emerge as partners to conversion reactions.[65] It is possible that Ignatia, so weakened, unconsciously averted her deepest inner feelings by permitting physical trauma to disguise her more deeply injured soul.

That bleeding ulcers also complicated her medical diagnosis suggests that physiological deterioration did indeed result in part from sleep and food deprivation. But situational, community-related factors were also involved in her breakdown.

In the Catholic religion of the 1920s, a long code of *never*s dominated the conduct of nuns. Nuns were expected to never complain, never say no, never disobey, and never think of themselves. Although these seemed to be worthy goals to strive toward, over time the directives often became exaggerated in actual practice. Unremitting service, obedience, and conformity to a literal, intellectually limited interpretation of the *Rule,* rather than to its intended *spirit,* often spelled disaster when they were used to measure a woman's holiness, commitment, and worth. For sensitive and creative types of women, community preoccupation with the literal practice of the *Rule,* rather than concentration on its deeper spiritual meaning, often frustrated, undermined, and stifled personal and spiritual growth.

Stimulated by the fact of Ignatia's physical and emotional complications—ulcers, anxiety, isolation, fear, and hysteria—a question comes to mind: Was a spiritual upheaval contributing to her breakdown too? It seems so. In hindsight, the mystery surrounding her later recovery suggests that something of the mystical applied to her illness as well. And in view of her later impact on the lives of millions of compulsive drinkers, examining her breakdown as a wholly physical or psychological event omits reference to the probable role of Providence both in her misfortunes and in her being healed from them.

Since Ignatia seemed destined to live for a purpose higher than one she could then envision, and since heroic, extraordinary people discover new opportunities for love from their own human suffering, what event better than a breakdown would provide the impetus for her dramatic change in direction? Why would God inflict Ignatia with a debilitating breakdown that totally incapacitated the musical talent essential to her life's work? And lacking divine intervention, why would Ignatia deliberately choose to journey down a darkened, solitary path if the course she was pursuing in 1927 fulfilled her and accomplished God's will for her life?

The answers seem precisely why Providence suddenly struck Ignatia: to redirect her course of action; to rechannel her creative drive and energy; to refine and purify her spiritual path; to reintegrate her physical, mental, and spiritual natures; to teach her the power gained by letting go of self; and to open her heart in preparation for a new direction. Thus a total breakdown for Ignatia might be better likened to an illuminating *breakthrough* that finally allowed truth and a living vision of the will of God to reawaken and quicken her spirit.

Surrender Brings Recovery

One of the most instrumental people ever to influence Ignatia's life was a physician named Frank Doran.[66] When Ignatia was admitted to St. John's Hospital, Doran came to her aid and saved her life. However, Frank Doran was not an ordinary physician by anyone's standards. In addition to being a skilled diagnostician and internist, Dr. Doran was an excellent psychologist, well versed in psychiatric illnesses and their remedies.[67] Accordingly, he augmented his interest in psychiatric medicine (not then a bona fide medical specialty) with his early memberships in the American Society of Medical Psychiatry and the American Society of Clinical Hypnosis. Doran's progressive intervention, which likely included his special skill in hypnosis, helped Ignatia identify and release some of the internal pressures that might well have been overlooked by a physician trained in the science of physical medicine alone. With the help of a few sisters who had been schooled in psychiatric nursing the previous year, Doran began a systematic treatment imposed to reverse the effects of Sister Ignatia's breakdown.

While the broken nun balanced precariously between life and death, Doran dealt first with the immediate physical emergency posed by Ignatia's bleeding ulcers. When that threat had passed, he faced the more difficult task of preventing a recurrence of the hemorrhaging. To do so, he addressed the underlying tensions that had aggravated her physical condition, straightforwardly telling Ignatia that recovery from her breakdown required her complete cooperation and the willingness to examine her life and habits. Then she would have to remedy them, one by one. Healing would come faster, he told her, if she would do as she was told and not resist the changes required of her for good health. Hopeful of recovery, she trusted both his medical judgment and his wholistic approach, accepting her Irish doctor's challenge to learn how to live again. The long healing process slowly began once she wholeheartedly gave herself up to the care of the strong, compassionate doctor.

Starting with the basics, Doran advised Ignatia that to begin correcting her problems, she must establish a healthy order to everyday life. Together, they reassessed her personal habits. Wellness demanded that she eat regular nourishing meals and add many extra hours of rest or, better yet, sleep to her day. A new lifestyle had to replace the ingrained harmful habits that had robbed her of the physical strength needed to cope with her other anxieties and even her deeper spiritual needs. To restore balance to her life, Ignatia would need to learn how to practice prudence, accept her own limitations, and better integrate her personal needs with her community responsibilities.

Next, psychological restoration required Ignatia to review her compulsion for overworking and her strong need for perfection—characteristics often linked to a deeper fear of failure. Through use of the hypnotic state—a deep relaxation of the body and mind—Ignatia and Doran began healing the emotional scars that contributed to her illness. Gradually, she let go of the deep fear and shock that had immobilized her during Sarah's ongoing attacks and the break-in at the orphanage. Her troubles with Bishop Schrembs, her obsessive career demands, and her belief that willpower alone could overcome anything—all slowly dissipated.

Convalescence afforded Ignatia the time and opportunity to spiritually renourish herself too. In the protective atmosphere of the hospital and its comforting chapel, she redefined her spiritual values, this time honestly integrating the physical realities of her life as well. She balanced prayer, self-examination, meditation, and the comfort of spiritual readings against the physical and psychological realities of her life. Ignatia no doubt stood on hard testing ground as in midlife she exchanged her youthful idealism, vigor, and obsessive compliance with meaningless rules for a mature and realistic relationship with God.

Sensation and movement soon returned to her arms. Six months later, the worst of her crisis had passed, and quiet reintegration into the mainstream of life began for her. Ignatia was released from the hospital but continued her therapy while living at the hospital's convent. For the next year, Dr. Doran prescribed simple jobs at the hospital, partly for occupational therapy and partly to keep the fragile nun from becoming discouraged over her slow though steady progress.

Fortunately, Ignatia was a model patient. She followed Dr. Doran's well-planned treatment regimen to the letter, but the extent of the changes required of her were not evident until well into the second year of her convalescence. Although she had made steady progress in her recovery, the complexity of Ignatia's breakdown troubled Dr. Doran, as did the strong possibility of her having a relapse. To date, the tough but frail nun had done everything he had suggested. He reasoned that she sincerely wanted to get well and that she had strong, caring people supporting her. After all, many of the sisters prayed and compassionately tended to her every need. Even her elderly parents had uprooted themselves from their East Side home, rented an apartment across the street from the hospital, and made themselves available to their daughter whenever she needed them.

Still, the depth, severity, and totality of Ignatia's sickness convinced the worried physician that a total lifestyle change would offer Ignatia the only chance for a lasting recovery. Perhaps even nudged by a whisper from Providence, one day late in the summer of 1928, Frank Doran posed a history-changing question to Ignatia: "You can either be a live nun or a dead musician. Which will it be?"[68]

With great difficulty, but even greater faith and courage, Sister Ignatia surrendered her music, her career, her identity, and her entire will first to Dr. Doran, next to the Divine Physician:

> Hold up your limp arms, steady your trembling knees, . . . the injured limbs will not be wrenched, but will grow strong again.
>
> Heb. 12:12–13

Then the miracle happened. Total surrender freed Ignatia and transformed her life. The healing graces of a second birth strengthened her spirit and opened her wide to be used for God's divine purpose.

Three

Spiritual Connections

In the total mystery of creation all the parts connect, even apparent opposites, as in the orchestration of a symphony. In searching for God, man, as a musician with a distinct theme, is drawn into the silence of his mystery to find the beginning note that will for him connect all the measures of his search.[1]

—Father Samuel R. Ciccolini
Founder, Interval Brotherhood Home
Akron, Ohio

The stockbroker from New York and the physician from Akron collaborated on methods of evangelizing and then coercing alcoholics to join their society. Meanwhile, Sister Ignatia, their non-alcoholic counterpart, worked in the wings of AA's first hospital.

Before 1939, like Bill and Bob, Sister Ignatia had sought effective ways to reach the pain of suffering people. The darkness of her own breakdown, now long past, awakened her to compassion for the broken. Her career in music had also found rest within the context of her transformed life.

By the time Smith sought her help, many of Ignatia's insights into wellness had paralleled Bill's and Bob's. All three, after all, had survived major life reversals, personal humiliation, illnesses, and spiritual storms. As in the cases of the two men, Ignatia's surrender to her own collapse had precipitated acceptance, but wholeheartedly extending herself to others guaranteed her recovery. God had demonstrated in a forceful way that his will for Ignatia's life was far stronger than her own.

Almost miraculously Bob, and then Bill after him, discovered Sister

Ignatia. Dr. Bob had opportunely studied her spiritual bearings and exemplary traits at the hospital. Soon enough, their first notes of friendship would grow into an enduring relationship of service to others. Inasmuch as both had found immeasurable strength from crippling weaknesses, the ex-alcoholic and the ex-musician embarked on AA's journey together.

Bill Wilson later declared that it was "a divine conspiracy" when AA's triangle of founders and figures met and merged their needs. Of that time he wrote:

> Never before or since those early Akron days have we witnessed a more perfect synthesis of all these healing forces. Dr. Bob exemplified both medicine and AA; Ignatia and the Sisters of Charity of Saint Augustine also practiced applied medicine; and their practice was supremely well animated by the wonderful spirit of their Community. A more perfect blending of Grace and talent cannot be imagined.[2]

The Hospital's Viewpoint

Though many hospitals occasionally accepted alcoholic patients prior to AA's inception, most did so rarely and only under duress. Institutions providing alcohol-related medical care concerned themselves mostly with patients in severe medical distress due to DTs, alcoholic psychosis, pancreatitis, cirrhosis of the liver, and other medical emergencies. Some facilities even provided emergency drying-out beds for seriously intoxicated patients. Rehabilitation services and successful methods for disrupting the obsessive drinking patterns of the common dipsomaniac did not yet exist, however. Caregivers resigned themselves to their inability to reform compulsive drinkers, leaving such hopeless work to Bible-toting evangelists in city-mission soup kitchens, proprietors of local flophouses, or law enforcement officials in the city jails.

Indeed, hospitals had numerous reasons for denying admission to alcoholics. One prime consideration—habitual relapse—characterized alcoholic sickness. Like the chronic sufferers of tuberculosis prior to the discovery of antibiotics, alcoholics who required medical care soon became chronic hospital patients who seldom recovered. Though doctors knew little about diagnosing or treating alcoholism, they recognized the self-perpetuating pattern of alcoholic illness at once. Just as quickly, they discovered that alcoholics sought hospital care only as a last resort when they felt too sick to drink. Also discouraging was that when some alcoholics felt better, they left the hospital and drank until they became sick again. Thus, bouts of alcoholic drinking led to bouts of drying out; bouts of drying out then led to renewed bouts of drinking. Even so, some hospitals admitted a few trial patients, naively gambling that a *sober* alcoholic's willpower would override the compulsion to drink.

By the late 1930s and the early 1940s, Ohio's Akron City Hospital, Just-A-Mere-Home (later called the Green Cross Hospital), Evangelical Lutheran-Deaconess Hospital, East Cleveland Clinic, St. Vincent Charity Hospital, and St. Thomas Hospital had been tapped for beds by the earliest AA pioneers.[3] In many cases, these hospitals listened to newly sober AA members and tried to support their patients. However, when the alcoholics could not pay their bills and repeatedly broke their promises to do so, hospitals made economically based decisions regarding the use of their very limited bed space. Needless to say, hospital officials felt justified in reserving beds for revenue-producing patients who suffered from so-called legitimate diseases and illnesses. Alcoholism was not construed as such. Rather, it was viewed as a self-induced condition, attributable to weakness or moral failure. Most agreed that the treatment of such a malady had no place in modern, growing medical facilities.

A Last Plea for Help

These were some of the dilemmas plaguing Dr. Bob on August 16, 1939, when he timidly approached Sister Ignatia with an earnest plea for a bed. He gambled on her sympathy because so many of the new AAs had held him spellbound with stories of her kindness toward them during their hardest-drinking days. Many had awakened from alcoholic stupors to find that Sister Ignatia had hidden them for a few hours in the corridors and closets of St. Thomas Hospital, where she nursed them through drunken escapades and allowed them to sleep off their demons. Thus Smith knew well of Ignatia's longtime sympathy for alcoholics. He hoped against hope that he could entice her into becoming an advocate for AA at Akron's Catholic hospital. When he walked into the admitting office, the deeply disillusioned doctor felt he had entered the court of last resort.

Even so, his visit with Ignatia went better than he had expected. A lengthy conversation revealed that each had independently procured part of the solution to the serious problem of alcoholism: Ignatia had the hospital beds, and Smith had the successful curative medicine of AA. Together, they could fully address the problem. From Ignatia's perspective, Smith's scheme for doctoring alcoholics answered her own frustrated prayers. Had she not groped for ways to transform problem drinkers into respectable members of society for the last five years? Although she had the vision, compassion, and good sense to come to the aid of such unfortunates, she had not yet determined the full formula for success in helping them recover. Smith appeared to have answers and a plan for treating inebriates, so his strong plea for beds roused her interest.

But what astounded Ignatia as she listened to Smith was the curious fact that this doctor embraced a *spiritual* approach to restore the health of alcoholics. She recognized this fact when he spoke of the alcoholic's need for unconditional surrender to a powerful, vital life force, a God of his or her own choosing—one who could replace the fear and emptiness left by alcohol. Smith said he could not fully explain the steps to sobriety, because they involved spiritual forces over which neither he nor the alcoholic had any control. He told Ignatia that he had repeatedly witnessed that once an alcoholic admitted his or her problem and surrendered alcohol and its accompanying unmanagability wholly to God, a seeming conversion occurred. Often this was extraordinarily dramatic in its effect on the alcoholic's entire lifestyle and mental outlook. Gone were alcoholic denial, guilt, and remorse—the useless emotions that froze alcoholics in their own revealing symptoms. In place of these wasting emotions stood acceptance, honesty, and willingness to change.

Proud egos, humbled by their own powerlessness, collapsed and became teachable.

It was at this point that the kinship of those who experienced similar hopelessness supported the floundering alcoholic and taught him or her the Twelve Steps to freedom. The support of other recovering people at the outset of sobriety was crucial to the healing. Their willingness to share and relate to others with the same problem marked the difference between whether the alcoholic isolated himself or herself and fell again or opened himself or herself to the endless opportunities for the growth and maturity offered by sobriety and fellowship. Then, when physically and mentally strong enough, the new convert would help the next alcoholic. All that stood in the way of the miracle was the dry alcoholic's choice to believe that God and others could and would help, if he or she let them.

From Smith's testimony that day, Ignatia grasped the dynamics of alcoholism. A peculiar demanding thirst filled alcoholics one moment and then emptied them of all values the next. In the life of the alcoholic, drinking diminished reason, sanity, responsibility, and God. The liquid anesthesia drowned loneliness and eased emotional pain, but in doing so, like a mercurial devil, alcohol took final possession of its victim's body, mind, and soul.

Perhaps Ignatia's thoughts momentarily traveled back to 1927, when her own humiliating illness had seemed hopeless. Recovery had occurred slowly with the help of a dedicated physician, hospital treatment, caring friends, a loving God, and a great deal of time. Was the physical paralysis of a musician's arms really much different from the numbing, deadening effects of alcohol on the human spirit? Were bleeding ulcers so different from bleeding hearts?

Ignatia's recollection of encounters with Sarah proved a case in point. Sarah had also been entangled in a morass of problems brought about by a disturbing obsession by a demon spirit. It seemed that whatever the cause of nervous breakdowns, demonic obsessions, or addictions, the end result was the same. A broken human spirit and loss of dignity could be mended only by spiritual intervention, sometimes provided freely by God, and other times, intuitively, by people who cared, who knew, who had been there too.

The Practical Side

These were just some of the problems that surfaced when Dr. Bob approached Sister Ignatia in 1939. By then Ignatia knew the administrative workings of the hospital and the ins and outs of admissions. Listening to the doctor, she realized that over the years, AA had haphazardly snatched hospital beds whenever and wherever they could be found. The AAs had no plan, no expertise, no knowledge of how to work within the system to achieve their needs. It was apparent to her that their quick reactions to alcoholic emergencies had blinded them to the possibility of finding a permanent solution to the hospitalization problem.

Understanding and then empathizing with the doctor's distress, she admitted Dr. Bob's patient. However, as part of the hospital's administrative staff, she also brought the situation a new perspective—she was acutely aware that only practical solutions would forestall future curtailment of alcohol admissions in any great numbers.

After giving the matter some thought, Ignatia remembered that at Cleveland's Charity Hospital, Sister Isabel secretly admitted alcoholic priests to private rooms.[4] Isabel had been drying priests out, sobering them up, and hiding them from their bishops for many years. Ignatia coupled this knowledge with Dr. Bob's AA Steps and envisioned a treatment program that could reach all alcoholics. She made her practical decision to approach alcoholism as a treatable disease worthy of hospital care.

At great personal risk, the savvy nun initially protected Dr. Bob and his patients from medical higher-ups in much the same way that Sister Isabel protected priests from their bishops. However, Ignatia's situation differed in one remarkable way. The priests went to Sister Isabel in scattered numbers, but Dr. Bob's patients appeared at Sister Ignatia's admitting office with demanding regularity. Later they returned to her as sober men bringing other alcoholics who needed hospitalization too.

Trial and error, more than administrative guidelines or treatment plans, taught Ignatia to admit the men two at a time into double rooms. Then they and their visitors could counsel and console one another privately without disturbing other hospital patients. However, she also had a practical reason for grouping alcoholic patients together. Usually the partnership helped the men to quiet each other's fears, thus preventing their discovery by the none-too-sympathetic nursing staff. In this way, the treatment of alcoholism had an official but small beginning at St. Thomas Hospital during the late summer of 1939. In a letter to Bill Wilson, Ignatia described this period:

> We coasted along very slowly from that time on. First of all, because AA was rather closely connected to the Oxford Movement [Group] and we did not care to become involved with a [religious] sect of some kind. Secondly, we had our trials and tribulations with the patients we did admit, partly because of the inexperience of personnel; even resentment of some towards intoxicated patients. Fortunately, as I was in the Admitting Office, and Dr. Bob was on our staff, I, personally, put them in under varied diagnoses, such as medical observation, nervous breakdown, or if they had a black eye, I would use "possible head injury," etc. I would place them in different parts of the house, sometimes on one floor and then another. I feared that admitting too many of them in one spot would bring about open rebellion and probably interfere with the work.[5]

Once Sister Ignatia saw alcoholics recovering under AA's program, she prepared to make alcoholism treatment an official service of the hospital. But in the early fall of 1939, just as her work with the AAs was getting under way, another personal crisis collided with her plans and threatened to delay the program's progress.

Family Sorrow Tests Resolve

For the past twenty-five years, Ignatia had honored her preconvent promise to care for her aging parents. Furthermore, the family became even closer following her own illness. Though the Gavins were advancing in years by the time Sister Ignatia moved to Akron, they left Cleveland to join her. Living in a rooming house close to St. Thomas Hospital, her father worked as the hospital's gardener; between recurring bouts of illness, Barbara Gavin mended sheets and gowns in the sisters' sewing room.

Throughout the years, the Gavins maintained close family ties. Perhaps because they were such a small, tightly knit family, when one member suffered, all suffered together. Ignatia had only one nephew—Raymond—who died unexpectedly sometime during 1939 when he was only twenty years old.

Later in the year, tragedy struck the family again. Pat Gavin had been vulnerable to upper respiratory ailments throughout his lifetime. In the early fall of 1939, he suffered an attack of acute pneumonia. Death came swiftly on October 8, less than two months after Ignatia began her work with AA. The deaths, in the same year, of both the oldest and the youngest members of the family greatly challenged the faith and stability of all the Gavins.

Fortunately, the lessons of life had already taught Ignatia to overcome crippling emotions by trusting in God, helping others, and immersing herself in constructive work. The outcome of the AA mission no doubt benefited from Ignatia's exhaustive emotional energy and intense grief. Thus, while lamenting her losses, she abandoned herself into the midst—and confusion—of the fledgling alcoholism treatment endeavor. And deeply sympathetic, Dr. Bob and the AAs helped the easily shattered nun grieve and eased her through the crisis.

In a philosophical sense, endings often precipitate new beginnings. Accordingly, Pat Gavin's death provided the impetus for an important step forward in his emotionally fragile daughter's life. Indeed, in the throes of deep sorrow, Ignatia might have turned away from her difficult, uncertain mission. Facing the painful aftermath of death offered Ignatia a God-provided pause, one last chance to walk away from AA's challenge. Instead, she chose to embrace it.

AA Work Becomes Official

Back at her hospital station soon after her father's funeral, Sister Ignatia immersed herself in the workings of Alcoholics Anonymous and studied alcohol admission protocol in depth. Knowing that medical authorities did not consider alcoholism to be a disease, Ignatia saw a real danger. St. Thomas Hospital had no obligation or commitment to regularly serve a population that generally could not pay for the clinical care of a nonillness. For this reason, administrative officials were able to justify the exclusion of alcoholics from their policy statements and charters. Thus, the rights of alcoholics to receive quality medical care went not only unrecognized but also unprotected. Reflecting on those days, Sister Ignatia told Bill Wilson:

> Hospitals did not usually admit alcoholics as such, rather only if they had been in an accident or suffered from some serious illness. If they were admitted, they would often develop *delirium tremens* because doctors treated them for what they considered their major illness, sometimes overlooking the fact that they were also alcoholics who needed tapering off.[6]

Sister Ignatia told Dr. Bob that somehow hospitalizing alcoholics had to be made a matter of regular admitting policy. The only solution for AA lay beyond secretly pirating hospital beds wherever and whenever possible. Ignatia's practical and farsighted wisdom changed the course of AA by demanding that medical assistance be guaranteed for alcoholics who needed and wanted to recover from their sickness.

A few months later on a cold November day, Ignatia and Smith agreed to seek a permanent base of operation at St. Thomas Hospital. First, however, an important obstacle had to be overcome: They needed the hospital's permission to continue their present work. Her official capacity as admitting officer convinced Sister Ignatia that the only way to stop the hospital from refusing admission to alcoholic patients was to approach administration with an honest statement of the alcoholics' needs, proof of Dr. Bob's successful treatment methods, and a well-developed operational plan. Knowing of the administration's financial concerns, Ignatia shrewdly suggested a plan by which the recovering men agreed to finance one another's care.

Before they could approach administration, though, Ignatia and Smith had another area of potential conflict to resolve. Because St.

Thomas was a Catholic hospital, some clarification was needed on
AA's affiliation with organized religions—namely, the Oxford Group.
Perhaps the hope and opportunity of establishing a recovery haven in
a Catholic hospital was exactly the impetus Dr. Bob needed finally
to consent to AA's formal split from the religiously suspect Oxford
Group. Thus, once the alcoholics separated their meetings from the
Oxford Group (November 1939) and convened at King's School (January 1940), formal clarification of AA versus religion was achieved. To
make certain that no further questions remained to confuse AA's
spiritual message with religion, Ignatia sought the counsel of a
nearby priest:

> Alcoholics Anonymous was not well known. But we were
> ready then to try a few [alcoholics] here and there. So it was
> then that I thought that I'd better make definite plans and
> check into the movement a bit before I went into it to any ex-
> tent. For that reason, I asked a little priest [Rev. Vincent P.
> Haas] in a neighboring parish near King's School if he would
> stop over there [King's School] some evening and listen in on
> the meeting. As you know, at that time they were closely al-
> lied with the Oxford movement [Group] and I was quite fear-
> ful . . . [that] I would be called on the carpet for getting mixed
> up, somehow. Although we were nonsectarian and it didn't
> matter what denomination people were, it still seemed to me
> that one had to put a certain personal effort into this if any-
> thing was to be accomplished. Father Haas was impressed
> and predicted that if they carried on as they were planning,
> Alcoholics Anonymous would probably become one of the
> greatest movements of our age in attempting the conquest of
> alcoholism.[7]

Father Haas observed the AA meeting for Sister Ignatia, if perhaps
for no other reason than to humor the worried nun. To his own surprise, the depth of the fellowship's nonsectarian approach to living
awed him. He returned to Ignatia and confirmed that AA was indeed a
unique spiritual movement toward recovery from alcoholism. Not

only did AA achieve the stated objective of sobriety, but also it respected people of all religions and excluded none. Catholics, Protestants, Jews, and agnostics gathered under one spiritual umbrella—AA—and yet continued to live according to their individual religious beliefs.

Father Haas's affirmation of AA's universal spirit was the ammunition that Sister Ignatia needed to plead their case with her superior. Soon after, she arranged a meeting with Dr. Bob, a few selected AA members, and Sister M. Clementine, the hospital administrator. Ignatia and Smith confessed to Sister Clementine that they had been secretly treating alcoholics at the hospital and then introduced their recovering addicts as sober citizens, proof of the success of their fledgling program. Sister Ignatia's recollection of that momentous conference confirmed the first major victory for Dr. Bob and the AAs:

> She [Sister Clementine] was in favor of setting up a definite hospital program for the care of these patients. I recall one remark the Reverend Mother made to the members of the committee: "There was a time in years gone by when alcoholics were a great trial to us. We worried lest they jump out of a window, or get in some other serious trouble. Today, under this treatment, things have changed. Evidently, Dr. Smith knows how to take care of these patients."[8]

Next, with Sister Clementine's hard-won respect, influence, and permission supporting them, the small band of AA advocates sought and received official approval for their proposed alcoholism policies from both the hospital trustees and the local diocesan authorities. To everyone's relief, permission to treat alcoholics as legitimate hospital admissions was granted, and *St. Thomas Hospital became the first religious institution in history to officially adopt a permanent policy that recognized the rights of alcoholics to receive hospital treatment.* The combined medical care and AA indoctrination pioneered by Sister Ignatia remains the hallmark of respected alcoholism treatment programs today.

Wasting no time, they organized their unpretentious methods of care into simple hospital procedures that permitted them to carry on their work while maintaining the program's integrity. Ignatia later reminded Bill Wilson:

> It was not until, probably, January, 1940 that a definite working agreement was achieved with the knowledge of my superior, Sister Clementine, Dr. Bob, and probably, the Chief of Staff. Had we proposed it to the whole staff, at that time, you may be sure that we could not have gotten a foothold. In fact, it is quite difficult to convince staff members, even today, of the necessity of hospital care for these patients.[9]

Admitting Office: The Key to Power

At first Ignatia kept news of the newly approved program well guarded. Though she and the AAs felt victorious over winning their initial encounter with the administration, Ignatia correctly deduced that if word of the hospital's agreement to provide hospital beds for alcoholics became entangled in grapevine gossip, adverse professional and public sentiment would crush the fragile plan before it could emerge. To protect the first alcoholic patients from premature discovery, she made brilliant use of her singular source of worldly power: the admitting office.

As she updated the daily census, the resolute nun transferred regular admissions freely, thus creating space for Dr. Bob's patients as needed. Practically speaking, a small measure of patient sobriety allowed her some added flexibility in making room assignments. If necessary, Ignatia could then admit alcoholics anywhere in the hospital with little fear of detection by unsympathetic staff members.

Sobriety as an early criterion for admission served another function: It permitted the unobstructed charting of medically acceptable diagnoses such as avitaminosis, gastritis, or amnesia to mask the unacceptable primary problem of alcoholism. Even so, she defined sobriety loosely for admitting purposes. Affirmative answers to questions such as "Can he stand up by himself? Can he speak coherently? Can he write his name?" usually satisfied Ignatia's requirements.

Though Ignatia and Smith used common sense and some flexibility when defining the sobriety standard for their admissions, the two were far more rigid when they assessed their patient's spiritual state. It is in this primary regard for the alcoholic's spiritual well-being that the work of this pioneering hospital team has never truly been duplicated. Thus, they always examined their patient's motivation for receiving treatment.

Both Sister Ignatia and Dr. Bob required that alcoholics who sought admission to the hospital also exhibit their intent to stop drinking and change. The toughest test for admission came when they asked the patient whether he wanted their entire program of sobriety. Their standard admitting policy relied on making the key distinction between needing the program and wanting it.[10]

The two hospital pioneers measured the answer with strict criteria—for the good of the patient as well as the program. Besides preventing people from developing a habit of repeat admissions and setting a bad example for patients who wanted sobriety, they could not afford, practically speaking, to waste scarce hospital beds on alcoholics who were not committed to long-term sobriety. Ignatia referred relief-seekers who only wanted what she called "defrosting" to local "jitter-joints" and rest homes for drying out.

So simple as to be artful, the clever nun created a twofold plan: First, restore sobriety and, second, learn a new way of life without drinking. There were therapeutic reasons for admitting relatively sober, stable patients too. Less intoxication meant more patient awareness of the treatment opportunity, and it assured a better chance to prepare himself for the somewhat extreme life changes that sobriety demanded. On the practical side, boisterous, screaming inebriates drew attention to themselves and jeopardized continuation of the effort.

Preadmission Assessment Guidelines

To foster a high level of patient care and a successful outcome of treatment, Ignatia collected preadmission data that weeded out insincere candidates from highly motivated ones. Thus, to be accepted, first the patient had to demonstrate the *need* for help with his or her drinking. The drinker's passage from normal, social drinking habits was easily determined by unpredictable, compulsive patterns. Compulsion and unmanagability were the glaring signs of addictive drinking. But three other guidelines hinted that the patient had crossed that imaginary line of control from social to problem drinking: if patients drank long after they knew they had had enough; if drinking controlled their life socially, economically, and morally; and if they became powerless over alcohol in any quantity or circumstance.[11]

Second, Ignatia and Dr. Bob required that the patient *want* the program. They determined this by interviewing the patients themselves or through a preadmission screening done by a practicing member of Alcoholics Anonymous. Interviewers sought "evidence of the patient's sincerity of purpose to get alcohol out of his life on a permanent basis." Those seeking physical relief or protection from angry family members, employers, friends, or civil authorities certainly demonstrated evidence of a problem; however, these were superficial circumstances and did not constitute proof of one's "sincerity of purpose."[12]

In cases where individuals needed hospitalization for the physical effects of their drinking but did not want the sobriety offered by the program, the hospital treated only the immediate, life-threatening complications of the disease. Ignatia confined such temporary relief-seekers to another area of the hospital, where they could not adversely affect recovering alcoholics who were learning the AA program.

Admission to the alcoholism ward was a serious decision made in concert with the patient, the sponsor, and the admitting clerk. The standing rule allowed only one admission per patient. Occasionally, an overly zealous sponsor tried to readmit a person whose first treatment had been unsuccessful. In these instances, and especially if names had been falsified to disguise a previous admission, Ignatia transferred the patient from the AA ward to a medical division and denied further sponsoring privileges to anyone who had acted deceptively.[13] There was always a lesson to be learned from Sister Ignatia. She held the AAs wholly accountable for their actions and thus taught them valuable lessons in personal responsibility. Thus, the integrity of both program and patients was preserved.

Even so, rare exceptions to the stringent policies occurred. Sister Ignatia herself sometimes overlooked a previous admission. Second admissions reflected her own difficulty in rejecting human suffering. Now and then, frustrated sponsors and family members criticized her procedures because they did not yet grasp the dangers inherent in trying to rescue an unmotivated alcoholic from his or her misery. Even Sister Ignatia had to learn through experience that when alcoholics manipulated others into pitying and taking care of them, they won the war to keep on drinking. That is why most often Ignatia wisely permitted no exceptions to the admitting rule. AAs learned that they had better not ask the determined nun for help unless they wanted help!

From time to time, Ignatia encountered unusual situations requiring a different approach. For instance, some individuals wanted the AA program but did not really need it. Occasionally people confused drunkenness with alcoholism, frequently overreacting to an isolated episode of intoxication or a frightening, alcohol-related incident. Others had emotional disturbances and feigned alcoholism to gain attention. In such cases, the deciding factor for admission rested on the compulsiveness of the drinking pattern as determined in the preadmission interview. Lastly, wives or other concerned persons sought admission for spouses and loved ones who, despite some convincing facts, were not yet ready to emancipate themselves from drinking.[14] Cases like these did not meet the admission standards and were respectfully told so. Nevertheless, all requests for help demanded an assessment of the problem, explanation of the policy, and compassionate recommendations for appropriate help.

Triple Effects, Triple Treatment

With the advent of Alcoholics Anonymous, Ignatia found hope for treating alcoholism and acknowledged new concepts about the illness. She witnessed alcohol's triple effects on the body, mind, and soul. The results of drinking were easily assessed by the alcoholic's

inability to control either the amount of spirits consumed or the de-
structive consequences that often followed. The exacting nun also
gauged the seriousness of the triple illness by contrasting the desired
outcome of drinking (escape, relaxation, avoidance of problems, relief
of boredom and loneliness) with the actual results of intoxication
(anxiety, physical illness, broken marriages, job loss, insanity, incar-
ceration, and despair). Comparing the momentary effect of drinking
with the actual outcome of drunkenness provided a forceful tool of persuasion for convincing the alcoholic of his or her addiction.

"What did you expect alcohol to do for you?" she might ask a resistant patient. And he might answer, "I was having trouble on the job,
Sister. Times are tough, and lots of the boys are getting laid off."

"You were worried about losing your job, so you drank for three
days to forget about it? Well that makes sense. Now you don't have a
job to worry about. You were fired for not showing up! See what your
drinking bought you?" Methods like that confronted reality and drove
home the insanity of alcoholic drinking.

Before long, the popularity of both AA and the St. Thomas Hospital
program necessitated Ignatia's frequent reminder to the public that
there was no known cure for alcoholism. So that their program would
not be misconstrued as such, Ignatia formalized the hospital's original policy and procedure guidelines:

> Because the alcoholic is a man (woman) sick in mind, soul,
> and body, it follows that only a program aimed in these three
> directions can hope for success. The *treatment* at St. Thomas
> aims to do this, as the following lines will help to make clear.
> Since the first humble beginnings, over six thousand men
> have taken the *treatment* (Emphatically, it is not a cure; at this
> writing, there is no cure.) which aims to do two things, pri-
> marily: one, to clear up the worst physical symptoms of
> drunkenness; and two, to indoctrinate the patient in the prin-
> ciples of the AA program.[15]

Her constant reinforcement of the fact that alcoholism could be
treated but not cured began the later custom among AAs of referring

to the hospitalization portion of the recovery process as "treatment." Today *treatment* is a widely utilized term that identifies the institutionally managed phase of recovery. However, the term itself came about accidentally, when Ignatia saw the need to dispel the myth of a cure. Old-time AA members remembered scenarios occurring somewhat like this:

> "Sister Ignatia, my friend needs to take the cure."
> "Oh? Well, there is no cure. We simply take these men and treat them."
> "Well, then my friend needs to take the *treatment*."

Ignatia's great success with Alcoholics Anonymous only increased with each passing day. It seems logical to assume that eventually operating the alcoholism ward would become her full-time assignment. However, this never happened. For thirteen years, Ignatia tended to AA activities during her spare time, all the while maintaining her official position as the chief registrar. It is likely that at some point, administration offered to relieve her of the admitting office duties. Ignatia was both pragmatic and tenacious, however. She held fast to her power, since there would likely be no available beds for AA if she relinquished her control of the hospital census. How did she manage it? Only careful planning bolstered by her enthusiastic spirit created the time she needed to develop the alcoholism ward's policies and procedures, tend to its operation, and oversee the admitting office.

Nonetheless, it is astonishing that interspersed with all of her activities, this reputedly fragile nun designed and implemented an alcoholism ward that became the model of most twentieth-century, hospital-based alcoholism programs thereafter. She initiated treatment customs at St. Thomas Hospital in the late 1930s and early 1940s that emulators enthusiastically carried across the country, convinced that her model was the only AA hospital program that worked.

However, Ignatia's administrative style was hardly flawless. A serious shortcoming that continuously haunted her career was her failure to see that adequate and systematic fee collecting was necessary for good business practices. Whether she was naive, charitable, or both, she often ignored financial responsibility in favor of getting the program running and the work done. Indeed, her natural distaste for fiscal matters caused her superiors much concern.

Fortunately, hospital costs were low—fifteen dollars per day for a bed and five dollars for each doctor's visit.[16] Thus, in spite of her obvious dislike for financial concerns, Ignatia established a payment plan that covered the normal five-day stay.

Meeting the Cost of Recovery

Ignatia's newly designed, official ward policy called for payment of 50 percent of the estimated charges at admission, with the balance due at discharge. On paper the policy looked good. However, Ignatia made exceptions so frequently that the ward was often thousands of dollars in arrears to the Sisters of Charity of Saint Augustine. The sisters, in turn, absorbed AA's debts to keep the ward open. The advent of hospital insurance helped defray costs to some degree, for Ignatia stressed to the carriers that according to her policy, the treatment of alcoholism was a one-time expense. Even so, in the early days of treatment, most patients had not yet acquired medical insurance. But those who had acquired it had already lost it due to their drinking. Shrewdly, she wrote an exception into her own reimbursement policy, making it acceptable to collect cognovit notes—IOUs, in effect—for "special cases."[17] The hospital administrator sent acid reminders to her that a drawer full of cognovit notes held no market value to the hospital's creditors.

When indignant AA sponsors questioned the hospital's financial demands, Ignatia was sympathetic and accepted the promise of payment at a later date. But unpaid bills mounted quickly from this practice and threatened the stability of the entire operation. A partial solution to the problem came from the AAs. Grateful former patients who had been unable to pay for their own care assumed financial responsibility to repay a new person's debt. Unfortunately, however, not even the generous reciprocity of recovered patients could always relieve the ward's financial strain. Sometimes even the sponsors created problems by refusing to respect the hospital's need for payment, then directed their anger at Ignatia. In response, she wrote into AA policy:

> To the indignant sponsor who demands to know why sobriety is to be denied to a poor man, it can be responded that there simply is no such thing as an unpaid hospital bill; the goods and services which the bill represents must be paid by someone or they cannot be extended to the next patient. Sometimes a request that the sponsor, if he is a reputable citizen, cosign a cognovit note with his patient will do much to impress the realities of life on sponsors who sometimes wish to make generous gestures with someone else's money.[18]

Occasionally, Bill Wilson organized fund-raising dinners to help defray the costs of treatment, and Sister Ignatia could always confide the ward's financial problems to reliable friends. Within hours of sharing her woes, the AAs raised enough cash to ease her administrative pressures. For that reason, the AAs and administration often exasperated one another. The alcoholics had difficulty understanding the administration's stance on fiscal realities, and the administration was equally frustrated by the AAs' swift ability to pay their debts when the ward's stability was threatened. Hospital authorities, still ill-informed about alcoholism, wondered why sobriety did not effect a quick return to financial responsibility. The oversimplified answer from Ignatia was that all that sobriety begot was sobriety; it took *time* for newly sobered AAs to discover their character defects and change. Fortunately, the sisters usually understood and forgave the alcoholics. The AAs, immersed in the newness of being sober and caring for one another, never realized the problems caused by their procrastination.

The Preadmission Interview

Assuming that no difficulties arose while securing financial accountability for the new patient, the admission procedure followed a well-practiced pattern. However, the process differed from traditional hospital practices in one very significant way.

Unlike every other hospital department, the AA ward did not accept patients referred by physicians. AA sponsors—never doctors— brought alcoholic patients to the hospital when they required inpatient care. And just as doctors provided diagnostic information to the regular admitting office, AA sponsors supplied Dr. Bob and Sister Ignatia with their patient's preadmission data. Along with both the patient and the sponsor, Ignatia assessed the information for clues to the patient's physical condition, emotional state, motivation for sobriety, previous alcohol-related confinements, and spiritual or religious disposition. Then came the most important questions, "Do you *want* to be here?" and, "Why do you think *you* deserve one of these beds?"[19]

Though seemingly harsh, such screening tactics were essential because hospital beds for all patients were scarce. Dr. Bob and Sister Ignatia adamantly agreed that the ward could not waste valuable beds and time on individuals who did not want to stop drinking. Nor could they appease well-meaning family members or friends who sought detoxification for alcoholics who themselves were uninterested in sobriety. Admission requests made by someone other than the sponsor were routinely handled by informing the petitioner that only an AA sponsor could refer patients to the ward. Now very much a lost practice, this early technique of immediately and thoroughly involving the sponsor in the patient's care drove home the message that hospitalization itself would not arrest alcoholism. Only daily contact with the sponsor and the AA program ensured the alcoholic's chances for recovery. Without those AA links, St. Thomas Hospital would not accept alcoholics for treatment.

Next, Ignatia informed patients of the ward's rules, briefed them on the conduct she expected, and clarified their rights and responsibilities as AA patients. A senior patient on the ward, whom she traditionally called "the Mayor," took charge of the new admission immediately. The Mayor introduced the new patient to the rest of the patients, who oriented the individual to the ward.

First, the copatients took the person to the shower room, where they exchanged the individual's street clothes for hospital attire.

Then they escorted the patient to an empty bed, pushed it against the wall, and raised the opposite siderail to prevent him from falling out if he got the shakes. Meanwhile, others wrote the person's name on a board kept beside the ward's main door to thus inform the doctor and other hospital personnel that the alcoholism ward had received a new patient! Following this, the Mayor logged the individual's and the sponsor's name in a large record book so that all AA visitors would have the opportunity to find and indoctrinate the newest patient. In a last admitting function, the Mayor delivered the patient's chart to the nurse in charge. There was nothing sophisticated or complex about their effective methods. With only a few staff members to rely on, the patients took care of one another. The story of Pat R. illustrates this process and provides an insight to an Akron patient's recollection of "taking the cure" and meeting Sister Ignatia:

> I was taken into St. Thomas Hospital, sober. I was very sick and shaking. In those days they had a straight chair in there on the other side of the door. My first thought was, "I've got to get out of here as soon as possible." I had my children with my mother and they were ready to probate me. I told Sister Ignatia that I had to make a living, and she told me that I'd so far made a mess! In a very insistent way, she told me, "We are not going to worry about making a living, we're going to worry about why you are here." Then the Mayor and a couple of the boys in pajamas got my bed and my clothes. In came the nurse. She gave me a quick checkup, and in came the doctor. Sister Ignatia was there the whole time. The doctor said, "Bring him a drink," and I said, "I don't want a drink, I'm in here to *stop* drinking." My sponsor was standing there and he told them I didn't want a drink, either. But Sister Ignatia said, "This is the doctor, Pat. You do as he asks, please. I want you to take it." So this doctor said, "You let me be the doctor. Do as we ask you to do, and you'll walk out of here in five or six days able to eat and sleep again." I drank the "St. Thomas Cocktail"—a mixture of alcohol and an awful-smelling sedative [paraldehyde]. So then they put me back in

bed, gave me a couple of shots in the arm, and another one in the hip. It was a big needle, and I didn't care for that one, but I think they deliberately gave it to let you know who was running the show. Anyway, it was the first time I had stretched out in over a week, and boy, did that feel good!

The only thing that worried me was that I didn't think I'd make it. I knew in my heart that everyone would make it but me. There was a priest in there at the time, Father X.; they put him in a monastery down in New Mexico, but he got kicked out of the priesthood and busted over again. Sister Ignatia said to him, "This bird, Pat's got a bad problem. He's agnostic, I think. Maybe you could help him." And he did. They had a long table in the room where we ate, and then a couple of smaller tables in the hallway. And Father X. would say, "Why don't you and I eat there?" So, he talked to me about God. And he did have one thing to say to me that I bought. He said, "You know, whether you believe in God or a Higher Power, He would help you for the asking. You'll never know unless you try. You can't lose. When you go to bed tonight, just ask Him for the sake of asking. If you want, pull the covers over your head, and thank God for the day; you've been under the weather, you've had three meals, and you haven't had a drink. Ask Him if He'd help you tomorrow." The next day he said, "Did you do it?"

"Yeah."

"Do you feel any better?"

"Nope."

"Do it again."

Then finally after three or four days, this is what got to me. He said, "I'm not asking you to believe anything, all I'm asking you to do is *assume* that there is a God, and that He'll help you if you ask Him. You just do this from now on. It doesn't hurt you any. When the day comes that you leave this world, if there is a God, you'll find out. And if there isn't, you'll never know the difference, so how can you lose?" Well, I could understand that. And I hung on to that. Then Sister made it very clear to all the boys in the ward, for as long as I knew her, that, "You have faith in no one, no living being, just God." And then she'd add, "You'll never get in trouble again."[20]

Spiritual Approach Essential

Sister Ignatia had an unshakable belief in the spiritual power of the AA program to disrupt even the most stubborn alcoholic's addiction. Neither she nor Dr. Bob long tolerated those who balked at the spiritual program of recovery. When patients at first complained that they could not grasp AA's "spiritual angle," Dr. Bob and Sister Ignatia confronted spiritual denial with the facts: AA's entire philosophy and program was spiritual—no part of it was not. To miss the spiritual angle was to have missed the thrust of the entire program.

Ignatia and the cofounders were wholly convinced that AA's spiritual power was the element that disrupted chronic alcoholism. Their philosophy assured alcoholics that they had a sickness for which the program of Alcoholics Anonymous was the only known medicine. Regarding the strong medicine of AA, Ignatia told her resistant patients:

> Even the most marvelous of the so-called miracle drugs will perform no miracles unless the patient *takes* them. The AA program has not failed anyone who *took* it sincerely and wholly.[21]

She guided patients into this belief by providing them with literature, talks, recordings, and her own daily thoughts and meditations. Also plentiful were AA visitors who guaranteed a constant din of AA conversation and a powerful example of hope and recovery. Consequently, once Ignatia had detoxified patients, she thrust her energy into transforming their cynical—or absent—spirituality. Placing the emphasis on the alcoholic's spirit, she wisely sensed that recovery would not occur unless a powerfully enticing substitute replaced the alcoholic's intangible obsession with alcohol.

By now Ignatia knew that in the early stages of addiction, the alcoholic made the choice to drink and thus journey into powerlessness. But as the disease progressed, the variable of choice vanished, leaving only the feeling of powerlessness in its place.

Something more potent and compelling than alcohol itself had to replace the compulsion to drink. Something more cunning than chemical seduction had to seize the alcoholic's will and fill his or her urgent emptiness. Something had to transform alcoholic self-centeredness into spontaneous human concern for others. To accomplish this, someone had to introduce the alcoholic to a real power—one more potent than himself or herself. Who could accomplish this better than a Catholic nun, a visual symbol of spiritual commitment?

But Ignatia did not view herself as a spiritual power. She in fact resisted the temptation to preach God or religion. Instead, she used each recovered patient's spiritual experience as a tool that prodded spiritual awareness loose from those who had not yet found it for themselves. Pat R.'s reflection of Ignatia's influence on the ward continues:

> I really do credit Sister Ignatia for the spiritual strength of AA because they'd written the Big Book, they'd told all their stories, they'd gotten others involved. But they couldn't hold a candle to what she did. Her full-time job was in the admitting office. But that didn't slow her down any. She came to the ward many times every day. And early in the morning, at noontime, dinnertime, and before bedtime, she talked to us boys. She'd give us a lecture, short and sweet, but very firm. She never let us forget why we were there. That's why we didn't have radios, newspapers, or anything but AA books. The visitors were asked not to talk about the news or the ballgames. She said we weren't in there to play baseball; it was an AA ward, and we respected that. Her lectures always had a meaning and a purpose, and a pleasant one. That's why I think she's done more for AA than anyone else. You didn't hear those things from sponsors, and you couldn't hear that kind of talk at meetings. She taught us what to do while we were in the ward, like how to get our lives together, how to be together, how to help each other, how to get our contact back

with our Higher Power. If an AA visitor was there, she might ask him to answer questions, or she would refer to him in her own lecture and use him as an example of someone who made it. She asked us to remember all the people who were helping us, all the ones we couldn't even see . . . like the ones who made our breakfast, for example. Somehow, she always taught us to believe. What's more, there wasn't even any reason to be ashamed that we were in that ward, anymore than if we'd had a heart problem, or diabetes, or something else. She said, "You are sick people; you have an illness; alcoholism is an illness."[22]

Precisely because Sister Ignatia viewed the alcoholic as a sick person who was also spiritually orphaned, she created a caring atmosphere of love and support, a spiritual home in which the patients could retreat to find or regain a sense of self-worth. Seen through the eyes of an accepting "substitute family" of cosufferers, patients were not judged or demeaned for their shortcomings. Her spiritual insight into the alcoholics in her care was simple. She told Wilson, "Bill, I feel all these people run away from God. I tell them we are all God's children."[23]

Her spiritual advice to alcoholics was simpler yet: "Just tell Him in your own words that you have made a mess of your life, and ask Him if He won't take over from here."[24]

Ignatia's spiritual direction, however, was a gift, a letting go of self that proved to be the alcoholic's powerful surrender to healing: "Just tell Him that you are going to put your life in His hands, and have the serenity to accept His holy will, and all that He sends."[25] In these gentle, simple ways, Ignatia inspired her patients to change the things that they could change—their drinking habits—and to accept what they could not change—their incurable addictions. Brief conversations with their Higher Power would then supply the wisdom needed to know the difference.

That is why Sister Ignatia asked the patients to treat God as if he were a friend, worthy of their secrets and anxious for their company. When she sensed they were ready, she led them to the hospital's chapel and gently showed each embarrassed, doubtful man how to bend his knees and pray. Tough men lost their pride and knelt down on the floor beside her. Many said that they first found God that way.

Ward Expands Despite Hospital Resistance

Recovering men spread word of Sister Ignatia's love throughout the growing AA community. By 1941, requests for alcohol admissions mounted. Soon room 228, a four-bed ward, was assigned for permanent use by Dr. Bob's alcoholic patients. But despite Ignatia and Bob's success, trouble was never far away. One day, the superintendent of nurses complained to administration that her women had not become nurses to treat drunks. The new hospital superior yielded to her demands and told Ignatia to discontinue the AA effort since it could not be defined either as psychiatry or as medicine. Ignatia asserted herself and reexplained the medical and spiritual dynamics of AA work. Before she left the meeting, she asked the superior, "Why was our community established if not to administer to the body and reach the soul?" and the superior relented.[26]

Not long after, Ignatia acquired a double room across the hall from the four-bed ward, making a total of six alcohol beds grouped in the same hospital area. Trial and error had convinced Sister Ignatia that hospitalized alcoholics recovered best when they were clustered together. And, as victims of a stigma-bearing illness, they were roommates unwelcomed by other hospital patients. For these reasons, group identification and mutual support evolved into powerful components of the treatment process. The new men bonded together, and AA visitors sustained them with encouragement and hope. More vitally, AA ward visitors yielded living examples of lives rebuilt by following Alcoholics Anonymous's spiritual remedy. Patient visitation was such an integral part of Ignatia's program that an exception to the hospital's general visiting policy was enforced: AA patients were allowed AA visitors at any time of the day or night.

Sister Ignatia recalled many years later that "ordinary patients started wondering why they were not allowed the same privilege, so we decided we had better find another location for them [the alcoholics]."[27] As she was prone to do in making remarks about the past, Ignatia avoided any mention of the more distressing details involved in the move, but much actually happened at this juncture.

Blistering comments about the "privileged alcoholics" again earned the superior's notice. Nursing and medical staff members who were provoked at the situation made certain of that. This time the superior agreed that the troublesome AAs should be banned from the hospital. She called Ignatia to accountability for the professional staff's complaints about alcoholic patients.

Ignatia already knew all the reasons for the new antagonism. Many doctors and nurses criticized the hospital for serving "moral degenerates."[28] An ugly form of professional jealousy crept into their thinking. Other AAs took care of hospitalized alcoholics. The skills of doctors and nurses were not much needed in the specialized work, so most medical and nursing staff members wondered why the hospital wasted beds on alcoholics. Medical personnel failed to understand that the treatment of alcoholism required a support system that recovering AA members better supplied. However, Ignatia saw the deeper, underlying problem: Serving AA patients allocated desirable beds to undesirable patients. That fact, and the stigma, lay at the basis of the controversy.

Not caught off guard for long, Ignatia remembered one hospital section where both doctors and nurses disliked working. The area was isolated from the nursing station's view by a long hallway. Heavy double doors neatly concealed a seven-bed ward, a utility room with plumbing, and the door to the chapel's choir loft.[29] Ignatia schemed and bargained to procure the area for continued AA work. With six desirable beds bartered to the medical staff, the sister-superior consented to a renovation of the vacant area for AA use.

In retrospect, Ignatia felt the skirmish produced a blessing in disguise. Once remodeled, the new space offered the privacy of a specialized unit geographically removed from the hospital's growing scrutiny. Jubilantly, Ignatia realized that for the offering, her alcoholics had gained one more bed! But by far most crucial to the program's success, the new ward rendered immediate (and anonymous) spiritual support because of its proximity to the choir loft and chapel.

Growth Follows Death

Just as Ignatia's recurrent problems with the hospital administrator over AA escalated, Barbara Neary Gavin died of heart failure after nearly nine years of illness. And just as the death of Ignatia's father preceded the first challenge to AA's hospital program, so now her mother's death marked another milestone.

Early on the chilling morning of January 31, 1944, Sister Ignatia gently closed her mother's eyes and prayed her Irish soul Godspeed to heaven. Again bereaved and this time orphaned, death and loss tested Ignatia's character. Once more she coped by fighting for the rights of the alcoholics. Only this time, she truly understood their feelings of abandonment and their need for a secure home. Now she was determined to find them one.

The times of Ignatia's deepest suffering always seemed to be followed by her greatest accomplishments. Did her inner pain always find God's love and then erupt in spiritual intensity that transcended her problems? To the AAs, it seemed so. A few short months after Barbara Gavin's death, the section of St. Thomas Hospital designated by Bill Wilson as AA's "first permanent haven for treatment" opened wide its doors. The date was April 19, 1944. The alcoholics—and Ignatia—at last had a place to call home.

The St. Thomas Hospital Alcoholism Ward

The new ward had everything the men needed to begin physical, mental, and spiritual healing. There were eight beds (one was an emergency cot), a coffee "bar," visitors' lounge, refrigerator, and a private entrance to the chapel's choir loft. While encouraging supportive group interaction, Ignatia also stressed the importance of moments spent alone. She and Dr. Bob both knew that quiet reflections with the God of one's understanding ingrained an inner balance needed for sober living. Years later a grateful patient wrote a fictitious but factual account of his introduction to Sister Ignatia's quiet time in the AA ward:

> One thing especially impressed Tom: from time to time,
> one or another of the men in the room would slip quietly away

and be gone some length of time. At first, Tom thought nothing of this; then he noted that the men crossed the corridor and disappeared through a door on the far side. Once when the door was opened, he heard a faint sound of music, as if an organ was being played in the distance . . . During one of her trips through the room, when she stopped by his bed to ask if he was comfortable and looking forward to a good night's sleep, he asked her about the door across the corridor. "Come with me," she said quietly. They crossed the corridor and the Sister stood for a moment with her hand on the doorknob. "In coming to us," she said, "you took the first step. You admitted to yourself that by yourself you are powerless, that your life had become unmanageable for you. That was your first of Twelve Steps." She turned the knob of the door. "You are about to take the Second Step," she told him.

Tom followed the Sister into a dimly lighted room. As she closed the door behind them, he felt a sudden sense of quiet, as if the world had been shut away from him and he was alone with himself. He looked around . . . On the wall behind them, arched above a cross, were the inscribed words: "BUT FOR THE GRACE OF GOD." "Sit down, Tom. This is our little chapel. You do not need to come here again unless you wish to. But it is a quiet spot, a spot where you can think."[30]

Sister Ignatia had spent many moments reflecting on the addicts and their addiction. She thought about the alcoholics' spiritual symptoms, recalling endless stories of the alcoholics' compulsion and despair, their powerful longings, their unanswered prayers. Then by hearing Dr. Bob and the other AAs explain their illness and the familiar steps to recovery, she learned to communicate in the language of the alcoholic:

> . . . Her very blue eyes drifted swiftly over Tom from his ruffled hair to his scuffed shoes. She glanced at Mac. "He's not as loaded as some of the babies you bring in," she remarked. Mac chuckled, "I can see you're learning the vernacular, Sister."[31]

Alcoholics Sponsor Alcoholics

Adept at getting to the heart of the patients' problems, she met the
men on their own terms. They respected the compassionate nun because she was not a trained clinician holding only professional status
and credentials as proof of her ability to treat them. Sister Ignatia
never had to prove herself to the alcoholics. She was effective because she learned from their experience of alcoholism and listened to
their pain. Her great success came from her instinct to work *through*
the men, aiming her indirect approach subtly at each patient, coaxing
one man to help the next. Without knowing what prompted them or
what spirit had moved them, the patients passed their own experiences along and reached out to others like this:

> . . . Of course, it was silly to think that he was in any way a
> different man from the one who had crossed the corridor
> and entered the chapel, some twenty or thirty minutes ago.
> And yet . . . It seemed to Tom that he felt a sense of assur-
> ance that had not been with him then . . . He didn't feel alone
> now; and he didn't feel altogether helpless. His attention re-
> verted to the newcomer just a few feet away from him, and
> the thought struck deep into his mind: this man was as Tom
> K. had been only a few hours ago . . . That thought had mean-
> ing: it meant that Tom was now different than he had been.
> He did not feel superior to his companion but he experienced
> a feeling of maturity and of quiet strength. Something had
> happened to him, something that made for a changed out-
> look. Then Tom surprised himself. He said very quietly, "Tell
> me about yourself."[32]

Five Days to Recovery

Ignatia herself described the ward in a convention talk she gave to the
Catholic Hospital Association in 1951. At the Philadelphia gathering
she stressed the ward's simplicity. She told the assembled hospital
leaders:

Our alcoholic ward is not a great problem. It is simply a large
room with accommodations in one end for eight beds. The
other end of the room is a small lounge with comfortable
chairs, a davenport, a "bar," a coffee urn, and an ice box. To
the rear of this ward-lounge is a room with a lavatory and
shower into which the new man is brought for admission to
the ward. An important point is that he is helped out of his
street clothes and into hospital attire *by other patients in the
ward.* The advantage for the *new patient* is that, from the first,
he is in the care of understanding friends. The advantage for
the older patients who perform this duty is that they are thus
able to see *themselves* again as they were upon admission.
Administratively, an economy is effected by thus eliminating
the need for hard-to-get employees. Directly across the hall
from our ward-lounge is the choir loft of our chapel, which
permits A.A. patients to hear Mass every day if they wish and
to make visits in hospital attire when they so desire—all in
complete seclusion. Bearing in mind always that the alcoholic
is a person who is sick *spiritually* as well as *physically,* the
ready access he is thus given to the source of spiritual healing
is a powerful factor in his recovery. To return to the mechanical operation of the ward, it can be stated that it is almost
wholly self-operating. A nurses' aide comes in to make beds
and an A.A. employee does the heavier cleaning. The cleaning
of ashtrays, the making of coffee, the washing of coffee cups,
all of this is done by the patients themselves. Usually they welcome these small opportunities to busy themselves and thus
keep their minds off their problems. Activity eliminates
brooding, and the volume of such work is never great at any
time.[33]

The alcoholism ward's program required a minimum of five days
for completion. However, each patient's condition determined the actual length of stay. Though administered in a hospital setting, Ignatia
viewed the program as a five-day retreat from the outside world and

the habits encouraged there.[34] To each day's focus, she provided a spiritual action or theme.

Ignatia named the first day *Reception.* On Day One, the new patient concentrated on his own physical needs. He tapered off from alcohol and, if necessary, received the famous St. Thomas Cocktail sedative to quiet his nerves and permit twenty-four hours of rest. Doctors and nurses studied his physical condition and then made recommendations for health and dietary needs. After he was escorted to bed and sedated, intravenous nourishment began. Then he rested.

Soon other patients came to his beside, telling their own stories, and welcoming him to the ward. On this first day, physical comfort was the key objective. The alcoholic's need for medical attention and bed rest drove home the reality that compulsive drinking created real physical illness. Sponsors and AA members surrounding the new man were the instruments of his healing. Witnessing their sobriety and their concern for him stirred the thought that things could get better, and his confidence was born. Sister Ignatia summarized this day by saying, "Nothing is left undone to make the new man feel at home. This reception inspires hope in his heart."[35]

The next day's theme grew from the first day's work. With intoxication lifted, the patient's physical condition also improved. And sober AA visitors prompted the *Realization* (Day Two's goal) that people recover from alcoholism:

> He feels encouraged because everyone seems interested in him. Visitors call on him, telling him, "This is how I made it." Some of the visitors may be men with whom he used to drink. The power of example is a great incentive to the patient. He begins to say to himself, "If he can do it, so can I. But how am I going to make it?"[36]

A slow recognition of his own powerlessness and his growing need for the sponsor's guidance crept into the patient's consciousness.

Now, thinking more clearly, he noticed little things that happened and learned easy slogans to remember, like the word *HALT.* The other patients told him not to get too *hungry, angry, lonely,* or *tired.*

And true to their advice, when he was *hungry,* they gave him food to eat. When he was *angry,* they gave him lots of time to share his frustrations. When he was *lonely,* they gave him his own sponsor and the friendship of other recovering men. And when he was *tired,* they gave him rest in a warm bed. The AA visitors' spirit and helpfulness made it no longer possible to find contentment in his isolated world of one. He turned to his sponsor and laid bare his struggles with alcohol:

> He honestly admits that he has tried innumerable times to drink normally and has always failed. He is finally ready, honestly and humbly, to admit defeat.[37]

Sister Ignatia often told the men at this point that relinquishing alcohol's hold released the power of God into their lives. Only spiritual surrender—admission of defeat, acknowledgment of powerlessness—prompted the patient's search for God:

> This is the grace of God at work in the soul of the patient: to admit helplessness and to seek help outside of self. This may be the first time the patient has admitted the fact that he is powerless to help himself. The next step is to humbly turn to God. "Ask and you shall receive." Patients have often said that this is the first time they sincerely prayed. The "Our Father" takes on a new meaning at this point. They feel that they really *belong.*[38]

Hearing the stories of other people's lives inspired patients to review their own life story; praying the Our Father, or Lord's Prayer, in a group brought spiritual awareness, a strong sense of belonging, and a reflective frame of mind. It followed that on Day Three, called *Moral Inventory,* they examined their own past: "He used to drink because he felt like it." He acknowledged his problem with God, himself, and new friends. Between flashes of self-honesty ("I am an alcoholic") and sincere pleas for help, the patient taught himself about himself. He discovered the character traits that most harmed him:

He is finished with alibis and reservations.

"I am an alcoholic. What a joy to be honest! The truth will make you free."[39]

With the reality of alcoholism confronted, Day Four, called *Resolution,* followed. Senior patients encouraged the new man to leave the past behind ("accept the things I cannot change") and focus all mental energy on the present moment ("courage to change the things I can"). Ignatia reinforced the message with her own frequently repeated words, "Eternity is now. Right now. This very instant. Today is all you have."

The most challenging part of Day Four was Ignatia's key to wellness. She asked each man to think of those he had harmed with his drinking; then she instructed him to ask their forgiveness. Ignatia felt that the making of amends was the pathway to the alcoholic's liberation. With guilt cleared away, the present was freed for sober living. Excuses to pick up a drink vanished quickly when guilt was dissolved.

With thinking improved and feelings controlled, the alcoholic in treatment became a person of reason rather than the victim of strong and unruly emotions. For possibly the first time ever, he knew the truth about himself; as an alcoholic, he could not take the first drink, for that was the one that could lead to the bitter cup of his undoing. Sober, he could identify and remember his own strengths and weaknesses, and his fears of the future were now placed in a Higher Power's strong hands. The words of childhood prayers floated back to him, expanded in meaning:

> "Give us this day our daily bread." This is interpreted by the alcoholics to mean "I can surely stay sober today."
>
> This is usually followed by an act of complete surrender to God. The past is finished.
>
> "I am heartily sorry."
>
> "I'll try to make amends.". . .
>
> He has learned from his fellow alcoholics that it is more blessed to give than to receive, and that it is a privilege to help

others. What a joy, too. He is kept so busy helping others that he does not have time to even think about a drink.[40]

On Day Five, the patient prepared his *Plans for the Future.* Knowing that he would soon leave the safety of the alcoholism ward and the comfort of newly made friends, the patient steadied himself to face the real world without alcohol. Five days earlier, the mere thought of life without drinking aroused feelings of suicidal despair. But now, he held a plan for living that had worked for others worse than he.

Daily Visits Strengthen Sobriety

Though inpatient treatment officially ended after five days, Sister Ignatia encouraged all the discharged patients to return to the ward thereafter on a daily basis. Frequent patient visits were her way of extending the early recovery phase, reinforcing newly learned principles, and providing sober examples to the new patients. By using the ward as a home base for sobriety, the visitors reminded themselves of how they had felt when they were in pajamas, how far they had progressed by not drinking, and how quickly they could return to their alcoholic misery.

Additionally, all the men needed the support of sober people while reconstructing their lives, finding new jobs, and resolving domestic situations. Often in these early days, the men had nowhere to live when they left the hospital. If they were from out of town, they needed the strength gained from Akron's AA meetings before returning alone to areas where AA had not yet been established. Accordingly, many of Akron's early AA families housed newly released patients until their circumstances improved and their sobriety stabilized. Sister Ignatia frequently obtained lodging for homeless men at an early Akron residence home known as "Mrs. Mosley's" on nearby Ash Street. There the men received nourishing meals, camaraderie, and warm beds to sleep in. They filled their spare hours by helping one another, going to meetings, and visiting the AA ward instead of the neighborhood bars.

When relapse occurred—and it did—the alcoholic was rarely readmitted to the hospital as a ward patient. However, Sister Ignatia immediately encouraged the "slipper" to return to the ward as a guest. There he spent as much time as he needed in the visitor's lounge, grouped with other AAs. In this way, with the influence of sober people and the counsel of the ever-present Sister Ignatia, a second chance for sobriety was always available. New patients also benefited when relapsed men returned. Early in recovery they learned that outside problems and temptations could easily challenge new sobriety.

However, before an alcoholic patient left St. Thomas Hospital, he looked forward to one final interview with Sister Ignatia. Frighteningly new to him were self-knowledge and sobriety. With the future placed securely in a Higher Power's hands and the present shared with a sponsor, Ignatia repeated her cautions to "guard against pride, self-pity, resentment, intolerance, and criticism."[41]

Next, she reminded her listener to bear in mind that his sobriety was a treasure, earned daily by not drinking, by going to meetings, and by helping others. She presented him with a personalized copy of *The Imitation of Christ* by Thomas à Kempis, inviting him to return to the ward often.

Perhaps most significant to the patient was that in this final interview he received proof of his successful completion of the program. As her parting gift, Sister Ignatia awarded a small religious token called a Sacred Heart badge. The ritual was steeped in commitment, gratitude, and future responsibility. Acceptance of the small badge sealed an agreement between the two, for it signaled a promise made by the patient; he agreed to return the badge to Sister Ignatia personally (before ever picking up another drink) if he ever decided that abstinence was not for him. The promise was a grave matter, and the men respected it. Returning the Sacred Heart badge to Sister Ignatia before drinking stopped many reckless and impulsive relapses. Many of Ignatia's patients still carry the Sacred Heart badge in their wallets, a reminder of their sobriety and the loving woman who led them to it. AA's later custom of awarding chips and tokens for sobriety grew from Ignatia's thoughtful symbol of the trust she put in her patient's ability to stay sober.

Overflowing Gratitude

The alcoholics' gratitude for Sister Ignatia arose also from their knowledge that, in spite of St. Thomas's Catholic orientation, Sister Ignatia demanded that AA's philosophy of "God as you understand him" be held sacred. Although no specific religion was forced on anyone, she counseled all AAs to seek a spiritual solution to their alcohol problems. In these early days of alcohol treatment at St. Thomas Hospital, Sister Ignatia also pioneered the true spirit of a later-developed Catholic ecumenism by bridging religious differences and sectarian conflicts that otherwise could have obscured the process of spiritual growth and healing.

By the time Dr. Bob Smith died in 1950, the advances he and Sister Ignatia had made in alcoholism treatment were widely honored. Prior to Smith's death, AA presented St. Thomas Hospital with a plaque for the alcoholism ward that Sister Ignatia recommended be inscribed as follows:

IN GRATITUDE
THE FRIENDS OF DR. BOB AND ANNE S.
AFFECTIONATELY DEDICATE THIS MEMORIAL.
TO THE SISTERS AND STAFF OF ST. THOMAS HOSPITAL AT AKRON,
BIRTHPLACE OF ALCOHOLICS ANONYMOUS.

ST. THOMAS HOSPITAL BECAME THE FIRST RELIGIOUS INSTITUTION EVER TO OPEN ITS DOORS TO OUR SOCIETY. MAY THE LOVING DEVOTION OF THOSE WHO LABORED HERE IN OUR PIONEERING TIME BE A BRIGHT AND WONDROUS EXAMPLE OF GOD'S GRACE EVERLASTING SET BEFORE US ALL.[42]

But even in the wording of the plaque, Sister Ignatia made her spiritual imprint on the fellowship of AA, permanently reminding its members of the enduring value of AA's fundamental spiritual principle, anonymity:

Visitors at St. Thomas today often wonder why this inscription says not a word about Sister Ignatia. Well, the fact was,

she wouldn't allow her name to be used. She had flatly refused;
it was one of those times when she had put her foot down! This
was of course a glowing example of her innate and absolutely
genuine humility. Sister truly believed that she deserved no
particular notice; that such grace as she might have could
only be credited to God and to the community of her sisters.

This was indeed the ultimate spirit of anonymity. We who
had then seen this quality in her were deeply affected, especially Dr. Bob and myself. Hers came to be the influence that
persuaded us both never to accept public honors of any sort.
Sister's example taught that a mere observance of the form of
AA anonymity should never become the slightest excuse for
ignoring its *spiritual substance.*

Bill Wilson
AA Grapevine, August 1966[43]

Four

Akron's Magic Blend

And so the ministry of Dr. Bob, his wife Anne, Sister Ignatia, and Akron's early timers sets an example for the practice of A.A.'s Twelve Steps that will remain for all time.[1]

—William G. Wilson

Between 1939, when modern treatment for alcoholism officially began, and 1950, when Dr. Robert H. Smith died, more than five thousand alcoholics recovered from their affliction through the Akron program pioneered by Smith and Ignatia. Eager word of their successful endeavor extended throughout the United States and Canada, the message deployed by a growing army of enthusiastic recovering alcoholics. The living results of their efforts spoke for themselves.

Akron's magic blend—the scientific with the spiritual—succeeded where previous attempts to treat addiction had miserably failed. Smith and Ignatia addressed the recovery from alcoholism in the same selective, progressive manner in which the disease subtly ensnared its victims. Smith and Ignatia's physical, mental, and spiritual antidotes restored health, hope, and sanity, wholistically arresting the fatal course of addiction. For the first time in history, the threefold illness received threefold care.

Dr. Bob, Sister Ignatia, and Bob's wife, Anne—Akron's scientists and saints—exemplified recovery by their inspiring application of AA's principles in their own lives. Though far less sophisticated than their East Coast counterparts who were equally committed to the task of healing drunks but initially less successful, this exemplary trio leaned first on God and then on one another before they expended their energy on the suffering alcoholics in their midst.

As the cofounder of Alcoholics Anonymous, Dr. Bob deserves special mention. Perhaps more than any other life of a recovering alcoholic in AA's early history, Dr. Bob's life bears unusual distinction in several areas later important to AA's growth. Subsequently a pioneer and a role model in many respects, Smith was

- first with Wilson in cofounding Alcoholics Anonymous
- first with Ignatia in pioneering hospital treatment
- first physician to admit his addiction and recover through AA's spiritual medicine
- first husband and father to confront his addiction and recover along *with* his wife and children

Dr. Bob was fortunate on two counts—at the hospital he had the unyielding loyalty of Sister Ignatia; at home, his wife's and his children's love sustained him in his sobriety.

Anne Smith: AA's First Home and Heart

From the early June morning in 1935 when Bill W. awakened as the Smiths' first overnight AA guest, he discovered that the aroma of brewing coffee was Anne's subtle way of awakening a sober alcoholic's spiritual appetite. Along with coffee, toast, and whatever other offerings the Smiths' meager budget permitted, Anne Smith served God and Scripture to all who gathered at her daybreak meal.

Often, Henrietta Seiberling came to the home on Ardmore Avenue to provide and share in the spiritual nourishment. Together, she and Anne taught Bill and Bob to begin each glorious, sober day with a quiet time for prayer and reflection. As AA slowly grew, the Smiths housed many alcoholics whom the local hospitals turned away. Early morning prayers became a ritual for the alcoholics and the unspoken rule of Anne Smith's home. Wilson fondly reminisced about the summer of 1935 and his spiritual growth in Akron:

> I came back to New York after having taken a great deal from Akron. I can never forget those mornings and those nights at

> Smiths'. I can never forget Annie reading to us (and the two
> or three drunks who were hanging on) out of the Bible. I
> couldn't possibly say how many times we read Corinthians on
> Love, how many times we met the Book of James, how many
> times Annie told us "Faith without works is dead."[2]

As time went on, Annie gained skill, comfort, and the ability to self-
disclose as she shared her own thoughts and feelings with the alcoholics in her home. Though faith in God came easily to Anne, sharing
personal sentiments did not. Years of living with the embarrassment
and unpredictability of her alcoholic husband's behavior had greatly
diminished her natural spontaneity. Anne grew quiet, polite, sensitive,
and mistrustful of normal human relationships. While covering up
her husband's drinking, Anne had also camouflaged her own identity.
Communicating genuine and precious feelings became a lost art in
their alcoholic marriage. Anne clung tenaciously to what remained of
her own self-respect and sensibility.

During Dr. Bob's first summer of sobriety, Anne regained her
natural optimism by helping the very sick and confused alcoholics
who lived in their home. Soon the alcoholics' problems drew her out.
Years of unspoken thoughts and feelings tumbled from her heart. No
longer hopeless over alcohol's relentless grip on the human soul,
Anne began to grow and change. Accidentally she discovered that by
helping others, she herself gained strength and value. As she shared
what she had learned and experienced with all the men and their
wives, loneliness and depression faded. In their place, she found new
and lasting friends.

Day by day, Anne found and revealed more of herself to her new
and needy friends. In addition to reading passages from Holy Scripture to the newly sober men, she read from her own Oxford Group
notebook, disclosing the personally meaningful ideas and spiritual
guidance she had gathered over the years. On her journal's ninth
page, she unconsciously wrote a valuable piece of advice for the alcoholics, part of which became AA's simplified response to the newly recovering alcoholic's frequent question, "How will I *stay* sober?" In her
journal, she had written:

Be willing to live *a day at a time,* an hour at a time. Walk by
faith, not by sight.[3]

Many present-day AA practices, slogans, and ideals leap out of
Anne Smith's Oxford Group journal. Her notes and readings focused
topically on sharing, projecting, surrendering, and the Five Cs: confidence, confession, conviction, conversion, continuance. Some of AA's
most valuable advice on sponsorship came from a descriptive passage
Anne wrote concerning the fifth *C,* continuance:

> *Continuance.* Stay with the newly surrendered person until he
> grows up and becomes a life-changer. Laugh him out of his
> growing pains. When he becomes a life-changer, we need not
> fear for him, because other people's needs will drive him back
> on God.[4]

Anne was a spiritual, God-fearing woman who found much solace
and direction in scriptural passages and parables. She taught her husband and his new companions to inspire sobriety in others through an
example she found enlightening in the biblical story of the Samaritan
woman who met Jesus at Jacob's well (John 4:4–30).[5] Anne told the
men that because of her sins, her undesirable heritage, and her gen-
der, the Samaritan woman felt unworthy of Christ's friendship. Ex-
pecting his rejection, she was taken aback by his easy acceptance of
her and startled by his perceptive knowledge of her past mistakes.
His forgiving manner converted the Samaritan woman's suspicious,
negative spirit to one of joy and hope. Her Redeemer, and thus her
healing, had finally come, regardless of her past. Grateful, she spread
news of his presence to her friends throughout the town.

Anne's spiritual insights into this story exposed some key attitudes sober alcoholics needed to display when approaching practicing alcoholics who needed the program. In an example, she wisely
told the men that the same nonjudgmental, forgiving spirit of love that
filled the Samaritan woman with hope could also light the hope of recovery in new AA prospects.

Thus Anne thrust herself wholeheartedly into the spiritual core of the new recovery effort. She did not limit herself to helping the alcoholic men, however. When Bill and Bob claimed an attorney as AA number three on June 28, 1935, Anne offered immediate support to the new man's wife. Henrietta D. met Anne Smith the same day that Bill and Bob recruited her alcoholic husband. A quiet, unassuming woman, she absorbed a great deal of strength and direction from Anne.

Like their alcoholic husbands, Anne and Henrietta had traveled down similar paths. Both women were the long-suffering partners of professional men gone astray, men whose drinking had imperiled their careers, families, and reputations. Anne and Henrietta understood each other's deepest feelings. Shame, resentment, guilt, frustration, and inadequacy had reshaped their personalities. These were the emotional by-products of living amidst the chaos and confusion of unrestrained alcoholism. Humiliation had replaced all self-respect long before these two AA wives ever met. With their meeting, the strength gained of sharing hope transformed their mental outlooks.

Anne instinctively extended compassion and understanding to Henrietta D. and the wives of other new AA members. Who knew better than she what life with an alcoholic could be? And likewise, who if not Anne could convince new wives that sober marriages could be renewed and revitalized the same as sober people?

Not much written in AA's history credits Anne Smith's pioneering efforts with recovering alcoholics and their wives. In fact, what emerged after her death as Al-Anon had its earliest beginnings in Akron within days of AA's official founding. A more historical accounting would attribute at least the precedent for Al-Anon to the June 28, 1935, meeting of Anne and Henrietta D.—an event that occurred as Henrietta's toxic husband remained unstable and unconvinced that sobriety was the way of life for him. On that day, with or without her husband, Henrietta's recovery began when she joined forces with Anne Smith.

Thus, when Anne died in 1949, Henrietta wrote a letter to Dr. Bob in which she spoke of the early AA wives' gratitude for Anne Smith's genteel leadership. Preserved in AA's archives as a lasting tribute to Anne, Henrietta's letter said, "Anne taught me to love everyone; she said 'love of God is triangular—it must flow from God, through me, through you, and back to God.'"[6]

Henrietta's lengthy letter documents much of the work that Anne accomplished for AA wives. Of particular interest and significance is the remark that dates Anne's work with the struggling wives. In Akron, the earliest AAs and their wives may not have known what to call themselves, but they assuredly discovered all the elements that made AA successful:

> In the early part of 1936 Anne organized a "Woman's Group" for wives of alcoholics, whereby in her loving way, she tried to teach us patience, love, and unselfishness.
>
> She told me I should never criticize the remarks of the person leading the meeting as we do not know God's plan; maybe what that person says will meet the need of someone in the group.[7]

The Neglected Role of Women in AA's Early History

Akron AAs didn't spend much time in planning or discussing fool-proof strategies for sobriety. Rather, their great effectiveness—their unparalleled magic—resulted from their actions. Sobriety and the goal to carry AA's message to any and all who needed it defined their grassroots mission.

Thus the earliest AA days transpired in Akron. During the late 1930s, when Ignatia was secretly hospitalizing isolated cases of alcoholism and praying in the chapel for direction, Anne Smith was also hard at work breathing a lasting soul into AA's first trembling body of members. Anne spoke to the newly sober followers of the Samaritan woman's message, while Ignatia contemplated the familiar scriptural words for the good Samaritan. Engraved on St. Thomas Hospital's altar, the inscription "Go and do thou in like manner" was a biblical injunction that brought meaning to the searching men's lives too.

However, little has been documented regarding the rich contributions made by Akron's women pioneers, who in truth were the love and guts of the program. A number of reasons explain why. First, most history is written by men, who record the valorous deeds of other men, and AA's chronicles are no exception. Bill Wilson, as AA's first historian, simply followed precedent. When he wrote of women at all, he did so in glowing terms, no doubt meaning well but sometimes patronizing just the same. At other times, he made honorable mention of women in relationship to their supportive, secondary roles, often to enhance the image or the work of a male counterpart.

In truth, however, the earliest women involved with Alcoholics Anonymous (usually nonalcoholics themselves) did far more than just pour coffee for the men. The women who stood alongside AA's male pioneers injected sensitivity, spirituality, intuition, and encouragement into AA's message. Without them, it is unlikely that the great strength of AA's love would have flowed so naturally into service.

The male history writers are not entirely to blame for their minuscule coverage of Anne and Ignatia, however. Truthfully, neither woman sought or wanted public recognition for her good works. Each instead leaned heavily on her respective God, confident that his intercession would produce the desired fruits of their labors.

The two women met in person on few occasions. Except to attend meetings, Anne stayed at home, particularly after her eyesight failed in later years.[8] There were always plenty of new husbands and wives ringing her doorbell, drinking her coffee, or seeking her counsel. Likewise, Sister Ignatia's time was consumed at the hospital, working double shifts and caring for the alcoholics entrusted to her care. Moreover, the rules of community life permitted few visits outside the hospital's boundaries.

In spite of such restrictions, Anne and Sister Ignatia became involved in each other's lives through the marital and family problems of the hospitalized alcoholics. Anne's daughter, Sue Windows, recalled their frequent contacts:

> Most of it [their relationship] was over the telephone. I know she talked to Sister Ignatia at least once a day. Often Sister Ignatia called my mother about a man's treatment, relatives, loved ones, because they didn't allow the families there [in the hospital] in those days.[9]

Between the counsel of Anne Smith and the spiritual ministerings of Sister Ignatia, most alcoholic marriages were revived once the husbands stopped drinking. During the hospitalization period, Anne worked closely with the wives, listening, prodding, praying, and encouraging them to allow their marriages one more chance. Sister Ignatia then met with the wife on the last or second-last day of treatment. By that time, Ignatia knew the husband well and had knowledge of the wife through Anne. Ignatia remembered her alliance with Anne Smith this way:

> I didn't like to bother Doctor too much so I would call Anne, Doctor's lovely wife. Anne's advice was of great value to me. Her calm, soothing tone and sympathetic understanding was a source of encouragement. She always found the correct answer. In her diplomatic way, she would present the problem to the Doctor, then telephone me and advise.[10]

It was not long before Sister Ignatia began spending time with the wives too. In conjunction with Anne's preliminary work, Ignatia found clever ways to breathe new hope into disturbed marriages. Still, timing in marriage reconciliations often spelled success or failure. The hospital stay was brief, so Ignatia felt that the ripe time to work on the marriage occurred when the husband was sober enough to speak with his spouse but not sober enough to leave her. Likewise for the wife's sake, Ignatia intervened prudently with the alcoholic husband. Before most wives would reconcile, husbands needed to demonstrate their willingness to change; to be convinced to take their husbands back home, skeptical wives wanted evidence that their husbands' attitudes and behaviors had indeed changed for the better. Ignatia used coercive but effective tactics to reconcile marriages:

> And very often, when I have called the wife of an alcoholic [into the hospital] she'd say, "I just don't want to see him. I'm finished with him. I've applied for a divorce." I would tell her [that] if she would come to see me, she wouldn't have to see her husband.

I [would] tell her, "Now you have come a long way with him. How long have you been married?" (It might be six years, ten years, twenty or thirty years.) "Wouldn't it be worthwhile taking one more chance on this program? This is not just a sobering-up process. We wouldn't use valuable hospital space if we were in the business just to sober people up. The thing that is so heartening to us is that so many who come through here get the program and never have any more trouble. Now won't you, on the strength of that, just give him one more chance? If you can do this, if you can pull the curtain on the past and start off that way, I assure you we'll return to you the man that you married in the first place."

. . . After I finished talking with her, I said, "Of course you don't want to see him." And she will [would] usually say, "Well, perhaps he doesn't want to see me." [Ignatia responded] "Well, I'll see. Just wait here a moment. It's up to both of you. I'm not getting into any domestic troubles!"[11]

Leaving the wife deep in thought, Ignatia hurried off to begin negotiating with the husband. Her approach to him was similarly cagey:

So then I get him [the alcoholic husband] in the corner and say, "You know who I have up in the office? Your wife! But, of course, you don't want to see her, I suppose." He says, "Well, I'm ashamed to talk to her."

"Well, would you like to see her? Maybe she would [talk to you] if I talked to her." [So] I get the two of them together, I go in with him, and as soon as the ice is broken and I see that I have given a few little leads to them, and I see they are beginning to get together and talk, then I say I have to go out to answer the phone or do something, and [I] leave them. Then it's amazing.

Sometimes I give her a little badge, too. Of course, as you know, I give the patients the Sacred Heart [badge] which he is to return to me before he reaches for that first drink. But I have been giving her a little medal too, or a little badge, and

[I] say, "Now, I'll ask you to take this and you may keep it providing you don't bring up the past. Try it for a while." I've had hundreds and hundreds of those cases.[12]

Staging marital reconciliations for the alcoholics was Ignatia's specialty. Preserving family unity and encouraging husband and wife to work out their difficulties rather than separate were second in importance only to sobriety. Again, Ignatia's methods worked hand in glove with Anne Smith's advice, reinforcing consistent guidelines to the newly united spouses. A key thought for couples that Anne shared from her journal was this:

> The real test of a surrendered life is that we are nice to live with. Surrender takes away shame and gives us real life.[13]

Anne's work with early AA wives was so effective that in 1938 during the preparation of the manuscript for *Alcoholics Anonymous,* Bill Wilson wrote these words to Dr. Bob:

> My own feeling is that Anne should do the one [chapter] portraying the wife of an alcoholic.[14]

Anne, however, declined the honor, possibly in deference to the feelings of Bill's nonalcoholic wife, Lois. In fact, a comparison of the Akron and New York records shows a discrepancy as to the actual authorship of the chapter "To Wives."

Akron records state that the chapter was written by Akron's Marie B., wife of Walter B., who first joined the fellowship in September 1935. (Later, Walter relapsed and became the first officially registered alcoholic patient whom Dr. Bob and Sister Ignatia hospitalized at St. Thomas in August 1939.) However, of the chapter's actual authorship Lois recalled:

> Bill wrote it and I was mad. I wasn't so much mad as hurt. I still don't know why Bill wrote it. I've never really gotten into

it—why he insisted upon writing it. I said to him, "Well, do you want me to write it?" And he said no, he thought it should be in the same style as the rest of the book.[15]

Bill found himself in a dilemma over the authorship of "To Wives" for three reasons: his suggestion to Dr. Bob that Anne write the chapter; his own wife's strong feelings that she should write it; and the sensitive relationships between Akronites and New Yorkers that arose during the writing of the book. He attempted to cover all the bases by accepting Marie B.'s version. This he revised for the obvious reason explained to Lois—that the finished book needed continuity in his own literary style and form. His explanation seemed to solve AA's problems and salved the hurt feelings at home.

Alcoholic Women Join AA

Actually, Anne Smith had little time or interest in writing chapters for books. Not only had she taken on the counseling and advising of the first nonalcoholic wives, but also she and Sister Ignatia had inherited, by default, Akron AA's first alcoholic women. Anne and Ignatia had to intervene because neither male AA members nor their wives readily accepted women alcoholics into their kinship. Even Dr. Bob had difficulty extending the AA message of hope and hospitality to "fallen" alcoholic women, who were far more stigmatized for their drinking than the men. Thus, while Dr. Bob did not turn away the first alcoholic woman who came to him for help, he also did not greet her with the same degree of warmth extended to the men he doctored over the years. Men were often taken into the Smiths' home, sobered up, given a room, meals, fellowship, and an invitation to be a living part of the Smiths' family.

This was not as readily so with alcoholic women. In fact, the earliest women newcomers were enigmas to Dr. Bob. Though sometimes he housed them in his basement, he was uncomfortable in their presence. In context, his attitude is understandable. The early organization considered itself to be a *fellow*ship in the strict sense of the word.

Thus the male membership had not anticipated the presence of *fellow* alcoholic women in its swelling ranks, nor did it know how to fit them into its program.

The Hardships and Double Standards for Women Alcoholics

Accordingly, the first women alcoholics who presented themselves for help did not fare well in Alcoholics Anonymous. Unsupported by the male alcoholics and harshly judged by insecure and jealous wives, alcoholic women felt alienated and rejected. Understandably, with little acceptance of their illness to be found, many returned to the practice of drinking. The few women who recovered found sobriety through personal application of AA's principles and not from the *fellow*ship.

In the early days, the moral and social stigma associated with alcoholism affected everyone, men included. For alcoholic women, though, the stigma was further exacerbated by society's double standards, which vastly differed for men and women.

Although men who drank could be violent, cruel, dishonest, or unfaithful to their moral commitments, if they sobered up and reformed their ways, forgiveness and respectability returned for the asking. The same was not true of women who drank, however. A common misconception taught that only immoral, promiscuous, low-class women indulged in alcohol—especially in public. Even when women stopped drinking and sought help for their problems, no amount of sobriety easily altered society's preconceived opinion of them.

In the 1930s, Alcoholics Anonymous was merely another social group that mirrored society's double standards, initially treating alcoholic women with little regard and little equality. Proving the point, AA's own attitudes and slogans often demeaned women. New men in AA were (and still are) warned by old-timers that "beneath every skirt there's a 'slip.'" Indeed, blame for the alcoholic male's sexual philanderings and fantasies was indiscriminately (and conveniently) projected onto the nearest new female in the group. Given such attitudes and clichés, the alcoholic woman's path to sobriety was littered with obstacles arising from her sex, not her alcoholism.

Much to his credit, Dr. Bob struggled with the question of women in AA until he found a solution. The self-knowledge learned in sobriety had taught him what to do when a problem had him beaten. Now, as he struggled with the question of women in Alcoholics Anonymous, the practice of taking counsel with the God of his understanding guided him to seek the help of others. Accordingly, he turned the problem over to the two women who had lovingly supported him to this point. Though Anne Smith and Sister Ignatia were as much entangled in the double standard as he, they agreed that alcoholic women deserved help too. They found it difficult to understand how good women from good homes became addicted to alcohol in the first place.[16] However, having accepted the responsibility, they made good on the challenge to lead these female newcomers to sobriety.

The first AA woman whose sobriety "took" was herself a much-loved pioneer named Ethel M. Until her death in 1963, she was credited in AA's history as having the longest uninterrupted sobriety of any AA woman. Although Marty M. had joined the fellowship in New York a few years before Ethel, early on a relapse interrupted her sobriety, leaving the honor of "longest sober woman in AA" to Ethel M.

One reason for Ethel's good fortune was a practical one. Unlike other women who tried the program before her, she came to AA with her husband, Roscoe. Thus, as a married woman, Ethel was far less threatening to the alcoholic men and their nervous wives than were some of the single and divorced women who appeared earlier.

Nonetheless, Ethel's struggle to find sobriety as the area's first woman AA touches us with her courage and simplicity. When the Scripture-based, formal route to spirituality eluded her, she was determined to find the God of her understanding another way—and it worked. New in sobriety and spiritually isolated, Ethel found God in her flower garden and surrendered her alcoholism in a way that felt natural to her. Many years later, while recording her early memories of AA, Ethel testified:

I want to bring this in, how I found God . . . I planted a large
garden and in that garden I found my God. I learned to talk to
Him in the simplest way imaginable . . . I accepted the fact that
there was something spiritual, something much stronger than
myself that had to enter into this to help, but I didn't know
how to pray, and I didn't [pray]. I didn't know how to pray the
Bible way. You know, nature is a marvelous healer and I
needed healing that summer. When things disturbed me,
when I thought a drink was the answer, I got the hoe and I
went to the garden and I talked to the God I had found in the
simplest words anyone could find. I asked Him to help me, to
give me an understanding of what all these things were about.
I built up a spiritual strength that summer in that contact with
the God that I found, that I had never had before, so that when
the time came when I needed that spiritual strength, it was
there . . . I felt that I had found the spiritual strength. . . . I felt
that I had made a complete surrender and that I had really
turned my life over [to God] that summer.[17]

During times of trouble, Ethel turned to Anne Smith for advice and
to Sister Ignatia for spiritual strength. They in turn taught Ethel the
ways of AA sponsorship and provided her with their own examples
and personal support. She was such an avid student of AA's teachings
that not even her lone role as Akron AA's token female alcoholic
caused her much distress. Gratitude for her own (and her husband's)
sobriety surmounted obstacles that might otherwise have tested her
surrender to AA principles. Ethel advantageously used all of the tools
that God and AA had given her. When Ethel came into the program,
she weighed no less than three hundred pounds, a reality that sobriety permitted her to accept about herself and even learn to laugh at.

Fortunately for AA women to come, Ethel never considered her
sex, her addictions, or her weight to be a problem when dealing with
AAs. The first time she was invited to speak at an AA meeting, a well-
meaning male AA friend said to her, "Ethel, don't do that. The women
over there will tear you apart." With a quick and humorous retort,
Ethel replied, "Well, there is a lot of me to tear."[18]

Simple faith and a generous nature eased Ethel's spirit into sobriety. In addition, she learned early on how to rely on other people to ease her through some very troubled times. Personal hardships, losses, and misunderstandings helped turn her toward friends she could trust, friends who would share her down times, whether major tragedies or minor misfortunes. During times of her greatest sorrow, it was Sister Ignatia who lent the "presence and understanding"[19] that Ethel felt so characterized the St. Thomas Hospital nun. Of Ignatia, Ethel said:

> I am very close to Sister. She was very helpful to me. I now have a card and a note that she wrote when my brother was killed. It was one of the most comforting things about it [the death].
>
> He was dead when I got to the city . . . he was shot. They didn't tell me anything. I found out afterwards that he raised up and said, *"I'm sorry,"* before he died. What Sister tried to get across to me was *that;* and it was very comforting to me.[20]

Then, some years later, Ethel's husband, Roscoe, died, and again Ethel gained strength from Ignatia:

> She [Sister Ignatia] came down to the funeral home when Roscoe was there. That was a wonderful gesture on her part. She knelt on the carpet before the coffin, and sat and talked to me for some time afterwards. She has an immense capacity to bring peace to people, just by her presence. *Everybody loved Sister Ignatia.*[21]

While Sister Ignatia's friendship helped Ethel find peace of mind and soul, Anne Smith's cosponsorship lent another dimension to her recovery. With Anne's guidance, Ethel added traits of self-confidence and wisdom to her sobriety. Prone as she was to self-doubt and uncertainty when she came into the program, Ethel gradually overcame her habit of negating and demeaning her own feelings in the face of criticism or disagreement from others. The painfulness of her early emotional experiences and her initial dependence on Anne for affirmation of newfound feelings of self-worth were a crucial part of her new lifestyle:

> . . . Nobody will ever know how I miss Anne's advice about things. I would get into the biggest dither about something. I hadn't been in too long and one of the men's wives called me on [a] Sunday. She told me that she didn't think I had any part of the program. Well, I wasn't sure I did! I was awfully foggy, and I wept. I asked her what she thought I ought to do about it. She said she didn't know, but that I sure showed plainly enough that I didn't have any part of the program.
>
> . . . but I remember how comforting it was when Anne told her I was crying . . . Anne talked to me and laughed about it, and got me all over it.
>
> And another thing that was helpful to me: I used to think I was cowardly when things came up pertaining to the program that troubled me. I said to her many times, "Annie, am I being a coward because I lay those things away on the shelf and skip them?" She said, "No, you are just being wise. If it isn't anything that is going to help you or anybody else, why should you become involved in it and get all disturbed about it?"[22]

Ethel remembered that Anne approached new members with signs of affection, like a welcoming handshake or a few words of encouragement. These gestures somehow made alcoholics in early recovery feel recognized and worthwhile. Like Sister Ignatia, Anne had the ability to draw good out of people and to help them find the same good in themselves. As a result, the early women AAs were deeply touched by Anne's neighborly gestures:

> . . . the first Christmas card we got from them [the Smiths], she said on it, "To our dear new friends as dear to us as our old friends." I loved it.[23]

Anne Smith's Death and Legacy

Sending Christmas cards was one example of the way that Anne personalized her relationship with all the AAs. As her eyesight failed, this simple act of love became a hardship that was difficult to continue. Thereafter, when they received her greeting, each recipient knew of the time and effort Anne expended on their behalf and treasured her all the more for this caring effort. Now a close friend, Ethel offered support to Anne:

> I know she started early in the fall, working on those cards. She would think up things about these people that evidently she would feel fit into their lives. I told her many times that I didn't think she had any idea what that really meant to these people. I related this to her, trying to make her understand that her efforts weren't wasted, that she played a terrific part in people's lives.[24]

By 1948, along with her vision, Anne's overall health was failing. On one of their few social outings together, the Smiths drove Sister Ignatia and a companion, Sister Mercede, to Cleveland, where they visited the orphans at Parmadale Children's Village. The event was a singular but precious moment for the three pioneers. Sister Ignatia later wrote to Dr. Bob of the day's vivid and meaningful memories. In her words she reveals the rich, wide spirit that clasped together a trio of hearts:

> I recall the day you and Anne took Sister Mercede and me to Parmadale Children's Village. It was a beautiful day. The scenery was delightful. Anne, who loved nature, seemed to drink in the beauties of God's creation. We visited the cottages, listened to the band, and finally attended a program given by the children. Anne's kind sympathetic heart went out to the little ones. We often spoke of that memorable day and hoped that someday we would make another trip to Parmadale.[25]

Not long after, on June 1, 1949, members of Alcoholics Anonymous experienced the deep sorrow of Anne Smith's death. At the same time, they were coping as best they could with the knowledge of Dr. Bob's diagnosis of cancer, already in an advanced stage.

Just before Anne passed away, however, the Smiths made one last visit to their son in Texas. By that time both Akron leaders were gravely ill. Soon after they arrived, their son, Smitty, could see that the loving effort and travel had exhausted them. Wisely he suggested that his parents return to Akron and the familiar comfort of their home. Dr. Bob telephoned Sister Ignatia from the airport to make arrangements for Anne's admission to the hospital. By the time they reached St. Thomas Hospital, Anne had suffered a severe heart attack, quickly followed by heart failure and acute pneumonia. Observing Dr. Smith's extreme exhaustion when he and Anne reached the hospital, Ignatia admitted both spouses as patients. The tiresome journey home and concern over Anne's condition had driven Dr. Bob to the edge of physical collapse.

Personnel at the hospital soon realized that Anne's death was imminent. Word of her critical condition spread quickly throughout the AA community. Confusion due to the Smiths' sudden return to Akron added the rumor that Dr. Bob himself had died. Meanwhile, family and close friends gathered at the hospital, dividing their energy between comforting "Doc" and "Annie." Ignatia kept a vigil over the AA ward, adding balm to her saddened spirit. During the long nights, she hovered at Anne's bedside, soothing her fears of death away. In a final gesture of love and deep affinity for the generous, noble spirit of Anne Ripley Smith, Sister Ignatia baptized her friend conditionally in the water and words of Catholic baptism. Conducting the rite alone, Sister Ignatia whispered as she poured the water:

> *I baptize thee in the name of the Father, and of the Son, and of the Holy Spirit. Amen.*[26]

Did Anne Smith choose to become a Catholic during her final illness? No one knows for certain, not even her children. Ignatia's gesture, though secretive, was consistent with the practice of hospital nuns to baptize their dying patients. Even so, a spiritual bond had always existed between the two women. Both were keenly aware of each other's spiritual predispositions, likes, and dislikes. Knowledge of their strong friendship and respect for one another makes it plausible that in the last moments of life, Ignatia prepared Anne for her journey into eternity according to her own Catholic practice and felt comfortable in doing so.

After Anne's death, newspapers in all the major cities across the country wrote of the enormous contribution that Anne Smith had made to Alcoholics Anonymous. News articles, obituaries, and editorials for the first time openly printed the full names of Anne R. and Robert H. Smith, thus revealing their leadership in the movement that had made recovery from alcoholic addiction possible for thousands. The *Akron Beacon Journal* wrote:

> Mrs. Anne R. Smith, 68, silent partner in founding and developing internationally famous Alcoholics Anonymous, died early today at St. Thomas Hospital.
>
> . . . Dr. Smith said his wife was "of inestimable value in her encouragement and moral support to me and to the movement" back in 1935 when AA was coming into being.
>
> "She entertained many of the members in our home, and gave them the sympathetic understanding that played so strong a part in rehabilitating persons addicted to alcohol," he said.[27]

The *Akron Beacon Journal*'s editorial writer later referred to the preceding article but added his own mention of Anne's warmth:

> Nothing that an editorial writer might say of Mrs. Anne R. Smith could be higher tribute than the simple but significant statement of her husband, Dr. R. H. Smith, which revealed for the first time her great contribution to Alcoholics Anonymous.
>
> . . . It seems a pity that Mrs. Smith's wonderful work could not have received the public's recognition while she still lived.

But thousands of rehabilitated alcoholics were aware of their debt to her and her husband. She must have known the gratitude in the hearts of the many persons she had helped. No alcoholic herself, Mrs. Smith nevertheless, as her husband said, gave "sympathetic understanding" to those alcoholics who joined together to help each other and eventually to give hope and health to alcoholics everywhere.

Akron should always be proud of the AA movement which was born here and proud of the fine woman who did so much to foster that movement.[28]

In the latter months of 1949, Bill Wilson made frequent visits to Dr. Bob in Akron. He shared Dr. Bob's bereavement over Anne's death and fretted about his partner's terminal illness. Always a man of immediate action, Bill saw the historical importance of Anne Smith's life and attempted to preserve it. To members of Akron's fellowship he wrote:

AA might never have been without Anne Smith. Her loyalty and devotion, her deep love, not only of Dr. Bob, but of all of us, these qualities secure for her the highest possible place in our affections and in the history of our AA society. It seems most fitting and urgently desirable that those who knew her best take steps to prepare an account of her life among us; this to the end that succeeding generations of AAs may profit by her wise example and be inspired by her wonderful personality. Knowing her as you did, I am sure you will be glad to contribute to this effort. As a stimulant to your memory, there follows a list of the outstanding qualities Anne had:

Love, Courage, Loyalty, Humor, Patience, Thoughtfulness, Humility, Unselfishness, Understanding, Spirituality

If you meditate on these qualities, many of the things she said and did will surely come to your mind. Will you select one or two of the best incidents in your personal experience with her and then put them in the form of a letter or memorandum? Out of such material we would like to prepare a piece for the *AA Grapevine* and a much more extended account to be filed with the Alcoholic Foundation as historical material. So, will you lend us a hand as promptly as possible?

Sincerely, Bill

P.S. We would appreciate having this by Dec. 15th.[29]

Exactly on December 15, Sister Ignatia responded to Bill's SOS for memories about Anne. Ignatia's insight into history, human nature, and Anne Smith's importance to Alcoholics Anonymous is clear. She wrote:

Dear Dr. Smith

With the spirit of Christmas alive again, I cannot help but think of Anne and her generous giving of herself in so many ways and to so many people. In the early years of AA here at St. Thomas, Anne meant so much to me. I called her countless times about patients and she had the right answer or soon found it for me. Her judgment was most reliable. Her calmness and stability inspired hope and confidence . . . God has been good to have given us Anne for so many years. As the years wear away, her influence in the beginning and growth of AA will be appreciated more and more. Wishing you all the blessings of this Holy Season, I am very gratefully yours in Christ,

Sister Ignatia[30]

Dr. Bob's Last Year

After Anne's passing, Wilson increased his visits to Akron. With Dr. Bob grieving and in waning health, Bill activated old friendships in Akron and intensified his relationship with Sister Ignatia.

Akron was still AA's Midwest bastion of spiritual ideals, practices, and orthodox values. Although a few other AA hospitals had by then come into existence, the St. Thomas Hospital alcoholism ward remained AA's most notable, most viable hospital plan in the country.[31] No other hospital owned the dual distinction of having AA's physician and cofounder functioning also as the copioneer of AA's first hospital plan. Moreover, following Dr. Bob's death, the torch of unofficial leadership would undoubtedly pass to his popular, capable partner, Sister Ignatia. Bill himself recognized this as one more proof—and guarantee—that Alcoholics Anonymous would exist beyond the passing of its cofounders.

Ignatia always enjoyed a pleasant, comfortable relationship with Bill Wilson, notwithstanding her outright and fiercely loyal allegiance to Dr. Bob. Wilson saw at this point the obvious need to provide direction for the Akron AA community so that it might survive the upcoming trauma of a change in leadership. To that end, he made sure that his alliance with the doctor's heir apparent, Sister Ignatia, was on a solid footing.

Indeed, a loving and lasting association developed between Bill and Ignatia as together they shared the pain of supporting Dr. Smith in his last distressful year. With cancer invading and destroying his bones, Dr. Bob's physical agony was excruciating. Yet his exceptional sense of humor and his emotional composure in the face of consuming pain awed hospital personnel.

Now Sister Ignatia's religious vocation and background in music brought relief and comfort to the two men's last days together. It happened in the following way.

Some of the ailing doctor's brightest moments came when he and Ignatia visited the chapel. After making Dr. Bob comfortable, she seated herself at the beautiful organ. Then the soothing sounds and fluid rhythms of Ignatia's music flooded the tiny chapel and filled him with a needed measure of peace. On special occasions, Sister Ignatia played the magnificent bell chimes that Paul R., a Youngstown AA member, had donated to the hospital in 1948. Symbolically, the pealing chimes seemed to ring out AA's message of gratitude to Bill and Bob, loud enough, Sister Ignatia said, for all of Akron to hear.

> During this difficult time, Sister Ignatia brought Bill a new perspective on the suffering that accompanies the alcoholic experience. One day while visiting the hospital, he accompanied her to the chapel where Benediction was about to begin. Light from the golden monstrance momentarily illuminated Bill. He walked over to a wall carving that depicted the Seventh Station of the Cross, "Jesus Falls the Second Time," and Sister Ignatia stood beside him: "Bill, this is The Way of the Cross. We make it each day," she remarked. Pausing, Bill replied, "I wish you'd teach me about it and make it with me, Sister."[32]

Then, just as she so often had done when leading the patients from the alcoholism ward to the nearby choir loft, she seized her moment and directed Bill on a tour of the chapel, explaining the stations of the cross as they went along.

They made their way up and down the empty aisles, crisscrossing church pews to better scrutinize the symbols. Ignatia paused before each of fourteen stations and explained their Christian significance to Bill. As she voiced the concepts, Bill began to sense a relationship between the cross of Christ and the suffering of the alcoholic.

Ignatia and Bill lingered and shared their reflections in front of the eleventh station. Bill was deep in contemplation as he read the legend, "Jesus Is Nailed to the Cross." His eyes moved to the figure hanging outstretched before them. The remembrance of his own body, rigid, powerless, and restrained by leather straps, flashed into his consciousness. The unbearable cross of alcoholism seemed to him a modern-day crucifixion, both a way of suffering and a way of salvation.

Alcoholic agony and isolation returned in a rush of emotion. The pleas of the dying Christ—"I thirst! My God, my God, why have you forsaken me?"—seemed divinely prophetic of the despair uttered by the suffering alcoholic. It comforted him to know that perhaps in some small measure he and Dr. Bob together had discovered a way to release alcoholics from their misery.

Though they had gone to the chapel together before, this particular visit was a moving experience for Bill and Ignatia. They paused again at the final station, where "Jesus Is Laid in the Tomb." Perhaps they both felt the sadness of Dr. Bob's impending death and used this opportunity to create some human sense of it. The answers—in parallels—were there for the asking: After Christ's death, his *friends* carried his message to the world at large.

Bill and Ignatia also realized that Dr. Bob's grateful followers would communicate AA's fellowship and message across decades and generations to come. The very thought consoled them and forged their bond. A new partnership was born as they prepared to carry on without Dr. Bob.

From that day forward, whenever Bill traveled to St. Thomas Hospital, he visited the chapel with Ignatia. There an unnamed but compelling presence brought him to his knees. Still, Wilson remained a questioning man in search of a religion for the rest of his days.

Aside from Dr. Bob's illness, Sister Ignatia faced other monumental problems during the fall of 1949. First was a drawerful of unresolved AA debts. Ignatia knew that the ward's financial liabilities increasingly vexed the hospital's administrators. It was no surprise when, one day, Ignatia received a bill and an ultimatum: Pay the AA debt or lose the AA beds.

Ignatia's Problems of Money and Fame

Though she possessed extraordinary abilities to understand alcoholism and treat its victims, Ignatia had little aptitude for business operations. To the end, a total disregard for financial management and accountability remained a blemish on her otherwise accomplished record. In fact, she never bothered to learn the system. When in financial straits, she always managed to find a solution or, as some would say, an angel. When Ignatia needed money, she asked for it, and she received it. That system worked for her. Perhaps for that reason, she rarely concerned herself with finances. From the beginning, Sister Ignatia took the poorest of the addicted poor into the AA ward. Indeed, she considered caring for the poor to be the source of the hospital's spiritual wealth, believing that the presence of the poor guaranteed the goodwill of Providence. All AAs knew that they could count on her help, regardless of their immediate ability to pay. Equally, when the hospital administration periodically called on her to tighten up on her loose financial practices, she knew that one word of her distress mentioned to "her boys" would elicit a flurry of fund-raising activity.

That October she advised Bill Wilson of her latest financial predicament, knowing he would help erase the debt. True to her expectations, he appealed to Akron's AA membership. They rallied and raised the $4,500 needed to pay the debt and put Sister Ignatia's books in the black once more.[33]

Despite such stopgap measures, Ignatia's disdain for finances constantly vexed hospital administrators. Their real frustration with Ignatia stemmed not so much from her inattention to financial details but from the growing power of her treatment program. To further complicate the matter, the administration discovered that any open criticism of Sister Ignatia brought a rousing defense from the four thousand former AA patients who credited this "problem nun" with saving their lives. Indeed, the uproar of four thousand grateful voices tended to weaken and smother the sounds of administrative reproach. When, in frustration, the sisters attempted to transfer her, the outcry from the AAs was thunderous. In spite of many efforts to remove her, Ignatia stayed.

For a time during the middle to late 1940s Ignatia's behavior was in fact somewhat high-handed. Thus, some of the hospital's concerns over Ignatia's management style were legitimate. As her own fame and power increased, it is said that she would have given every bed in the hospital to the AAs, had she not been occasionally accountable to the administration. Doctors and nurses complained that truly sick patients could no longer obtain beds with Sister Ignatia functioning as the official admitting officer. Nor, as the medical staff saw it, did she always exercise impartial judgment when revising the daily admissions roster. Even the AAs proudly exaggerated reports that Sister Ignatia was known to turn away a patient with a broken leg or a woman in labor if an alcoholic needed a hospital bed. Although this was not truly the case, it makes a point about Ignatia's fervor regarding the alcoholism ward.

The truth is, her decisions can be both criticized and commended. However, one thing about her is certain: Sister Ignatia believed wholeheartedly that God had given her this work to initiate and accomplish, and she was not afraid to back her faith with action. All would agree that she committed 100 percent of herself to alcohol rehabilitation when it was an unpopular cause. In doing so, she practiced the love-centered spirit of her religious community, sometimes at the expense of their more conventional rules. In the true fashion of a founder or pioneer, this musician-counselor-nun sometimes seemed out of step to people of less spiritual intensity and vision. Precisely because Ignatia and her unorthodox ways were not always accepted by the medical staff or by her community, a circle of AA devotees stood ready to protect the spunky nun from angry moves by the administration. In fact, it was the growing number of reformed alcoholic companions that steadily increased her power.

With Dr. Bob terminally ill, some members of the administration thought their problems with Ignatia would soon be over. In fact, with Smith's death, most assumed that the AA movement itself would grind to a halt. But AA's spirit and unity were not to be stopped. As the movement grew, Sister Ignatia's popularity in the Akron area kept pace.

Because so many had already been saved by her at AA's first hospital, the small nun's reputation gained notice in distant parts of the country, carried swiftly by her out-of-town recovered patients. For example, AA's New York office received inquiries for the address of the "Ignatia Hospital."[34]

California reporters used their opportunity to interview Dr. Bob to garner quotable information about Sister Ignatia. During his final trip to the West Coast in 1949, they asked him, "What kind of a person is Sister Ignatia?"[35] Smith's AA traveling companion (Dan K.), who observed the press encounter, said:

> I'll never forget how humble he was when he answered. He told me later, "I looked down on that floor and I thought, 'God, help me give the right answer.'" And he said, "Gentlemen of

the press and fellow members of AA, in my book, Sister Ignatia is the type of person who's born once every hundred years in this world."[36]

As Sister Ignatia's prominence increased, so did the hospital's efforts to restrain her. With her removal from the hospital temporarily impeded by the AA supporters, the superior employed a private avenue of discipline: She turned to the Community Rule, and thus exercised her authority over Ignatia.

The one surviving page from Sister Ignatia's journal during this time is revealing of the conflict. Her brief notations suggest that difficulties *did* exist between her and the superior and that she was disciplined because of them. The entry for November 3, 1946, reads:

> Spent most of day (11:00 A.M.) in room in Obedience to Superior's order (voiceless). Complained to three sisters instead of accepting God's Holy Will; short with telephone operator. Try to cultivate instinctive Love for God—Love of Preference by giving up something I value for love of Him. Three Masses—no time for formal visit; mortification missed xxxx. Love God in All—All in God; Contemplation in Action.[37]

Days of recollection were important to Sister Ignatia's spiritual growth. However, popular acclaim for her AA work provided her with real opportunities to practice key virtues such as humility and obedience.

AA Awards Multiply

By now, AA was building a public record of its achievements. Articles about AA appeared in newspapers and national magazines with some regularity; the frequency of awards and honors granted to the fellowship increased.

The first major award cited in Alcoholics Anonymous's New York records was the Lasker Award.[38] This honor was presented to Bill Wilson and the fellowship of Alcoholics Anonymous on behalf of the twelve thousand physician members of the American Public Health Association. The text of the award states:

> Alcoholics Anonymous works upon the novel principle that a recovered alcoholic can reach and treat a fellow sufferer as no one else can. In so doing, the recovered alcoholic maintains his own sobriety; the man [woman] he treats soon becomes a physician to the next new applicant, thus creating an ever expanding chain reaction of liberation with patients welded together by bonds of common suffering, common understanding, and stimulating action in a great cause.
>
> . . . It enjoys the good will and often the warm endorsement of many medical and scientific groups—no mean achievement in itself for any organization run entirely by laymen.[39]

Bestowed in 1951 in a ceremony at the San Francisco Opera House, this award was recorded by Wilson as AA's first award. However, the Lasker Award was merely the first award Bill Wilson *himself* received on behalf of Alcoholics Anonymous.

Earlier, in 1949, the fellowship of Alcoholics Anonymous was honored closer to its Ohio birthplace. Founders Associates of the College of Steubenville, Ohio, awarded the first annual Poverello Medal to Alcoholics Anonymous for its distinguished pioneering efforts in the world of alcoholism. The Poverello Medal itself honors St. Francis of Assisi, patron of the College of Steubenville. In his lifetime, St. Francis was affectionately known as *Il poverello,* the little poor one, because of his love and work for God's poor. Etched on one side of the medal is a scene of St. Francis giving money and clothing to the very poor. On the opposite side, an inscription reads:

> In recognition of great benefactions to humanity, exemplifying in our age the Christ-like spirit of charity which filled the life of St. Francis.[40]

The medal was cast in steel to symbolize the ideals of Franciscan poverty, the steel industry (the major industry of the Steubenville area), and the strength of character found in those who exemplify St. Francis's ideals. A list of its first recipients between 1949 and 1954 is impressive: 1949, The Fellowship of Alcoholics Anonymous; 1950, Edward F. Hutton of Freedom Foundation; 1951, The Court of Last Resort; 1952, Lions International; 1953, Variety Clubs International; 1954, Llewellyn J. Scott, T.O.R., Blessed Martin de Porres Hospice, Washington, D.C.

Perhaps because a Catholic organization sponsored the award, Bill ignored its importance to the fellowship. Also, anonymity for alcoholics at the public level was still an unresolved issue for the cofounders. In any case, Dr. Bob was too sick to appear publicly, and Bill, for whatever reason, was not involved in the Ohio award.

However, another explanation for the low profile attached to AA's receipt of the Poverello Medal is possible. Letters from the president of the College of Steubenville to Sister Ignatia's superior suggest that Father Daniel W. Egan, T.O.R., and the Founders Associates had, as their unspoken agenda, the intention of honoring Sister Ignatia in the name of AA. By 1949, she was very well known, especially in Ohio and the surrounding states. Many people declared her to be the prime reason for AA's strong success and spiritual effectiveness. She had already been dubbed "the Angel of Alcoholics Anonymous" by the press. Her presence—not Bill's or Bob's—at the awards ceremony was clearly desired by the Founders Associates. However, at the last minute Sister Ignatia balked at participating in the event. Four days before the ceremony, Father Egan expressed his deep concern over the reticent nun's hesitation to Mother M. Carmelita, then superior general of the Sisters of Charity of Saint Augustine. On December 3, he wrote to the superior:

> Dear Reverend Mother:
>   Since my last communication to you I have learned that Sister Ignatia has become a bit concerned and perhaps rather frightened at the thought of coming to Steubenville for our Founder's Day dinner, and she now wishes to beg off.
>   I fully appreciate the fact that the initial publicity attendant upon the announcement of the awarding of the Poverello

Medal and its receipt by Sister on behalf of Alcoholics Anonymous caused her some concern. The interest in this Medal and its recipient this year has been amazing. In response, however, to Sister's request, we immediately instructed the publicity department to play down the use of her name so as to avoid any embarrassment. I believe that has been done.

All that Sister needs to do at the affair, and it is with the hearty approbation of the Bishop here in Steubenville, is to be in attendance and receive the Medal from my hand. She will not have to say even a word, but her presence is almost vital to the success of the program and it will cause considerable embarrassment if she does not attend. I am taking it for granted that it is only Sister's humility and her desire to remain in the background that is prompting her to try to have our plans changed. I think that when she realizes the tremendous effect this award seems to be having on the morale of Alcoholics Anonymous everywhere she will be glad that she cooperated.

We are arranging to have Mr. William V. H. of Kent, Ohio, who is highly regarded by Sister Ignatia, fetch her from Akron to Steubenville on Wednesday and back again on Thursday. He will also bring whatever companion is to come with Sister, and it would please us very much if you yourself could arrange to come. I hope that this will be possible.

With every expression of sincere gratitude, I remain,
Sincerely in Christ,
Daniel W. Egan, T.O.R., Pres.[41]

Sister Ignatia, pressured by the superior, received the Poverello Medal on behalf of Alcoholics Anonymous on December 7, 1949. With no mention in AA's official archives of Sister Ignatia's award of the Poverello Medal, New York historians seemingly overlooked the stature of both the prize and of the woman who received it. But the Poverello Medal was, in fact, the first public honor bestowed upon Alcoholics Anonymous.

Nonetheless, the distinction resulting from receiving the Poverello

Medal forced a change in Sister Ignatia's image. From the moment she accepted the honor, she became a public figure in her own right, separate from the fellowship and its cofounders. The presentation also coincided with her taking on increased responsibilities for the AA ward because of Dr. Bob's rapidly deteriorating health.

Not only was AA "coming of age," but so was Akron. By 1950, Dr. Bob's last year, many important transitions were under way in the fellowship. Worldwide expansion renewed public interest in the rapidly growing AA movement. The *Saturday Evening Post* published an updated article on Alcoholics Anonymous by Jack Alexander. He had written the first *Post* report on AA in the March 1, 1941, issue. In a second in-depth study nine years later, which was much less publicized, Alexander reviewed the matter of hospitalization. His writing illustrated spotty but generally improved hospital conditions for the victims of alcoholism. On April 1, 1950, he wrote:

> . . . Understandably, many hospitals are reluctant to accept alcoholic patients, because so many of them are disorderly. With this sad fact in mind, the society [A.A.] has persuaded several hospitals to set up separate alcoholic corridors and is helping to supervise the patients through supplying volunteer workers. To the satisfaction of all concerned, including the hospital managements, which find the supervised corridors peaceful, more than 10,000 patients have gone through five-day rebuilding courses. The hospitals involved in this successful experiment are: St. Thomas' (Catholic) in Akron, St. John's (Episcopal) in Brooklyn, and Knickerbocker (nonsectarian) in Manhattan. They have set a pattern which the society would like to see adopted by the numerous hospitals which now accept alcoholics on a more restricted basis.[42]

Alexander's article revived AA's spirits and so prepared the fellowship for the memorable Cleveland convention of July 1950. Awash in the sentiments of reviewing AA's fifteen-year progress and anticipating its future success, AA's First International Convention attendees took part in a historic, if not touching, moment before the conference ended. The last weekend in July, seven thousand participants unanimously approved AA's Twelve Traditions at Wilson's strong urging. Adding to the Twelve Steps, the Traditions sought to preserve operational unity as AA prepared for the loss of its Akron cofounder.

Dr. Bob's Farewell to AA

As if adoption of the Twelve Traditions were not an emotional enough issue for the convention fellowship to absorb, on Sunday afternoon Dr. Bob Smith made his farewell speech to the thousands of sober alcoholics gathered before him. His talk was necessarily brief. The spread of his cancer made it difficult for him to move or breathe, much less speak to a public gathering of thousands. But speak to them he did in his characteristic simple fashion. His gratitude for Alcoholics Anonymous, God, sobriety, and for those gathered reached out from the podium to unforgettably touch their hearts and bid farewell to all the membership present.

Never before had so many AAs witnessed such contrast in styles between their benevolent cofounders. Bill's talents for organization and public relations were evident in the well-planned guidelines for AA's ongoing philosophical and operational integrity. Dr. Bob's charismatic presence and simple but brilliant remarks summarized all that fostered AA's inner spirit. He told a mesmerized, tearful audience:

> I get a big thrill out of looking over a vast sea of faces like this with a feeling that possibly some small thing I did a number of years ago played an infinitely small part in making this meeting possible. I also get quite a thrill when I think that we all had the same problem. We all did the same things. We all get the same results in proportion to our zeal and enthusiasm and stick-to-itiveness. If you will pardon the injection of a personal note at this time, let me say that I have been in bed five of the last seven months, and my strength hasn't returned as I would like, so my remarks of necessity will be very brief.
>
> There are two or three things that flashed into my mind on which it would be fitting to lay a little emphasis. One is the

simplicity of our program. Let's not louse it all up with Freud-
ian complexes and things that are interesting to the scientific
mind, but have very little to do with our actual AA work. Our
Twelve Steps, when simmered down to the last, resolve themselves into the words "love" and "service." We understand
what love is, and we understand what service is. So let's bear
those two things in mind.

Let us also remember to guard that erring member, the
tongue, and if we use it, let's use it with kindness and consideration and tolerance. And one more thing: none of us would
be here today if somebody hadn't taken time to explain things
to us, to give us a little pat on the back, to take us to a meeting
or two, to do numerous little kind and thoughtful acts in our
behalf. So let us never get such a degree of smug compla-
cency that we're not willing to extend, or attempt to extend, to
our less fortunate brothers that help which has been so beneficial to us. Thank you very much.[43]

These were the final thoughts Dr. Bob publicly left with the fellowship. Over the next and last months of his life, he repeated the admo-
nition "Let's not louse it all up with psychiatry" to most of his final
visitors. Perhaps as a physician he saw more clearly than most the
dangers inherent in complicating recovery with professionalism.

Dr. Bob issued a timeless warning with that simple observation.
Moreover, by 1950, outside educators and prominent scholars of medicine and theology had come to notice AA's remarkable success in arresting alcoholism. Some traveled to Akron to meet the renowned
pioneering hospital team of Dr. Bob and Sister Ignatia, then returned
to their hospitals to replicate the work.

That fall, shortly before Dr. Bob passed on, the Rev. John C. Ford,
a Jesuit moral theologian, visited the St. Thomas Hospital alcoholism
ward where at last he met the "benign conspirators,"[44] Dr. Bob and
Sister Ignatia.

By 1950, Father Ford was well acquainted with Bill Wilson and
Alcoholics Anonymous through his own early writings and teachings
at the Yale School of Alcohol Studies. As the first prominent Catholic

theologian to speak out on the morality of alcohol use, Father Ford was a pioneer in the growing trend toward achieving alcoholism prevention through educational efforts. His visit with Dr. Bob was a memorable one. Three hours passed into history as the doctor charmed the priest with wit, wisdom, and his sage personality.

But the Akron meeting was important to Father Ford for another reason. At the time he was drafting his own scholarly treatise, *Depth Psychology, Morality and Alcoholism.*[45] From this discussion he vividly recalled Dr. Bob's warning, one reflecting his own philosophy of keeping it simple. Bob reminded the moralist, "Don't louse it up with psychiatry."[46]

Bob Smith's words left a lasting impression on the priest, and his mannerisms matched Father Ford's own congenial ways. Soon the two alcoholism pioneers were exchanging stories and sayings, including this quip from Father Ford's repertoire, which delighted Dr. Bob:

> At the punch bowl's brink
> Let the thirsty think
> What they say in Japan:
> "First the man takes a drink,
> Then the drink takes a drink,
> Then the drink takes the man."

> An Adage from the Orient[47]

Once more before he died, Dr. Bob raised his voice in warning to those who would carry on AA's work. Bill Wilson was the beneficiary this time. Having finally secured Bob's support for scheduling AA's World Service Conference,[48] Bill recalled their last parting:

> I went down the steps and then turned to look back. Bob stood in the doorway, tall and upright as ever. Some color had come back to his cheeks, and he was carefully dressed in a light gray suit. This was my partner, the man with whom I never had a hard word. The wonderful, old, broad smile was on his face as he said almost jokingly, "Remember, Bill, let's

not louse this thing up. Let's *keep it simple!*" I turned away, unable to say a word. That was the last time I ever saw him.[49]

As Bill anticipated, the AA membership reached out to Sister Ignatia for spiritual nurturance and leadership when Dr. Bob died on November 16, 1950. Following her example, Akronites rallied from their grief and loss. Together they memorialized Dr. Bob's great spirit with steadfast loyalty to the Oxford Group's four absolutes that had governed all his principles about sobriety: honesty, purity, unselfishness, and love.[50] Those were the four spiritual themes that underscored the legacy of Dr. Bob and underlay the sheer wisdom of his final important advice to Alcoholics Anonymous: *"Keep it simple . . . Honesty, Purity, Unselfishness, and Love."*

True to Dr. Bob's directives, Sister Ignatia carried on with their system of conducting the alcoholism ward at St. Thomas Hospital. Structured as before, the ward functioned smoothly, aided by the transition time his lengthy illness provided. Dr. Thomas P. Scuderi—the same Dr. Scuderi who had worked with Sister Ignatia at the beginning—now joined the AA team, treating the alcoholics' physical complications until his own retirement many years later. As the scope of her responsibilities increased, Sister Ignatia's role changed somewhat too. Most of her hours were still spent inside the hospital, but because of AA's increased publicity a growing portion of her time now went to answering requests for information from other hospitals.

Soon the Catholic Hospital Association of the United States and Canada invited Sister Ignatia to speak about alcoholism at their annual convention in early June 1951. In Philadelphia Sister Ignatia presented her first major speech, entitled "Care and Treatment of Alcoholics." She cited the happy cooperation of St. Thomas Hospital with Alcoholics Anonymous as an incentive for other Catholic hospitals to follow suit:

> We have hospitalized well over 4,000 AA patients at St. Thomas. They have come to Akron from Alabama, South Carolina, Michigan, Maryland, Texas, and many other distant parts. They would not have had to travel so far if their *local*

hospitals made it possible for them to receive the program nearer home.

Time and finances prohibit many from making such a long trip. . . .

. . . It is perhaps the best means by which the work of the hospital can be interpreted to the community. It gives the hospital a good name, not only with the reformed drunkard, his family, friends, and neighbors, but the whole community can point to something constructive which the hospital has done. These people are seeking truth; in other words, they are thirsting for God.[51]

Officials attending the hospital convention received Ignatia's prophetic remarks graciously but skeptically. In fact, several years would elapse before most health care facilities saw the profit in responding to her challenge.

Nonetheless, speaking at the hospital convention provided a momentous occasion for Sister Ignatia and for the fellowship as well. In New York, Bill Wilson acknowledged her speaking debut with a brief letter:

Your cordial note transmitting me your paper, "Care and Treatment of Alcoholics," which you gave at Philadelphia has just been read with deep interest. This simple, glowing testimony affects me more than I can say. It stirs memories of the past, it reminds me of your invaluable friendship, and it augurs for a bright future. Thank you so much, dear Sister.[52]

The Philadelphia speech was followed by another first-time experience for Sister Ignatia, namely a published article under her byline: "The Care of Alcoholics—St. Thomas Hospital and A.A. Started a Movement Which Swept the Country." *Hospital Progress,* the journal of the Catholic Hospital Association, featured the article in its October 1951 issue.

Ignatia Confronts Wilson

This move toward public speaking and writing enhanced Ignatia's pride in the early endeavors of the alcoholism ward of St. Thomas Hospital. A new self-confidence filled her. In turn it buttressed the courage and assertiveness she needed to deal with the occasional problems that originated in the New York AA office. For example, in early 1952, AA's journal, *The AA Grapevine,* published a brief article on AA's beginnings entitled "Historical Highlights." Some of the contents incensed Sister Ignatia and the Akron AAs. Accordingly, on January 24, she called Wilson's attention to the inaccuracies he published regarding the beginnings of AA hospitalizations. Clearly, Bill's habit of highlighting AA's achievements in New York at the expense of his fellow workers in Akron infuriated Sister Ignatia. In particular, when Bill's rambling historical narratives bypassed or downplayed Dr. Bob Smith's contributions to the fellowship, the fiery nun minced no words. She confronted Wilson's perceptions of history as well as his motives in the following frosty letter:

> . . . I direct your attention to two inaccuracies in that summary. The first is the statement that the first religious hospital open to AA was St. Thomas Hospital, Akron, in *1942.* The statement is inaccurate as to date. Our records establish that the first AA patient treated at St. Thomas Hospital, Akron, was admitted on August 16, *1939.* The physician was Dr. Bob of honored memory.[53]

Ignatia's letter continues:

> The second inaccuracy is the statement that the "First Hospital Plan" was inaugurated at Knickerbocker Hospital in New York in 1945. Unless the writer of the statement is using the word "plan" in a sense different from that which has common acceptance, this statement is also contrary to fact. As indicated in the paragraph above, St. Thomas Hospital has treated

AA patients continuously since 1939 and then, as now, we operated on a definite and specific *plan*.[54]

However, the conscience-pricking statement came in her next-to-last paragraph:

> I hope you will not think that I am inspired by any petty considerations in pointing out these two errors. I know you will agree with me that a prime requisite of good history, particularly when it deals with the relatively recent past, is accuracy.[55]

Basically, Sister Ignatia was intimating that Bill could benefit from a personal review of AA's principles:

> I do not raise the issue of Honesty, one of the Four Absolutes, because there is *no reason to* suppose that these two errors were made with any intention to deceive. In justice to St. Thomas Hospital and to Knickerbocker Hospital, however, I suggest you check the statements objected to. Knickerbocker Hospital would not, I am sure, desire distinctions incorrectly imputed to it.[56]

The closing of her letter is uncharacteristically formal and cool toward Bill and his fellow AAs in New York:

> I trust that you are enjoying good health and will find it possible soon to visit us again. With kind personal regards and all good wishes to yourself and your associates in AA, I remain,
>
> Sincerely yours,
> Sister M. Ignatia, C.S.A.[57]

Three weeks later, Bill responded. Apparently choosing his words carefully, he attempted to smooth over the upset:

> Your letter of January 24th caused me not a little distress. I am extremely sorry for *The Grapevine*'s error in this respect. As yet, I have not had an opportunity to run the situation down, but you may be assured that I shall do so. Naturally, I heartily agree with you that no one on the staff had any deliberate intent to misstate anything or intentionally wishes to put New York hospitalization in a more favorable light than Akron's.[58]

Then Bill shifted the focus from the dispute to a potential good that might arise from it. He was also attempting to placate the influential Akron nun:

> By implication, you have also drawn my attention once more to the need for getting our total AA story approximately straight in writing. It is my intention to devote a greater part of the years to come to doing just this. The very first book contemplated would be to describe AA's three Legacies of Recovery, Unity and Service in terms of our history. In such a book, great emphasis would be thrown on the origins of AA's Group No. 1 at Akron; also, the magnificent part you, yourself, played in its development. When the time comes to set these things down, you may be sure I shall check most carefully with you.
>
> I do hope that Providence will soon discover an errand which may carry me to Akron. For, now that Anne and Bob are gone, my foremost joy will be in seeing you again.

> In affection,
> Bill[59]

To further smooth the waters, Bill asked Virginia Burneson, then managing editor of *The AA Grapevine,* to review the situation and write to Sister Ignatia. She did so in a letter dated March 6, 1952:

> . . . Since its inception in 1949 the Knickerbocker plan has been widely discussed in *The Grapevine,* professional

publications, and the public press. In its early beginnings, much of the procedure of the Knickerbocker plan was based on the experience gained from St. Thomas and other hospitals working with alcoholics. It is obvious to us, as it is to Bill, that these misunderstandings will occur until such a time as the total AA story is in print. Bill has suggested that you can be of great help to him and to us if you told the AA story as you remember it. We are contemplating assigning such a story to a competent Akron writer. Would that meet with your approval? And do you have any suggestions as to who might be qualified to do the assignment? In order to avoid any future mistakes, both Bill and *The Grapevine* need this authentic information badly. Perhaps you will see your way clear to help us obtain it.[60]

Thus, for the time being, the matter of historical accuracy was put to rest. Clearly, efforts had been made to assuage the angry feelings Ignatia expressed on behalf of herself and Akron AA members.

For the record, the points made by Ignatia represented recognition of Akron's crucial contribution to AA's success on two counts: In addition to being AA's founding city, Akron had also offered the first legitimate AA hospital refuge and treatment. Periodically in the years to come, Sister Ignatia would reaffirm these points with those interested in AA history.

Cleveland Calls

But another development was in the works. Complications arising from the hospital's need to update admission procedures would end the standoff in Sister Ignatia's relationship with the hospital administration and result in her transfer, finally, to Cleveland's Charity Hospital in 1952. Such a move had been contemplated by administration earlier, only to be dropped when the AA membership roared to Ignatia's rescue. Now the plan would be resurrected and this time would be implemented.

The question of Sister Ignatia's transfer had been averted up to now by her standing as a major figure in the AA story. By 1952 she and AA had emerged from comparative obscurity and, accordingly, Bill gave her ready respect and valued her approval in most AA matters. However, the same success that raised her up to AA's notice caused the administrators at St. Thomas Hospital increasing alarm. The tiny nun had become a dynamo of might and power unto herself.

This time, her local clout would not stand up in the face of administration's decision to modernize the admission operations. With Sister Ignatia's commitment to her twenty-year-old method of manipulating hospital admissions for the good of AA standing stubbornly in their way, the hospital administrators opted to risk the wrath of the AA membership and moved, successfully, to transfer her elsewhere.

Ignatia's humor covered her pain at the prospect of leaving Akron. She explained, "We're just like the people in the Army, you know. We go to where we're sent. I'd often wondered whether I was off the mailing list or whether I was forgotten!"[61] Though Sister Ignatia rarely looked back, she did so at Bill's request for historical material in 1954. On that occasion, she elaborated on her exit from Akron:

> As you know, I was in Akron one month short of twenty-four years. We received our obediences on the first of August, 1952. Of course, the Sisters had been teasing me year after year, saying, "Well, are you packed and ready to go?" And I would always say, "Surely." My feast day of St. Ignatius was on the thirty-first of July, so I usually would pick up all the little junk I had around and wrap it up in tissue paper to get rid of it. Then I would put numbers on it and have the Sister draw them. So, of course, we went through all that the evening before. We got our obediences the next day. I put the little slip in my pocket because we were having an exposition of the Blessed Sacrament. I went to the chapel and forgot the little note. I didn't even open it. Finally, at about ten o'clock in the morning I thought I'd better look at it. Well, it said "Charity Hospital on the seventh of August," giving me just those few days to get all my things together.
>
> There was another Sister and myself who changed that

particular year, so I said nothing. I met one of the sisters in the hall and she said, "They say there are two changes and we know who one is but we don't know the other." I must have looked like the cat who swallowed the canary because she said, "It wouldn't be you?" Well, I didn't tell them until lunch time. Then I packed up and had an Irish Wake at St. Thomas. I said to the sister who was taking my place, "Sister Mercede, I think it would be nice if I could introduce you to the people. Probably Wednesday evening will be the King's School meeting, and then the people will stop in. I'll take you up to the ward and introduce you there." Then someone came in and said, "It might be better in the cafeteria because there won't be so much commotion." Well, by evening they had it announced over the radio, and they were coming from everywhere. There was just such a crowd. I called it an Irish Wake. And I left the next day and came here.[62]

Actually, Sister Ignatia's departure from Akron drew thousands of well-wishers. The evening of August 6, autos jammed the surrounding streets from every direction. The scene on the old Akron viaduct, a lengthy bridge that spanned the huge valley between Akron's suburbs and St. Thomas Hospital, has not yet been forgotten. Traffic came to a standstill as drivers flashed their lights and parked their cars on the bridge wherever they stood. Attending police officers looked the other way, oblivious to the snarled traffic. In paradelike fashion, friends inched their way to the hospital on foot just to shake Sister Ignatia's hand one last time. Reporter Oscar Smith wrote in the August 5, 1952, issue of the *Akron Beacon Journal:*

> The "Little Sister of Alcoholics Anonymous" here is leaving St. Thomas Hospital Thursday after twenty-four years of service.
>
> Sister M. Ignatia is being transferred to Charity Hospital in Cleveland to do similar work there, trying to rehabilitate victims of the liquor habit. She is in charge of admissions at St. Thomas.

"I thought I could leave Akron without any fuss being made over me," sighed Sister Ignatia.

But the A.A.s had other plans.[63]

Early on the morning of August 7, Sister Ignatia closed the door to her fifth floor room in the hospital's convent. A tiny smile crossed her face as one of Dr. Bob's humorous remarks flashed back: "It's a good thing you live on the top floor, Sister. That may be as close as you will get to heaven after spending all your time on earth with the drunks."[64] The memory of his spirit warmed her heart all the way to Cleveland.

1. An early home of the Gavin family in Cleveland, Ohio. They lived in the right half of the duplex and sometimes in the cottage far in the back, depending on their financial state. Picture taken in late 1985.

2. Sister Ignatia's parents, Patrick Gavin and Barbara Neary Gavin, circa 1920 (above)

3. A 1914 photo of Sister Ignatia (right) *just prior to her entering the convent. Pictured with her mother* (center) *and probably her cousin* (left).

4. St. Augustine's convent, girls academy (boarding school), and music studio, Lakewood, Ohio, circa 1923

5. *Sister Ignatia (bottom right) at St. Vincent Orphanage in 1923*

6. *Dr. Francis Doran, Sister Ignatia's physician during her nervous breakdown in 1927*

7. *St. Thomas Hospital, Akron, Ohio, 1930*

8. *St. Thomas Hospital Chapel—an important source of spiritual healing. The Alcoholics Anonymous ward was accessed from the choir loft.*

9. *The admitting office where Sister Ignatia worked, circa 1930*

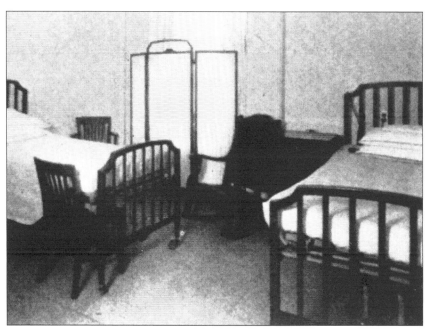

10. *A two-bed ward at St. Thomas Hospital, similar to the first wards assigned to Alcoholics Anonymous members, circa 1930*

11. *Sister Ignatia* (third from left) *at her Twenty-fifth Jubilee Celebration in Akron, Ohio, in 1939, around the time she began formally working with Alcoholics Anonymous*

12. Henrietta Seiberling in 1941 (above)

13. Sister Ignatia receiving the Poverello Medal for Alcoholics Anonymous at the College of Steubenville in 1949

14. First anniversary of Rosary Hall, Cleveland, Ohio, 1953. Pictured left to right: Sister Ignatia; Bill Wilson, cofounder of Alcoholics Anonymous; Father Otis Winchester, founder of Stella Maris (an alcoholism treatment center) and an early recovering alcoholic priest; and Madeline V., one of the first women alcoholics to recover.

15. Rev. John Ford, S.J., Fiftieth
Jubilee picture

16. The "cofounders" of Alcoholics
Anonymous—Sister Ignatia,
Bob Smith (left), and Bill Wilson
(right)—in St. Thomas Medical
Center, Ignatia Hall, Akron, Ohio

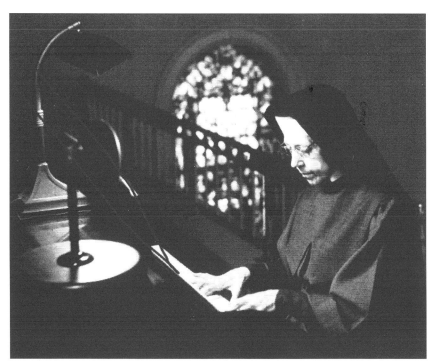

17. Sister Ignatia at the organ at St. Vincent Charity Hospital Chapel,
Cleveland, Ohio, circa 1954

18. *Sister Victorine Keller, C.S.A., and Father John B. McCarthy, S.T., who assisted Sister Ignatia at Rosary Hall during her final years there*

20. *Sister Ignatia at her desk in 1957. Photo is signed "To my esteemed friend Jack, Dec. 14, 1957, Sister M. Ignatia."*

19. *Sister Ignatia speaking to the Twenty-fifth Anniversary Convention of Alcoholics Anonymous in Long Beach, California, 1960*

21. *Home of Bob and Anne Smith and the early members of Alcoholics Anonymous, Akron, Ohio*

22. *Memorial Rock in front of the Akron, Ohio, home of Bob and Anne Smith*

23. *Congressman John Seiberling in 1991 in front of the gatehouse where Bill Wilson and Bob Smith met. The congressman's mother, Henrietta Seiberling, was responsible for the meeting of Alcoholics Anonymous's cofounders.*

Five

The Cleveland Frontier

October 6, 1952

Dear Bill,

You'll surely think that I'm lost in this big City of Cleveland. The truth of the matter is that I have been quite busy trying to find my way around. I have plenty to do even though we have not opened up a division for AA as yet. As you know they did have a four bed ward here for alcoholics at one time. The work was discontinued during the time they were building their new wing. I am hoping and praying that they'll give us a proper set-up in the near future. I am asking your prayers too, so that if it be God's Holy Will, we may be able to continue the work.

. . . Sister Mercede is taking good care of our patients at St. Thomas. The fact that Rev. Mother appointed a sister who understood the program as well as Sister Mercede did make my transfer much easier.

With kindest regards to yourself and your beloved Lois and eagerly looking forward to a visit with both of you in the near future, please God, I am,

Ever Sincerely Yours in Christ,
Sister M. Ignatia[1]

The "Little Sister of Alcoholics Anonymous" reported for work at St. Vincent Charity Hospital on August 7, 1952, with a heavy heart and a vague assignment. For all practical purposes, her mission with AA was momentarily suspended. Now sixty-three years old, Ignatia passed once more from success and prestige at one institution to the challenge of loneliness and uncertainty at another. Surely Ignatia could not help but wonder what new act of Providence lay ahead. At St. Thomas, she had held an important administrative job; at Charity, her position was unclear. The only instructions on her orders were to visit the patients on the second floor and work with AA. But in August of 1952, no AA ward existed at Charity Hospital. Ignatia had been involved with hospitals and convents long enough to suspect that a job change at her age might be the intended prelude to retirement.

Still, this did not matter to the feisty nun. The mere mention of AA on Sister Ignatia's official obedience kept her hopes alive. Nevertheless, severing twenty-four-year ties with her Akron life was painful. During the first difficult weeks of transition, Ignatia communicated with friends in Akron and practiced the spiritual principles and coping strategies she taught to the alcoholics. The Twelve Steps were often her salvation too. Like the alcoholics, she prayed for "knowledge of God's will for her life—and for the power to carry it out." Only her intense prayer, faith, and positive outlook empowered her to overcome the easy temptations of fear, self-pity, and resentment. Arising each day, Ignatia abandoned herself to her Creator and awaited signs of his will.

Her new duties were simple enough, requiring no special training. As the second-floor surgical wing's spiritual visitor, Sister Ignatia made certain that patients were comfortable, families were greeted, and priests were summoned for baptisms, confessions, and last rites. Beyond those duties, the spiritual counselor in a Catholic hospital consoled, encouraged, and prayed with patients who were seriously ill, depressed, or frightened. In a sense, spiritual visitors were official greeters, unofficial welfare workers. It was their special function to bring spiritual peace and comfort into the medical setting. Where white-garbed nuns walked hospital corridors, the patients' sense of well-being always increased.

Perhaps what patients remembered most about their spiritual visitor was the abundant contents of her pockets. At any given moment, hospital nuns reached deep into the folds of their skirts and produced holy cards, medals, rosaries, relics, and even a surprising selection of brightly wrapped candies. Their delightful gifts allayed children's fears and often brought smiles to the faces of the dying.

Ignatia performed these functions with natural ease and optimism. Offering comfort was, after all, her specialty. But it was the last vague words of her assignment that stymied her. They did indeed say that she was to *work* with AA, although there were no further directives or detailed authorization to do so. Did the reverend mother want her to care for isolated alcoholics who also happened to be medical patients? Or did she wish Ignatia to create an alcoholism ward at Charity Hospital? For the time being, Ignatia had no answers to these questions, and Sister Francetta, the hospital administrator, offered no concrete explanations.

On the chance that a call to open a ward would soon come, Sister Ignatia studied the local AA situation and compared it to the setup in Akron. There, the partnership with Dr. Bob had lent credibility to her AA work. But in Cleveland, that would not be the case. From the very beginning of AA, Cleveland had established its own leadership, and she knew that the AA tempo in the larger city was very different.

Cleveland's AA Origins

Ignatia already knew that in 1939 Clevelanders had openly refused to attend the Akron meetings, in part because of religious confusion over the Oxford Group. Clarence S., one of the Cleveland leaders who led the exodus from Akron and convened the first Cleveland meeting, boldly called himself "the Father of Alcoholics Anonymous." Shortly after beginning the first Cleveland group, Clarence persuaded Elrick B. Davis, a Cleveland *Plain Dealer* reporter, to write a series of six editorials in the hopes of publicizing AA's work and enhancing its membership. Davis treated AA's purposes, scope, and spiritual foundation in great depth, showing unusual sensitivity. Ecstatic, the fellowship praised his insightful articles. Of utmost significance, though, the Davis series focused on AA's wider spirituality, thus minimizing the threat of organized religion as a barrier to membership. Wilson himself acknowledged that the favorable publicity generated by Davis's articles heralded AA's explosive growth and convinced the early members that AA's message could indeed be marketed to the public. He wrote:

> At this point the Cleveland *Plain Dealer* ran a series of pieces that ushered in a new period for Alcoholics Anonymous, the era of mass production of sobriety.[2]

What did this mean for AA? For one thing, it meant that an opportunity existed for unprecedented growth. For another, it demonstrated that the idea of mass-producing sobriety had not occurred to the cofounders, who initially had believed that AA's message demanded individual promotion—one alcoholic to another. They had not been aware of the great market value of AA's *spiritual* message, now contained in its book. Wilson continued in praise of Davis:

> . . . Elrick B. Davis, a feature writer of deep understanding, was the author of a series of articles that were printed in the middle of the *Plain Dealer*'s editorial page, and these were accompanied every two or three days by red-hot blasts from the editors themselves. In effect, the *Plain Dealer* was saying, "Alcoholics Anonymous is good, and it works. Come and get it."[3]

Clarence and the Cleveland pioneers proved that membership could grow quickly if they relied on the philosophy found in the Big Book and helped others discover it. About twenty in number, the Cleveland group distributed copies of *Alcoholics Anonymous* to all prospective members. Recognizing that sobriety itself could not be mass-produced, these evangelizers mass-produced AA's bible instead. As a result, Cleveland became the fastest-growing AA town in the country. Of that hectic time Wilson wrote:

> The Cleveland pioneers had proved three essential things: the value of personal sponsorship, the worth of the AA Book in

indoctrinating newcomers, and finally, the tremendous fact that AA, when word really got around, could now soundly grow to great size.[4]

Excelling on its own merit, the Cleveland AA had quickly become a third faction of AA power. Proof of Cleveland's impact was borne out by membership statistics tallied in Akron's *General Bulletin,* October 1, 1940:

New York	150
Washington	100
Chicago	100
Los Angeles	100
Philadelphia	75
Akron	200
Cleveland	450[5]

Including the 258 members registered in fifteen other U.S. cities, the total national membership of AA came to 1,433. Of these, a little more than 30 percent of AA's membership resided in Cleveland, with 47 percent of AA's total membership living in Ohio.[6] Between its hospitalization opportunities, avid sponsorship, and mass evangelization, there was no mistaking that Ohio's formula for sobriety had achieved the greatest results.

Despite their geographic proximity to one another, communication between Akron and Cleveland members was surprisingly limited; members from both cities corresponded with Bill Wilson in New York headquarters more often than with each other.

Although Sister Ignatia was not well acquainted with the Cleveland membership as a whole, she knew individual AA members, because she had treated them in Akron. Thus even for her, Cleveland was a brand-new town, offering its own distinct challenge to her leadership abilities.

A few weeks passed. By the end of August, no AA assignment was yet clarified for Ignatia at Charity Hospital. Meanwhile, Akron still reeled from her transfer. At this juncture, Burr M. and some of the other Akron members approached Cleveland's Bishop Edward F. Hoban to plead for Ignatia's return; they were directed instead to the diocesan chancellor, who convinced them that nothing could be done to reverse Ignatia's transfer. However, the Akron party's visit with the chancellor left Cleveland clergy unmistakably aware of Sister Ignatia's standing and popularity among recovering alcoholics. Thus Burr's initiative pried open the door for Sister Ignatia's future relationship with the Cleveland clergy.

AA's Support in Transition

With the days passing, Ignatia confessed to some of her AA friends that she felt anxious about Charity Hospital's silence toward AA. These friends visited her often and helped to buoy her spirits. A Jewish member, Eddie G., spoke with her daily and remembered her anguish:

> I don't ever want to forget the start of my friendship with her. I don't ever want to forget going in to see her every day at Charity. She paced the corridor and said, "Eddie, I'll never have another place." And I said to her, "You're *going* to have another place."
>
> She gave her life for the drunk . . . she was the Protector of Drunks. She was in trouble from the time she came in because she had a heart. She took in those without any money. And then she'd say, "I am in trouble. What are you going to do to bail me out?"[7]

Men like Eddie supported Sister Ignatia with visits, phone calls, and letters. They encouraged her to make plans for the day when the new ward would open. Actually, the delay was probably beneficial, for it provided Sister Ignatia with ample time to prepare for her involvement in the Cleveland area. At the same time, her Akron AA friends suspected that the Cleveland AA organization might offer Sister Ignatia some resistance. One of them, Lou C., a former patient from Akron, anticipated the potential difficulties she might encounter and

quickly took the initiative to reinforce Sister Ignatia with dependable
AA advice. By September 1, he had written a course of action for her
to follow and mailed it to her. His lengthy letter made several observations and recommendations based on her earlier work:

> I called Tom N. yesterday and he said he would be glad to
> come down with Jack J. and Carl B. if possible, to help you in
> the arrangements of a tentative layout for your ward.
>
> I think that an overwhelmingly important detail to establish
> at the beginning of your enterprise is the question of control.
> You should, I think, make yourself unmistakably clear at the
> very beginning that control of all phases of the ward's activities
> rests definitely with you and your superiors. The Central Com-
> mittee of AA in Cleveland has a Hospital Sub-Committee
> charged with a duty of checking on the care given AA patients.
> Such a committee has its values but, as respects your Sisters
> generally, and in your own particular case, it can, if you let it, be
> a great deal more harm than good to your hospital and to AA it-
> self. It is proper to remind any of these gentlemen who may be-
> come disagreeable on this point that your Order has cared for
> the sick in this area for well over a century and needs no in-
> structions on this point from this Committee. Do not, under
> any circumstances whatever, permit any control over admis-
> sions or exclusions by any group of AAs, however attractive fi-
> nancially the "bait" for this control may seem. It is entirely in
> order to remind those whose thinking you are already familiar
> with (their line is that "Sister Ignatia, not being an alcoholic
> herself, simply does not understand these things") that your
> experience in this field *antedates* AA and goes back to a grass-
> roots connection with one of the movement's cofounders. The
> better elements in the movement will not presume to dictate or
> bargain for control. The noisier, less-informed elements
> should, from the start and thereafter, be put, courteously but
> very firmly, in their place. Many thousands of people all over
> the country not only approve but applaud your judgment in
> matters alcoholic and the only effect the years have made in

that judgment is one of seasoning it. The foregoing might suggest, to anyone other than yourself, that I am critical of AA. I
hope you will believe this is not so. It is because I have seen a
few tragic errors made in the past (some of them persist) as regards the hospitalization of alcoholics that I would like to see
these errors avoided in your new ward, both for your sake and
that of the real, long-range good of this great movement itself.[8]

The thoughtfulness of Sister Ignatia's AA friends is evident in their
offers of time and guidance. She took comfort as well from their firm
faith that another alcohol ward would soon be hers. Such gestures
made at this troubling time demonstrated that the AA men considered
Sister Ignatia to be one of them. They hovered around her, grateful for
the chance to return some measure of the love and encouragement
that she had extended to them at St. Thomas.

Those closest to her realized that anxiety was clouding her
thoughts and draining her self-confidence. Now that Sister Ignatia
was the human being in need of strength and personal support, she
demonstrably leaned on her friends until she regained her professional equilibrium. To help her along, Lou C. rehearsed some familiar-
sounding plans so that Sister Ignatia would feel confident and
prepared when and if the subject of an alcoholism ward surfaced. She
appreciated his help immensely. Though Ignatia knew well enough
what to do for hospitalized alcoholics, she had much to learn about
AA politics in Cleveland. And for that matter, Cleveland had much to
learn about her. She read on:

As to the mechanics of operation of your Ward, I believe that,
with whatever modifications circumstances make necessary,
the pattern of Akron will suit admirably. A curfew at night
should be set up and rigidly enforced, even at the risk of offending some AAs. A talk every evening, limited to 30–45 minutes, will help greatly in the indoctrination of patients. Visitors
should be restricted to members of AA and each visitor should
be required to register. To help you build up a reference list, it
might be desirable to ask for the address as well as the name

of each visitor. Visits of women AAs to men patients should be prohibited and vice versa, except in cases which you personally approve.[9]

So far, all of Lou's advice was a familiar reminder of what had worked in Akron. But a wise warning more pertinent to Cleveland's circumstances about the absolute separation of the AA work from professionalism became apparent in the next sentence:

> The acceptance of help from AA in the form of monitors, aides, guides, etc. should be done rarely if at all. . . . Where their services are utilized, as in the giving of talks in the Ward, let it be clearly understood that these services are done as a phase of 12th Step work on the part of the individual performing them and not as a gratuitous contribution of the individual AA to the operation of Charity Hospital.[10]

His next paragraph broached a matter of special concern to Sister Ignatia:

> One of your sorest problems, due to the physical location of your Ward, will be the spiritual one. The alcoholic, as you have often said, is a man [woman] spiritually sick. At Akron you had an almost ideal set-up in the fact that the organ-loft entrance was located right in the AA Ward. A small oratory is a possibility that should be considered as a make-do for the Akron arrangement. A curious fact about the chapel at Akron was that the non-Catholics appeared more drawn to its use actually than the Catholic patients as a place for meditation. How to make available for your patients the maximum spiritual assistance, which they need so badly as a corrective for the selfishness which is a part of their trouble with drink and other faults, is a problem that will challenge your greatest efforts.[11]

Ignatia filed the thought away for later consideration. Lou was correct in his assessment of the physical layout at Charity Hospital. In the space that would probably be allotted for an alcoholism ward, no ready access was available to the main chapel on the floor below. Even so, Sister Ignatia philosophized that if God provided a ward, he would also provide a place of worship where his spiritual healing could begin. She continued studying Lou's detailed plan:

> In the field of indoctrination [education], I think a primary step is to establish to the patient's satisfaction that he is, indeed, an alcoholic. The small questionnaire should be given to each patient shortly after his arrival. If he is not an alcoholic he should be dismissed as soon as possible, else you reduce your ward to the status of a mere "defrosting" station, about on the level with the dozen or more drying out places in Akron. Though these places perform a function of some value, I most emphatically do not think that the operation of one of them is fit work for a Sister of Charity or a proper use of hospital space.[12]

Sister Ignatia agreed wholeheartedly that the value of treatment was surely lessened by repeaters who took their drinking, but not their sobriety, seriously. She had no quarrel with Lou's concern for AA's valuable hospital beds. But his praise of her great value to the program no doubt embarrassed her and caught her off guard:

> As to indoctrination by reading, I believe that most alcoholics are not great readers and that the best results are gained by the use of the smaller pamphlets rather than by undue insistence on the reading of the Big Book, valuable though that undoubtedly is. More important even than the reading matter or talks by AAs are the talks you yourself gave to these men singly and collectively. It was in these talks, even more than in any of the many other things you did at St. Thomas, that you showed the one vital difference between your type of hospitalization and that of any other, Catholic or non-Catholic. Running through all these talks was a clear *will* to get the patient sober and to keep him that way. It was this *will* for their sobriety that

prompted you to supply the vitamin service and the lounge privileges that meant so much to so many of us.[13]

He recalled other aspects of her work in Akron, so unique to her alone:

> I know of no other hospital or, for that matter, no other depart-ment of your own hospitals which went to the limits you did to maintain the degree of moral and physical health to which you initially restored the patient sick with alcoholism. Your pa-tients always got much more than they ever paid for, even in the purely physical sense, in the many post hospitalization services you rendered them. You were farsighted enough to see that hospital visits are both an essential part of the mental and spiritual therapy which the patient needs and a powerful protection against relapses into drinking *for the visitor himself.* Instead of placing unreasonable restrictions against visiting you always encouraged it to the greatest extent consistent with proper hospital care of the sick man and with proper hos-pital administration. That this is not so in other institutions, even Catholic ones, I know very well.[14]

So well thought out were Lou's instructions that he even provided suggestions for ward decorations:

> As to the furnishings of your Ward, I think that a full size replica of the plaque at St. Thomas and the oil painting of Dr. Bob are two things you should have, not as trophies of your successful career in the treatment of alcoholism, but as silent reminders to patients, visitors, and staff that you can speak with authority on the AA program. Framed copies of the Twelve Steps (not of the Twelve Traditions, which are a bit vague and misleading in spots, in my opinion) could well be placed in strategic places. One of the "But For The Grace of God" signs could be used properly also. Copies of the AA prayer might also be placed conveniently. I know this has no

imprimatur but you could try to get a good canon lawyer to tell you some way to use it. I always thought it was tailor-made for an alcoholic.[15]

In closing, he stressed:

If I can help in any way to get your ward started off on its best foot please let me know. I think this goes for almost anyone in Akron, but I'll let them speak for themselves. Forgive this rather untidy letter and be careful to whom you show it as I have stepped on a few important corns in places in it. I hope that at least some of the above may be useful to you as a very small token of a huge debt that I owe you.

Sincerely and respectfully yours,
Louis C.[16]

With a detailed outline for Charity Hospital's future alcoholism ward locked in her mind and her self-confidence restored, Sister Ignatia set out to investigate the hospital's previous AA connections.

Charity Hospital's AA Roots

The earliest stories about past endeavors in the field of alcohol treatment concerned a physician named Dr. Harry Nash and his occasional cohort, Sister Lucille. The doctor was a member of the surgical staff; Sister Lucille worked on Ward F, the main corridor of Charity Hospital's second floor.

In 1941 Dr. Nash encountered serious objections to his habit of mixing surgical practice with alcohol indulgence. He was in surgery, about to open an abdomen early one day, when the assisting resident surgeon startled him: "Turn the knife around, Harry. You're not going to operate!"[17] The voice belonged to a young and exasperated Dr. Victor D. Ippolito, and he was appalled that Nash was attempting to make an incision with the top side of the scalpel's blade. More surprising yet, Dr. Harry Nash complied with this junior assistant's order, handed him the scalpel, and staggered out of the operating room.

Later that morning the two encountered each other again. Dr. Ippolito made it emphatically clear to Dr. Nash that even as a junior staff surgeon, he would not tolerate, protect, or condone drunkenness in the operating room. Then in what might have been the first professional intervention, physician to physician, in AA history, Dr. Ippolito convinced Dr. Nash to visit the physician and nun in Akron who knew how to arrest alcoholism. Dr. Harry Nash was hospitalized in St. Thomas's alcoholism ward that day. He never drank again.

Dr. Nash no doubt might have heard of AA's miracles from Father James A. Nagle, who had become chaplain in 1937. Nagle's own father had been hailed as one of AA's early Cleveland pioneers, so the priest had close personal experience with AA's first successes. Gratitude for his father's recovery prompted his quiet praise and support of AA in hospital circles, soon earning him the title "Friend of AA" from the local membership.[18] Nagle must also be considered one of AA's early supporters and, thus, a part of Cleveland's history.

Several months after he recovered, Dr. Nash returned to Cleveland and promptly went about treating alcoholics himself. With the help of Cleveland AAs, he cared for so many patients at the East Cleveland Clinic that members named Dr. Nash "the patron saint of Cleveland AA."

In his treatment of alcoholics at Charity Hospital, Dr. Nash tried to follow the lead of Dr. Bob and Sister Ignatia's partnership. With the help of Sister Lucille, he admitted alcoholics on a scatterbed basis and detoxified the casualties in Ward F. However, his teaming with Sister Lucille was short-lived and did not produce the same results as the Akron model.

One reason that Nash's early program at Charity Hospital did not succeed was that he did not indoctrinate the hospitalized men with a sufficient dose of AA medicine. Instead, Dr. Nash focused his treatment on physical detoxification, enhancing the effects with his own favorite remedy (known as Dr. Nash's Formula) of castor oil and egg soup. But also impeding his progress was a greater need for secrecy in treating alcoholics at this larger, more sophisticated, and less sympathetic hospital.

Before he could fully establish a program for alcoholics, Nash's work was interrupted in 1942 by World War II. Like many middle-aged, draft-deferred but patriotic physicians, Dr. Harry Nash voluntarily enlisted in the U.S. Medical Corps. However, less than three months later, Captain Harry Nash suffered a fatal heart attack as he was preparing to go overseas. In his absence, the AA effort at Charity Hospital ceased for lack of a sympathetic doctor.

A physician assumed the duties of Dr. Nash, but he failed to win the support of AA members. Later, Dr. Victor Ippolito took over the task of ministering medically to the AA patients and swiftly won the wholehearted approval of the membership.[19]

Seeking additional hospital support for the alcoholism effort, the AAs next approached a young nurse named Sister Victorine Keller. In September 1942, Sister Victorine was a new graduate of Marquette University. She had recently been assigned as the head nurse on Ward L, a medical-surgical floor, around the corner from Ward F, AA's previous second-floor location. It was there that she became acquainted with Dr. Ippolito.

Before long, two AA members, Frank W. and Jack S., approached Sister Victorine and asked whether she would set aside a few beds for alcohol detoxification. Knowing nothing about AA or alcoholism, Sister Victorine referred the two men to her superior, Sister Paul Johnston, for approval. The superior was indignant at the men's request and emphatically stated, "No beds for alcoholics. Hospital beds are for sick people!"[20]

About a year went by. During that time, Sister Annette, who worked in the admitting office, accepted alcoholics with a doctor's consent. Two physicians—Dr. Victor Ippolito and Dr. Frank Hanrahan—actively admitted alcoholic patients to the hospital. With admission diagnoses of "evaluation, observation, and avitaminosis," they treated alcoholic patients on Sister Victorine's Ward L for nearly two years before the hospital granted them permission to do so in an AA ward.

Meanwhile, to assist the hospital's wartime efforts and to secure a presence within the hospital, the AAs formed a small corps of hospital volunteers:

> . . . During World War II, AA members organized a group of men to assist on Ward L, as volunteers, and a crew was formed to work in the Accident Department. In both of these departments, AA volunteers were on duty nightly. It was their duty to enforce the regulations of the hospital, particularly insofar as the visiting hours were concerned.[21]

The AA volunteers made themselves indispensable to the hospital and soon secured another meeting with Sister Paul. There is some discrepancy as to the exact date, but Sister Victorine's personal records placed it in January 1944. She remarked:

> Present were Father Nagle, Sister Annette, Sister Victorine, Dr. Hanrahan, Dr. Ippolito, and a group of AA members. Among the AAs was a man named "Paul J." Coincidentally, Sister Paul Johnston had a favorite brother by the same name. The AA named Paul was very handsome and personable; Sister Paul took a liking to him.[22]

The first of three such conferences that spanned a period of fifteen months, the meeting disclosed the following AA action plan:

> Paul J. and Roy W. outlined the hopes of the Fellowship to Sr. Paul.
> They called attention to the increasing demand for beds for alcoholics and suggested that a separate department in the hospital be designated for exclusive [AA] use.[23]

In their plea, they voiced the AA Hospital Committee's opinion that the Cleveland AA program's most effective work was being accomplished in Charity Hospital and cited the following reasons:

- diligent supervision
- expert medical care and a thorough understanding of the problem of alcoholism
- spiritual counsel
- careful sponsorship

Sister Paul was forced to hold her decision in abeyance until the critical bed shortage in the hospital was alleviated, but in early April 1945, she gave her approval to the plan and designated Room 231 in Ward L for exclusive use of AA patients.[24]

Ward L Annex

On April 20, 1945, the new Ward L annex was outfitted with four beds and miscellaneous furnishings; added later was a two-bed ward with a cot. Women patients were occasionally treated in a private room no larger than a closet, set apart from the men's ward.

On April 24 another meeting outlined the operating relationship between the AA program and the hospital. Devising the guidelines, governing policy, and procedure were Father Nagle, Sister Annette, Sister Victorine, Dr. Victor Ippolito, Harry D., Paul J., Dewey S., and Roy W. Immediately afterward, the AAs began holding evening meetings for their patients in Ward L's kitchen.[25]

Reflections made in 1985 on those early days elicited thought-provoking observations from Sister Victorine. She reminisced:

> There was no treatment program. The men were detoxed and sent on their way. They were given medical attention, vitamins, and an AA sponsor. Emphatically, there were more successes then (because of intense sponsorship) than there are now with formal treatment programs. AA volunteers took care of the patients in the hospitals.[26]

According to Sister Victorine, the procedure she followed with AA patients relied on AA members for its success. First, AAs referred their alcohol admissions to her on Ward L annex, the space allotted for AA's use. Sister Victorine then notified Sister Annette in the admitting office that she had a request for an AA bed. The admitting office contacted Dr. Ippolito or sometimes Dr. Hanrahan, who then issued the medical order to admit the AA patient for "observation." Once the alcoholic was hospitalized and medicated, AA sponsors stayed with the patient and provided twenty-four-hour care and support.

Simple policies and an unsophisticated program were in place at Charity Hospital by the next winter. All methods were based on the successful strategies developed by Sister Ignatia at St. Thomas Hospital. Coincidentally, long before Charity Hospital approved an AA ward, Sister Victorine educated herself about alcohol treatment as practiced at the AA ward in Akron. As a result, a similar alcohol policy emerged at Charity Hospital, as her account details:

> The policy was that only first time patients were admitted to the alcoholic ward. Patients stayed four or five days, and brief, informal meetings were held every evening in the diet kitchen in Ward L.
>
> Gradually, the regular meeting program was formalized. In January, 1946, former patients of Charity Hospital and representatives from other AA groups met to discuss a plan for more thoroughly acquainting patients with the AA program. They adopted the procedure of holding nightly half-hour meetings conducted by the volunteer workers on duty. Regular meetings of all workers were to be held on the last Friday of each month in the Nurses Auditorium. Two years later, in 1948, these meetings were open to all AA members, and have been conducted regularly ever since.[27]

The official program approved by Sister Paul in April 1945 was effective but short-lived. Later the following year, the community reassigned Sister Victorine to the position of sister superior (administrator) at St. John's Hospital, another of their Cleveland health facilities. Her transfer, coupled with a postwar building expansion at Charity Hospital, led to the close of the AA ward. Yet even in her absence, the AAs continued holding weekly meetings in Ward L's diet kitchen. In fact, when Sister Ignatia arrived in 1952, signs of the ward and the AA meeting place on the second floor were still apparent.

AA at St. John's Hospital

After Charity Hospital formally discontinued alcoholic admissions, the AAs followed Sister Victorine to St. John's Hospital. As the official administrator there, she authorized the opening of a four-bed alcohol ward. Thus, a small number of Cleveland AAs received their hospital care at St. John's during the 1946–50 period. Soon, however, the added pressures of hospital administration prevented Sister Victorine from personally overseeing the AA ward. Accordingly, she delegated the ward's responsibilities to the floor supervisor, Sister Mercede.

The AAs found the new sister to be a caring and capable woman who was also sympathetic to AA's needs. Not all staff members were. At the same time, the Sisters of Charity recognized Mercede's growing expertise with the alcoholic population. Therefore, when the question of replacing Sister Ignatia in St. Thomas Hospital's alcoholism ward arose in 1952, Mother Clementine found Sister Mercede to be experienced and thus the natural choice. Sadly, with Sister Mercede's transfer to Akron, the short-lived alcohol treatment services at St. John's Hospital ground to a halt as well.

Although much of the Sisters of Charity of Saint Augustine's enormous success with alcohol-related illness relied on courageous women of vision like Sister Victorine and Sister Ignatia, the fact is that their work depended on their superiors' approval and support. There existed a providential chain of events in community affairs during the start-up phases of alcoholism treatment at both St. Thomas and St. Vincent hospitals.

When Sister Ignatia initiated the plan for alcoholism treatment early in 1940, Sister Clementine was the first hospital superior to grant official approval of the project. Later in 1940, Sister Paul Johnston replaced Clementine as the St. Thomas Hospital administrator. Two years later, in 1942, the community named Sister Paul administrator of Charity Hospital. The following year Sister Clementine, who had first sanctioned AA in Akron, became the major superior of the entire order, a highly effective position for helping Ignatia's AA hospital mission.

With the experience they had gained during AA's pioneering years in the early 1940s, both Sister Paul and Mother Clementine were instrumental in expanding the role of AA in hospitals and in the community at large. Sister Paul served as superior at Charity, from 1942 to 1948, when Sister Victorine began her initial AA work. Sister Paul's familiarity with AA in Akron carried over and helped open the hospital doors in Cleveland. Then Sister Eleanor Adams replaced Sister Paul as the St. Thomas Hospital administrator between 1942 and 1947. She was also sympathetic to Sister Ignatia's AA work.

Altogether, the support of Mother Clementine, Sister Paul, and Sister Eleanor provided Sister Ignatia with administrative strength and protection in the face of general hospital staff disapproval. However, in 1947 in Akron and in 1948 in Cleveland, new superiors were named, reducing administrative support for alcoholism treatment at both hospitals. So the question arose as to who or what would ensure that AA hospital programs could continue as before.

The answer came from the order's open-minded, consensus-style leadership emanating from the top. Sister Ignatia's longtime friend, Mother Clementine, permitted local administrative disapproval of AA hospital work, but she never sanctioned the total discontinuance of alcoholism treatment. Indeed, when she agreed to Sister Ignatia's Cleveland transfer, the St. Thomas alcoholism ward was too well established to be phased out. Fortunately, thanks to Sister Victorine, Sister Mercede was experienced enough to carry on the work in Sister Ignatia's absence. As things worked out, Mother Clementine gambled and won that Sister Ignatia's tenacity, experience, and dedication to AA would stand up to the administrative disdain for alcoholism treatment that existed at St. Vincent Charity Hospital.

However, a practical reason was also at work in the timing of Sister Ignatia's transfer to Charity. In 1952, Sister Francetta Morrison, Charity Hospital's administrator, faced both a critical shortage of nursing personnel and an overabundance of empty hospital beds. Though she was personally indifferent to alcoholism treatment and possibly even opposed to it, she was nonetheless a sharp administrator who saw the potential benefits in filling her hospital beds with AA patients who did not require skilled nursing care. An immensely practical and crisp-mannered woman, Sister Francetta was also a professional nurse. As hospital administrator she developed creative special-care hospital units to compensate for the nursing shortage. The intensive care and surgical recovery room units that were her innovation effectively pooled nursing resources and concentrated nursing coverage; at the same time, they provided more efficient patient care.

Thus, Francetta's ultimate decision to open an AA ward did not arise solely from humanitarian reasons. For the most part, granting AA the use of a hospital ward was a shrewd administrative decision that all but guaranteed filling hospital beds without further draining nursing resources.

Rosary Hall Emerges in 1952

Word of administration's upcoming plans for an AA ward came on the heels of Ignatia's letter to Bill Wilson concerning the hospital's silence on AA matters. Somewhat unexpectedly, Ignatia received an urgent summons to report to Sister Francetta's office. The date was October 7, 1952, known on the Catholic Church calendar as the Feast of the Holy Rosary. Ignatia arrived to find the administrator, an architect, and the director of nursing deep in the study of blueprints for an alcoholism ward. As she answered their questions and listened to their plans, Ignatia's hopes alternately rose and fell. Realization of medicine's all-too-familiar professional ignorance of alcoholism swept over her.

"What do you want for this alcoholic ward?" Sister Francetta asked her.

"Are they violent?" queried the nursing supervisor.

"Are they intoxicated?" fired the supervisor.

"Will they need to be put in cages?" shot the architect.

Sighing deeply, Ignatia said, "How would it be if I drew up a sketch of what I want?"[28]

The hospital's building committee was scheduled to convene soon, so for the sake of time, all three agreed to her suggestion. The next day Sister Ignatia presented her own plans to Sister Francetta, who received them coldly. "I am not personally interested," she flatly informed Sister Ignatia. "But I am also not opposed."[29]

With Francetta's lukewarm agreement obtained, Ignatia sent her plan to the architect. As part of the ward's setup, she requested a coffee bar for the patients, similar to the one in Akron. However, a board member who reviewed the plan questioned the need for it. He returned the plan to Sister Ignatia and scribbled, "A table will have to do." But even as close as she was to having a new ward, Ignatia would not compromise. She knew what she wanted for the AAs, and she put the future of the ward on the line with her reply: "Let's forget about it if you're not going to give us the proper setup."[30] The coffee bar remained in the drawings.

Hearing that plans for an alcoholism ward at Charity were now official, many former alcoholic patients from Akron and Cleveland swamped Sister Ignatia with offers of help. Father Otis W.,[31] one of AA's early recovering priests, solicited community support for Sister Ignatia and the proposed ward. At the St. Agnes AA meeting, he made a speech and told the members, "It's up to us to get her organized."[32] That very evening, AA enthusiasm sparked the formation of the "bucket brigade," a group of men who assembled hordes of AA members to wash down the walls and woodwork of their prospective ward.

The formation of the bucket brigade signaled only the beginning of AA's rush to Ignatia's assistance. Next followed an almost miraculous outpouring of time, materials, and money—the foundations on which Charity Hospital's alcoholism ward was built. Responding to the AAs' generosity, one hospital administrator contributed a supply of old, unused shower units for the ward. But the problem of where and how to install them forced the architect to consult a plumber. He telephoned Spohn Plumbing Company for professional advice.

Spohn Plumbing sent Charity Hospital a plumbing consultant named Keith C. to design and oversee the installations. When Keith arrived, the architect introduced him to Sister Ignatia, who by now had become the real designer of the ward. Keith was taken aback when he shook her hand. Startled, he asked her, "Are you the same sister who worked with Dr. Bob?"

"The same," she replied.

"Well, there would be many people interested in helping here. I am in AA; let me see what can be done."

Keith C. returned to his employer. "Would you mind if I chipped in some of my own time to help Sister Ignatia?" he inquired.

Receiving an affirmative response, Keith appealed to friends who were local material suppliers. They donated bathtubs, showers, sinks, commodes, and all of the fixtures needed to outfit the ward. After securing the supplies, the recovered plumber recruited AA friends to volunteer the labor. They worked after hours, long into the night, installing, repairing, and completing the plumbing restoration.[33]

As work moved toward completion, the question of a name for the new alcoholism ward was on everyone's minds. Though she hadn't said so, Sister Ignatia had already decided to name it "Rosary Hall Solarium," only later explaining why:

> The day they [hospital officials] came was on [October 7] the Feast of Our Lady of the Rosary. That's how we came to call it Rosary Hall. When I was moved there I thought, "I'd love to have this in memory of Dr. Bob." Rather than call it the alcoholic ward, we'll call it Rosary Hall. All I need is an "S," and I'll have Doctor's initials, "R.H.S.," Robert Holbrook Smith, so we called it Rosary Hall Solarium. The insignia on the door is R.H.S. This [ward] was granted by the hospital authorities on October 7, 1952, Feast of the Most Holy Rosary.
>
> I feel that people, whether in the Catholic Church or not, no matter what denomination, when they see a rosary, it always means prayer. So, I think that this [Rosary Hall] is the result of someone's prayers. The Grace of God comes through someone's prayers, for sure. The insignia ultimately expresses the efforts of the Sisters of Charity of Saint Augustine, a religious order that joins forces with the members of AA, a strictly

nonsectarian movement, in an attempt to rescue men and women of all creeds from the bottomless pit of alcoholism.[34]

Naming the new ward accomplished one more step toward fulfilling Ignatia's—and the AAs'—dreams.

Caught up in the AAs' infectious enthusiasm, the architect himself offered to supply paint for the refurbished hallways. But the AAs had already anticipated the matter of painting; a business agent for the local painters' union sent two professional painters to Sister Ignatia. They brought their own paint and, in two weeks, the entire ward was redecorated.

Carpenters, electricians, plumbers, and painters donated their services and their materials to build Sister Ignatia's dream ward. Work progressed so rapidly that Sister Ignatia could hardly keep abreast of the daily changes. One afternoon a former patient from Pittsburgh telephoned her from the Cleveland airport while awaiting a connecting flight to his Philadelphia offices. He asked how things were going and inquired how he might help. Ignatia told him of the scores of volunteer workers at Rosary Hall adding, "Oh, Charlie, if I ever needed a construction engineer, I need one now."[35]

Charlie placed one phone call to a Cleveland friend, Tommy O. M., and Rosary Hall's haphazard renovation had an instant project manager. Tommy organized the painters, the plumbers, the carpenters, and the electricians into a team. For her part, Sister Ignatia provided ample food and coffee to bolster the volunteers' strength through the long nights as the work progressed. Night after night, the routine was repeated. These laborers of love built Rosary Hall in record time to please the well-known sister who saved alcoholics and promoted AA's work. Almost every AA in Cleveland and Akron joined the massive group effort required to ready the hall in time for its December 7 dedication date.

Everyone involved contributed something. Those men and women who lacked skill or time donated large amounts of money to the building campaign. With their offerings, Sister Ignatia purchased building supplies, furnishings, robes, pajamas, slippers, medicines, and coffee. Everyone worked toward Sister Ignatia's goal to open Rosary Hall to the public on December 8, the Feast of the Immaculate Conception. The formal dedication of the hall would come on the preceding day. Moments before the ceremony began, grateful AA workers proudly hung the sign above the entrance doors that expressed Sister Ignatia's prayer for those whom Rosary Hall Solarium would shelter: "Take Hope All Ye Who Leave Here."

For the next two days, Rosary Hall's jubilant open house introduced the concept of alcoholism treatment to inquisitive hospital trustees, doctors, nurses, hospital personnel, church officials, and Cleveland's community leaders. But the greatest testimony to the success of Sister Ignatia's AA work was in the striking monument of Rosary Hall itself, readied and built by those who had personally conquered the hopeless spiritual infirmity of alcoholic addiction. Theirs was a witness of love and example—and a startling course in public education—that would positively publicize the curative powers of a mixture of AA, science, and religion in the Cleveland area from this time on.

That weekend in December, one newsman reported the miracle of Rosary Hall's beginning with a touch of awe:

Charity Hospital Readies AA-Built Alcoholic Ward

A center for Alcoholics Anonymous, built by AAs and their friends, will be opened Monday in St. Vincent Charity Hospital . . .

. . . Hundreds of AAs and their friends, rallying around with traditional generosity, have cooperated in creating Rosary Hall Solarium, either working on it personally, or donating materials or funds.

A woman sent $1,000. Businessmen contributed fixtures, furnitures, paint and what not. Unions gladly gave permission to members to work in their spare time.

One union even hired a couple of carpenters and sent them to Rosary Hall to speed up the final touches. An attorney and his wife took charge of the oratory. In St. Vincent Charity's Rosary Hall here last week, AAs of all kinds of occupations were hurrying the work to completion, dropping in with donations or suggestions, and bringing news of new benefactions.

Among them were Jews, Catholics, and Protestants. Sometimes they choked up as they told what a stay in St. Thomas Hospital had meant to them and their families.

An AA, they said simply, will do anything in his power for Sister Ignatia and Rosary Hall, because an AA knows out of what depths he was lifted—how his whole life was remade.

In Rosary Hall, all the rooms but one are for more than one patient, because it is not good for an AA, usually, to be alone. There is one private room for difficult cases in the worst stages. Sister Ignatia, a woman so frail as to be almost transparent, calls it, with a twinkle in her eye, "the defrosting room."

Rosary Hall did not exactly "just grow" like Topsy, but there was a Topsy-like quality in the way it came to be. As soon as word of the project spread among AAs, they swarmed in and took the details out of Sister Ignatia's hands. "Just let us worry about that" became their repeated injunction to her.

After one businessman had dropped in, conferred with other AAs, and departed to arrange for furnishings for one room, Sister Ignatia inquired anxiously whether he had quoted a price. She lifted her hands helplessly when told, "There is no price. He's donating everything."

All that Sister Ignatia could say was, "Well, that's the AAs for you. They're like that. And their relatives and friends are like that. Really, I haven't anything to do with all this. It's Our Lady and the AA who are doing it."[36]

Throughout the first week of December many more news reports carried glowing accounts of Sister Ignatia, Rosary Hall, and the charitable works of the recovering alcoholics who made the ward's opening possible.

Sister Ignatia spent one more week tending to last-minute organizational details before she accepted Don L., Rosary Hall's first alcoholic patient, on December 15. On that date, fourteen beds for men and two beds for women were ready to accommodate Cleveland's alcoholic citizens.

Rosary Hall's Immediate Success

From the outset, Rosary Hall captured the community's instant respect as evidenced by its first year's statistics. The rapidly expanding census proved how deeply Alcoholics Anonymous had penetrated the public's consciousness and the hospital's awareness of alcoholism's treatability. Sister Ignatia tallied the monthly census in her small black record book:

Month		Census
December	1952	37
January	1953	70
February	1953	68
March	1953	83
April	1953	83
May	1953	98
June	1953	87
July	1953	87
August	1953	94
September	1953	79
October	1953	84
November	1953	73
December	1953	75
TOTAL		1018[37]

Numbers do not lie. Ignatia's statistics revealed that Rosary Hall was treating ten times as many alcoholic patients as patients suffering from tuberculosis.

The ramifications of alcoholism also needing attention included family disruption; marital discord; poverty; unemployment; deterioration of physical, mental, and spiritual health; and loss of faith, ideals, and self-esteem. Thus, the large number of patients combined with her increasing awareness of the societal effects of the disease convinced

Sister Ignatia to increase the length of stay from five to six days during Rosary Hall's second operating year. Still, there were exceptions. She evaluated and treated patients on an individual basis, since some conditions required longer-than-usual periods of sedation. Following the custom in Akron, Rosary Hall's official policy permitted no repeaters.

The treatment of alcoholism at Rosary Hall followed the same sequence of practices instituted in Akron by Sister Ignatia. An exception revealed itself in the AA sponsorship policy. At Rosary Hall, Sister Ignatia required sponsors to earn one full year of uninterrupted sobriety before she allowed them to carry their message to a new alcoholic under treatment. This new rule recognized AA's evolution—the fellowship was now seventeen years removed from its Akron beginnings. In contrast to the earliest days, many of the members now had five, ten, and fifteen years of sober living experiences to share with brand-new patients.

Experience taught Sister Ignatia that the sponsor's crucial role of sharing AA's way of life with newly detoxified patients hinged on the powerful example of his own sobriety and mastery of the program. Consequently, she had little patience for those with only an intellectual grasp of the Twelve Steps and AA's slogans, literature, and Big Book. Sister Ignatia knew that a sponsor's sobriety would prove unconvincing to the new candidate if unaccompanied by distinct evidence of hard-won changes in attitude and lifestyle, made possible only through prolonged abstinence and the practice of AA's Twelve Steps.

The determined nun's spiritual presence and personal magnetism combined with Cleveland's unique, evangelistic AA spirit to generate an unsurpassed level of caring at Charity Hospital. In all, Ignatia's thirteen years of formal apprenticeship with alcoholics in the hospital setting had their effect. Her understanding, respect, and especially her love for the alcoholic were now fully mature. When linked with Ignatia's early expertise in the hospital treatment of AAs and her single-minded drive, the result produced a unique magic. Though other hospitals carefully duplicated her methods, none could draw upon the spiritual force that Sister Ignatia projected—a force that, in the end, explained her enormous influence on AA.

Under Ignatia's direction, Rosary Hall was much more than a professionally administered treatment program. It was a kind of recovery mecca where physical medicine, spiritual nourishment, and brotherly love regularly produced miracles of recovery. AA members rarely questioned Sister Ignatia's reasons or methods; her success spoke for itself. Sister Ignatia herself was Rosary Hall's breath and spirit. Each time she walked into a room, spoke to the men and women, or laughed and prayed with them, she imparted an experience of love and compassion, of hope and good humor. Some said that visiting with Ignatia was better than taking a drink. Indeed, a good number of alcoholics returned daily for a fresh dose of her healing medicine. To many she was a saint; to most she was AA's spokesperson and spiritual anchor.

One year after opening, Rosary Hall celebrated the first of many anniversary parties. Afterward, Bill Wilson described the occasion and reminisced about the early days in Akron and Cleveland in an article, "Another Fragment of History," which he wrote for *The AA Grapevine.* His attendance at this party moved Bill to capture Rosary Hall's unfolding drama for AA's worldwide readership. He attended the function despite his reluctance at the time to travel. The published article began as follows:

> Because a tribute from all of Alcoholics Anonymous was due, Bill made a special trip to Cleveland to attend this particular meeting which he describes below. But he wishes us to say for him with regret, that this does not mean he is once more available for general travel and speaking.[38]

Bill was a specialist in public relations and AA politics. In a grand way he capitalized on every occasion he deemed important to the fellowship's success and history. However, such tributes were also his way of conveying his pride and gratitude to AA's otherwise anonymous groups and leaders.* Some of this was conveyed in Bill's following vivid account of Sister Ignatia, Rosary Hall, and the Ohio AA:

---

*Officially, there are no leaders in AA.

It was December 13, 1953. The occasion was the first anniversary of the opening of Rosary Hall, the newly remodeled
alcoholic ward at Cleveland's famed St. Vincent's Charity Hospital. It had been a great AA meeting. The small auditorium
was crammed with alcoholics and their friends. So was the
balcony. One thousand people now rose to their feet, clapping
wildly. The slight figure of a nun in a gray habit reluctantly approached the lectern's microphone. The uproar doubled, then
suddenly subsided as the little nun commenced to give her
thanks. She was embarrassed, too. For had not the program
she'd helped write for the occasion definitely stated that
"The Sisters of Charity, and the members of Alcoholics Anonymous who have assisted, decline all individual credit." Sister
Ignatia's attempted anonymity was busted wide open, for no
one there wanted to let her get away with it this time. And anyway, she was just about as anonymous in that part of our AA
world as baseball's Cleveland Indians.[39] This was a tribute to
her which had been years in the making.

As I sat watching this scene, I vividly remembered Dr.
Bob's struggles to start Akron's AA Group Number One and
what this dear nun and her Sisters of Charity of St. Augustine
had done to make that possible. I tried to envision all the vast
consequences which have since flowed from their early
effort.[40]

Then Bill proceeded with a lengthy though somewhat inaccurate
account of Cleveland and Akron's earliest AA hospital stories and
growing pains. Wilson also credited the Cleveland membership with
its all-important contribution to AA's pioneering days:

> . . . There soon evolved the great idea of organized per-
> sonal sponsorship for each and every new man and woman.
>   Meanwhile Cleveland's membership soared to hundreds
> in a matter of months. There at Cleveland in the winter of 1939,
> they proved that mass production of sobriety was a glad fact.

This is Cleveland's great and rightful claim to distinction as a pioneer group.[41]

The article concluded by recapping the personal sacrifices of time and money that went into the creation of Rosary Hall the previous December:

> Money, and much more flowed in. With special dispensations from their respective unions, AA carpenters, plumbers and electricians worked long nights . . . A plumbing inspector summed it all up when, after looking at this astonishing result, he remarked: "This was no professional job. The folks who worked on this thing had their hearts in it." More than $60,000 in funds and night work was thus expended on this urgent labor of love . . .
>
> Is it any wonder, then, that the anniversary meeting of the opening of Rosary Hall was turned into a declaration of our personal love for Sister Ignatia and all her works? If the plumbing inspector had been present at this great meeting, he would have again exclaimed, "This is no professional job. It comes from the heart."[42]

Dissension at Rosary Hall

In spite of the successful outcome of their first year's efforts together, Sister Ignatia and some of the old-time Cleveland members were slightly at odds over the anniversary festivities. Here Sister Ignatia demonstrated her strength and leadership to the old-timers, who were upset because their lengthy sobriety did not secure their right to run the show. Sister Ignatia stood her ground in the presence of their boisterous efforts to control the anniversary program. Instead, she had favored the participation of newly sober men who had been recently treated at Rosary Hall, thus allowing them to help plan the anniversary. In this way she bestowed on them the honor to participate and the opportunity to openly express gratitude for their sobriety.

Though some older AAs were disgruntled for a short time, they soon recognized her wisdom in encouraging the new graduates to participate and thus become a part of Rosary Hall's extended family. The small fracas, though characteristically intense, was soon forgotten.

Minor incidents and dissension could be expected in the new ward. Start-up phases often offer opportunities to change the basics of successful programs. Countering this, Ignatia exhibited unshakable adherence to the policies and procedures she had initiated in Akron, holding fast to the traditions that both she and Dr. Bob had pioneered.

In spite of some professional objections and mistaken AA attempts to make a good ward better, Sister Ignatia held tenaciously to her own tested guidelines. When some AA members wanted to extend the length of stay to solve *all* the alcoholic's problems, Ignatia reasserted her objectives: to get her patients sober and help them find God. To her way of thinking, those two accomplishments completed the inpatient treatment process. Life's other problems could be addressed at AA meetings or therapy, if needed. Thus, by keeping the focus somewhat narrow by modern standards, Sister Ignatia accomplished her task; most patients truly found sobriety and experienced the beginnings of a spiritual life.

Another practice she refused to change was her rule regarding unnecessary distractions and non-AA reading materials during treatment. Her reasons for controlling reading materials and prohibiting non-AA visitors, television, and telephones were based on her considerate and realistic expectations of the alcoholic in treatment. Ignatia knew well that patients undergoing detoxification had clouded, drug-affected minds. This made it hard to concentrate on the important information they were receiving in AA lectures and meetings. Patients who were still in the throes of addiction were easily distracted and distressed. Thus, interference from outside sources simply impeded progress and removed the patient's focus from sobriety. To avoid this problem, Ignatia insisted that alcoholics in treatment remain temporarily isolated from the world and, thus, free of outside influences. Her primary concern in this area had little to do with patient abuse of such privileges. Quite to the contrary, Ignatia believed that television, radios, newspapers, and telephone abused patients by wasting their time, money, and opportunity to recover sobriety.

Although patients sometimes balked at her rules for the hall, most often they were still under the influence when they complained. Many actually experienced relief and a sense of protection emanating from Sister Ignatia's plan to insulate them. Soon enough, those who objected came to realize that Sister Ignatia aimed every effort toward the alcoholic's long-term benefit. Following treatment, a newspaperman from Michigan described his own experience, and naiveté, to a friend:

> When I arrived at the hospital that Monday night, Sister met me, called for a wheelchair, and summoned a fellow named Brownie to take me to the ward. They took me up. Naturally I was very low in spirits. I was repelled by the looks and talk of the men I met. I meditated the possibility of getting a private room. The whole world stunk. I lived to laugh later in the week about that first night mood and many other things. As I told Sister I enjoyed some of the deepest diaphragm laughs I had known in a long time. There was an auto dealer from Akron, a Pittsburgh newspaper man (they have quite a few journalistic customers), a tough-talking steel worker from Cleveland, a tool-maker, an Italian-American from Pittsburgh (a handsome guy), a theatrical man from New Philadelphia.
>
> I had taken my typewriter down with me, blithely thinking I might help pass the time by getting out some work. On my arrival, Sister impounded the typewriter, my wallet, and two newspapers I carried and I didn't see them until I left. It is probably just as well, otherwise I might have missed some of the camaraderie of the week—maybe the tough steel worker would not have taken me by the shoulder as he was leaving and said, "Cheez, yer a good guy, I hate to say goodbye."
>
> I find helpful some very brief prayers. In the morning I say, "Dear God, I give you this day." At night, "Dear God, I thank you for returning me this day, whole; Oh Sacred Heart, stay near me."[43]

Such testimonials of a sincere and deeply felt love for the Irish nun multiplied day by day. Some of the letters of acclaim blossomed into national recognition of her work. Instead of accepting personal awards, Ignatia praised the AA programs and her religious community. But her fame grew despite all her efforts to contain it.

Sister Ignatia touched everyone she met in a special, unforgettable way. Once she opened the doors of Rosary Hall, it seemed that Cleveland's larger metropolitan area alerted the entire world to Sister Ignatia's charisma. AAs who moved or traveled to Cleveland from other parts of the country immediately sought her counsel and became as devoted to her as the hometown patients she treated.

Frank M. was one such man who had joined AA while living in New York City in the early 1950s. A few years later, business moved this chief executive officer to Cleveland. He looked up Sister Ignatia soon after his arrival and quickly became one of "her boys." Familiar with AA hospitals in New York, he offered these comments and comparisons:

> There were none of these fancy places like there are today. In fact, there were very few. In New York where I lived in the early fifties, we had Knickerbocker and Towns hospitals. Rosary Hall was larger than both put together, larger than all the treatment in New York. The Hall was talked about everywhere in the country and *her name* was known to be that of a magical lady. The alcoholics coming into the hospital, industrialists I knew in other cities, had heard of her.
>
> She had a power that reached them before they ever got there. It was like magic in the air. She had that reputation. If you went there, you were probably going to get the cure and you were not going to get away with anything, not even in her later years. She was one step ahead of the best of the con artists who went through there. Those guys needed a strong-willed lady, and she was a one-of-a-kind. She knew everything an alcoholic would say and all the innuendoes they would use to cut a deal. But somehow, she always had the answers.

There was a mysterious liaison between her and the problem. She was born with it, and she was gifted.

Sister Ignatia had a chemistry with anybody. She was even able to get to a person who violently disliked her. I saw that happen. I literally saw a man who had been on the ward before say, "Keep her away from me, I don't want any part of her." She said to the men, "You let me handle that," and she somehow reached him in her own way. There was a Godlike atmosphere with this woman that I can only describe as a presence. It worked.

She was sent by a Higher Power to run this thing. That's the kind of person they needed, and I wish there were more of them around. The only one I can see in my later life who ever compared to her was Mother Teresa, in India; she also has the ability to reach both the C.E.O. and the common person.[44]

Thus, the hard work of initiating treatment in Akron with AA's founding fathers now flowered into the miracles of recovery in Cleveland's Rosary Hall. One little step from music school to hospital admissions in the life of Sister Ignatia ended in a giant leap forward for Alcoholics Anonymous.

Six

An Unfinished Mission:
Alcoholism and Catholicism

Nothing great is ever done without much enduring.

—inscription on the Catherine of Siena Medal
awarded to Sister Ignatia, June 28, 1954

By 1954 Sister Ignatia had earned considerable public recognition for her acclaimed work among alcoholics. After only fifteen years of aiding drinkers to sobriety, nearly every major American city boasted of citizens recovering from alcoholism who had been treated by Sister Ignatia and sustained by Alcoholics Anonymous. Her past work at St. Thomas Hospital and her present effort at Rosary Hall drew extensive media—and Catholic Church—attention.

It came as no surprise to Bill Wilson when, one day, he received the following inquiry from a Cincinnati woman, Mrs. James G. Manley:

> At the suggestion of Mr. Herbert H., Cincinnati, I am writing you to learn the details of Sister Ignatia's contribution and work with alcoholics. Her name has been mentioned as a candidate for a national award to an outstanding Catholic woman, and I have been asked to assemble the facts. I am anxious to verify two unsupported statements that have come to me. One, she was the first to recognize alcoholism as a medical situation, and the first to set aside hospital facilities for treatment of alcoholism. Two, she had a part in the founding of AA.[1]

Elated that Sister Ignatia would finally be recognized by her Church, Bill answered the letter at once. His response thoughtfully detailed the pride the AA fellowship held for Sister Ignatia and his own high esteem for her:

Dear Mrs. Manley:

Seldom do I receive a letter containing more pleasant news than yours bore—the possibility that Sister Ignatia may be in line as the outstanding Catholic Woman of the Year. Though, of course, not an alcoholic, she is already rated among us as a saint in AA's pioneering time and since has played an invaluable role.

Now respecting your specific questions, no, she was not the first to recognize alcoholism as a medical situation. So far as AA is concerned, that was the contribution of Dr. William D. Silkworth of New York City, but she was the very first to offer Catholic hospital facilities for the treatment of alcoholism by admitting us to St. Thomas Hospital, Akron. Respecting your second question, I would most emphatically say *she played a considerable part in the founding of A.A.* [author emphasis].

Dr. Bob began to shop around for hospital facilities and placed the dilemma before Sister Ignatia, then in charge of Admittance at St. Thomas Hospital in Akron. This was sometime in 1939, I believe. While it is true that a great amount of pioneering work had already been done, we had never been able to solve the actual problem of hospitalization, either at Akron or New York. Sister Ignatia stepped into the breach and began to admit alcoholics at St. Thomas.

I enclose a piece that I recently wrote for *The Grapevine* which is an historical sketch describing her benign activity and the celebration which many of us attended at Charity Hospital in Cleveland this spring. I have no words good enough to describe the magnificent devotion of this truly saintly woman, nor could any human being begin to estimate what her work has meant in terms of souls saved and alcoholics released from their thralldom. And should she be named Catholic Woman of the Year, I can think of nothing that would please our members more, especially those in the Middle West, to whom she has administered and who know her so well.

Gratefully yours,
Bill Wilson, Cofounder[2]

Wilson's letter satisfied the questions asked by the National Council of Catholic Women's (NCCW) Selection Committee. Ignatia was stunned to receive a congratulatory letter from Mrs. Clare J. Steigerwald, national president of the Theta Phi Alpha chapter:

Dear Sister Ignatia,

It is an honor and my happy privilege as National President to officially announce to you that you have been selected as the 1954 recipient of National Theta Phi Alpha's St. Catherine of Siena Award.

This medal is awarded by our fraternity to an outstanding Catholic woman of national distinction. Some of our former recipients include Mary Norton, Congresswoman; Miss Jane Howley, nationally known social worker; Mrs. Anne O'Hare McCormick, ex-world journalist; Frances Parkinson Keyes, Authoress; Dr. Helen White, scholar, author, clubwoman; Sister M. Madeleva, C.S.C., President of St. Mary's College, Notre Dame; Loretta Young, actress; Anne Laughlin, former Chief of the United Nations International Children's Emergency Fund in Bulgaria; Dr. Elizabeth G. Salmon, first woman president of the American Catholic Philosophical Association. As you can see, the recipients represent a wide range in public and religious service . . .

Your name was selected by the selection committee in recognition of your outstanding achievements in one of the major problems affecting our country today—alcoholism.

Your fame as "the Little Sister of A.A." has spread far and wide . . . We sincerely hope that you will be able to be present and that you will say a few words in acceptance of the award.[3]

Sister Ignatia attended the June 28 ceremony in Cincinnati with a companion from the community, Sister M. Bridget. Her acceptance of the Siena Medal signaled another turning point in her career—but one fraught with new implications and problems. Before this date, AAs had spread Ignatia's reputation by word of mouth, primarily among themselves. Now, however, receipt of the Siena Award brought national interest to Ignatia's work and a new dimension—publicity— to her life. The National Catholic Welfare Conference News Service released news of the award to all the Catholic newspapers in the country. From coast to coast, Catholic readers learned of Sister Ignatia's work with Alcoholics Anonymous and Theta Phi Alpha's demanding criteria for selecting her:

The Siena Medal is awarded in honor of the 14th century social reformer Saint [a woman] to "a Catholic woman who has made a distinctive contribution to Catholic life in the United States."

Sister Ignatia was singled out for "outstanding achievement in one of the major problems affecting our country today—alcoholism." But she refused to admit that she of herself had achieved anything.

"Credit for any achievement," she said in an interview, "belongs to the members of our religious community who have encouraged this work, and to the hundreds of men and women who have been helped, and having been helped, returned that help to others." To the thousands of AAs who have been helped, Sister Ignatia is regarded as *"The Little Angel of the AAs."* Her name is well known not only in Akron but in AA circles throughout the country.

Writing in the current issue of *The Catholic Nurse,* edited by Archbishop Richard J. Cushing, a member of Alcoholics

Anonymous wrote of her: "It was a nursing nun in a Catholic hospital in Akron who gave AA its first impetus. She understood alcoholics. She sympathized with them. She let Dr. Bob, cofounder of AA, bring his alcoholic patients to the hospital although the other doctors objected, and she helped to indoctrinate the patients with AA."

Sister Ignatia now admits that what seemed to her at the time as a routine act in her job as hospital registrar, may have been the beginning of this chapter in medical rehabilitation.

. . . Sister Ignatia, who 40 years ago entered the religious life, was attracted to the Sisters of Charity of Saint Augustine because of its work among orphans. She feels now that she is still working among orphans, for as she has said: "Many of those who come to Rosary Hall, are estranged from family and friends, and are alone. They feel rejected."[4]

Estranged, alone, rejected: These were Ignatia's chosen words to describe the emotional climate of the alcoholics she helped. Often enough, though, the same words applied to her life too. The Siena Medal thrust Sister Ignatia into the limelight and brought new publicity to the cause of alcoholism. For Ignatia, however, national fame cast a shadow over her personal life. Her community allowed her work with AA to progress, although not everyone understood or empathized with it. Publicity elicited disparaging remarks and critical judgments from some of her community members. Still, others who had been personally touched by the recovery of a relative or friend praised Ignatia's talents.

Thus newspaper publicity only complicated her relationship with peers and superiors. Although none of the sisters denied that Ignatia's work was constant and determined, many still questioned its necessity. To avoid unnecessary conflict, Sister Ignatia moved away from community dissent and relied on God and the AAs for personal support. Because she was sensitive to the personal ramifications of publicity, Ignatia carefully accepted praise and awards in the name of her religious community. Invariably, her speeches and news articles diminished her own role and instead reflected her gratitude to the community for allowing her work with AA to continue.

For a brief time after the Siena Award and its accompanying acclaim, Sister Ignatia was invited to speak before various organizations and conventions. Usually the invitations came from church-related groups requesting information about alcoholism. Actually, though, her formal presentations were few. This was unfortunate, since as an acclaimed Catholic spokeswoman she had much knowledge and insight to share about addiction and many methods of prevention to offer her listeners.

One outstanding speech, delivered to the National Council of Catholic Women in Akron in 1954, shows the expansiveness of her knowledge of alcoholism. In it she offers solutions and exhibits prophetic awareness of the problems that unarrested alcoholism would undoubtedly lead to in the future. She began by telling the members of NCCW:

> Alcoholism is a matter of great public concern today [1954]. According to Father Ford, S.J., in the *Catholic Encyclopedia,* there are about five million alcoholics in the United States. This is appalling when we think of it in terms of family disruption, poverty, deterioration of body and mind, collapse of moral and spiritual values. There may be another three million problem drinkers in the United States, that is, heavy drinkers who may easily become alcoholics. These problem drinkers, too, affect the lives of others with whom they come in daily contact. Then there are episodes of drunkenness such as office parties, anniversary celebrations, weddings, class reunions, and escapades of teenagers and college students.[5]

In her remarks she carefully detailed the triple deterioration—physical, mental, and spiritual—that accompanied alcoholism, while outlining the proper medical and spiritual treatment. Further on, she spoke courageously on the Catholic Church's failure to responsibly address alcohol use and abuse among the young:

In years gone by, in our Catholic system of education, considerable respect was paid, and attention given, to various Catholic temperance organizations, but, as a result of the dislike of the Volstead Act [Prohibition] in the middle of this century, it may be that our Catholic system of education got too far away from the subject of alcoholism, and neglected to bring out, for the benefit of our youth, the evils that are always present with alcohol and which were so greatly emphasized in our schools previous to prohibition.

Much of my training has been in hospital work. I do not profess to be an educator, but I cannot help hoping that our Catholic educators will give serious thought to the possibilities of injecting into their curricula some study, or at least discussion, of the evils which may result from the excessive use of alcohol.[6]

This was a concise, instructive speech that offered concrete facts and solutions for approaching the subject of alcohol use in Church and society. Normally, Ignatia's speeches were disappointingly brief—simple compositions that left a charmed audience hungry for more of her wisdom. But this presentation offered more. Significantly, Ignatia produced a simple yet comprehensive overview of the need for treatment, prevention, and education that remains worthy of today's study and implementation. In that sense, there is a timeless quality to her words.

Ignatia challenged her Church audience to address alcoholism on a spiritual level as a necessary part of the solution. After long years of hard work with alcoholics, she had come to realize that perhaps only the powerful effect of collective prayer would one day raise the Church's consciousness of this spiritually deadening disease. In addition, only by changing public values toward drinking and attitudes concerning the use and effects of alcohol would potent spiritual solutions come. The 1954 speech continues:

Universities and welfare groups have expended millions of dollars in an attempt to find the cause of alcoholism. No one has been able to place his or her finger upon the exact cause. However, it is the consensus of opinion among the great minds that have attacked the problem that a lack of proper spiritual application on the part of the victim is at least a primary cause. The cofounders of Alcoholics Anonymous believed that the solution of the problem for many was to be found in the merger of the forces of science and religion.[7]

The speech next cites a special area of concern for Ignatia; its mention is surprising in the context of the 1950s and sadly is still applicable and inadequately addressed today:

> The problem of the American woman and alcoholism is much greater than any of us like to admit. The problem has many causes, one of which should not be overlooked. With our high standard of living in America, there results considerable leisure time.
>
> Today, narcotics in the form of sleeping tablets and sedatives, easily obtained, are too frequently administered to the American woman by doctors . . . well-meaning men. These sedatives, used with moderation, may have their place, but excessive use of them creates a serious problem, to say nothing of their combined use with alcohol, where the result is all too often catastrophic. It may well be that when the history of our age is written, it will be referred to as an *Age of Sedation* [author's emphasis].[8]

Next, Sister Ignatia spoke of ways that parents could guide their children in the use of alcohol and offered advice for dealing with youthful excesses. Evident are her strong views on the crucial role of the family unit in supporting alcoholism recovery, though her tone should be viewed in the context of the 1950s sociological climate:

> In the home where there are growing children, alcohol should be referred to as a gift of God, intelligent use of which is a blessing to many; but by the same token, to many people

it is a terrible curse. The fruit of the vine is a harmless stimulant for many; in the hands of the alcoholic it turns to poison. In many homes, especially the mother will over-emphasize the evils of alcohol in raising their children. When the children begin to grow up and find that successful, law-abiding Christian people use alcohol with no apparent harm, they decide that mother and father were entirely wrong.

It is my considered judgment after observing thousands upon thousands of cases through the years that the father and mother who drive the alcoholic child from the home, unless as a last resort, are making a very serious mistake. Likewise, the husband or wife who thinks legal separation or divorce from the alcoholic spouse is the answer, also is making a very serious mistake. The family unit may be the last ray of hope for the floundering alcoholic.[9]

Indeed, family support during early sobriety has proved to be one of the strongest predictors of long-term recovery. Without a solid family unit supporting an alcoholic's sobriety, chances for long-term recovery are negligible. Even so, Ignatia anticipated her listeners' question, "What do I do with an alcoholic?" and outlined a simple plan of action:

How would you proceed if you were confronted with an alcoholic who asked for help? Avoid nagging him. The first thing to do is to pray for him. Do all that you can to help the individual to sober up physically, and urge him to pray for God's help. Encourage carbohydrate intake by means of fruit juices and sweets of any kind. Often the aid of a doctor may be necessary. If the patient really wants help and is in a receptive mood call a member of Alcoholics Anonymous (referred to as a sponsor). Nearly every city has a central office listed under Alcoholics Anonymous in the telephone directory. Let him take over. He knows all the tricks of the trade because of personal experience. The sponsor will know when hospitalization is advisable.

A priest once told me that the A.A. program is the most fruitful source of conversions. Many return to the sacraments who have been away for years. Many who have never prayed, learn to pray.

One may get the program "the hard way" as they put it, without hospitalization; but the [consensus] . . . is that one learns more during five or six days of hospitalization than he would in attending meetings for a year. Persevering prayer and sacrifice bring grace and final results in God's Own good time.[10]

Speaking at a crowded Catholic women's conference presented a rare opportunity for Ignatia to lobby on behalf of negligible Church- and community-based alcohol education and prevention activities. Advantageously, she appealed to the group's moral decency and com-passion—their feelings rather than merely their intellects—espousing a humane rather than the prevailing punitive approach to alcoholism.

Ignatia as spokeswoman fortuitously urged society also to set limi-tations on alcohol beverage advertising. The determined nun shared her own extensive treatment and educational resources and proposed forming children's early attitudes toward alcohol consumption around the Christian-oriented premise that sobriety is a choice as well as a virtue to be learned and practiced. Her own words express her message best:

What can an organization such as yours do to prevent the spread of alcoholism? If anything is to be accomplished it must be intelligently approached. A misinformed world is a mis-understanding world. The alcoholic is extremely susceptible to the attitudes of those around him. Attitudes in the early days of recovery make or break the individual's progress. Lack of confidence in the possibility of recovery is very damaging.

Public education is necessary. Ignorance produces hostil-ity in many cases. Our laws are a reflection of public opinion towards alcoholism. Other illnesses produce behavior symp-toms, such as brain tumors, cerebral accidents, diabetes, etc.

Yet these people are not placed in jails. Commercials on radio and television advertising alcoholic beverages, neon signs, and [other] advertising should at least be curtailed.

Several of our priests are very well informed on this subject. Reverend John Ford, S.J., Weston College, Massachusetts, is probably one of the best authorities living at the present time. He has made an intensive study of the subject.

[Others are] Rev. Edward Dowling, S.J., of St. Louis, Rev. Ralph Pfau of Indianapolis, and locally, Rev. Vincent Haas of St. Thomas Hospital. Invite a member of AA to address a PTA meeting for instance. I have a bibliography here which could be used as study club material.

There is a Catholic Youth movement which was started in Baltimore during the last year called The Crusaders. The purpose is total abstinence for Catholic youth in honor of the Sacred Thirst and Agony of Our Lord. It is not based on the evils of drinking but, rather, that "it is good to abstain from a good thing for a good reason."[11]

In her concluding remarks Ignatia reemphasized the Catholic Church's untapped power of prayer in resolving the spiritual illness of alcoholism. A spiritual remedy for a spiritual disease seemed to her only logical. Along with treatment, prevention, and education, prayer was a powerful prescriptive for jarring loose intellectual resistance in accepting alcoholism as a disease. Sometimes it drove an enlightening wedge of awareness into the stubborn rationalizations and misconceptions of the uninformed and interrupted harmful drinking patterns of potential victims. Other times praying relieved the sense of helplessness experienced by the alcoholic's loved ones.

Encouraging the use of prayer was also a powerful but nonthreatening way of elevating the alcohol awareness of the clergy and the faithful while subtly promoting the temperate use of alcohol. Thus Ignatia was in full accord with the Catholic position proposed by moralist John Ford: Teach the practice of sobriety as a desirable virtue to be cultivated by clergy and faithful *together.* Accordingly, Ignatia saw no reason why church groups could not offer prayers, as well as programs, to combat the growing global epidemic of addiction. She continued forthrightly, relating prayer and divine help to the alcoholic's experience:

> We have in our meeting room a sign which reads, "But for the Grace of God." I have seen almost miraculous reformation through prayer for the alcoholic. There are those who advance these reasons: that the reformation of the alcoholic may be used by God to show the power of prayer, because of all the sinners [in the world] the drunkard is the one who *displays* his weakness and his deficiency for all the world to see. When prayer accomplishes a reformation in him, God therefore teaches us a lesson on the power of prayer.
>
> I usually give the patients a little talk after breakfast every morning. Sometimes I use this very theme . . . some loved one has been praying for you or you would not be here; someone has been praying and making sacrifices for you, because grace is obtained only through prayer and sacrifice. Many of the patients come to me after my little talk, with tears in their eyes and say "Sister, I know that my wife has been praying for me, or my sister. . . ."[12]

Archbishop Limits Ignatia's Outreach

As a speaker Sister Ignatia was neither spontaneous nor dynamic. She read her speeches almost word for word and rarely deviated from the text. However, her growing reputation, bashful manner, wispy Irish voice, and intense interest in her subject commanded the audience's attention. If her voice was frail, strength rose from the meaning of her words.

Sister Ignatia had much inspiration and experience to offer as a spokeswoman for alcoholism treatment. Sadly, however, her speaking engagements were limited in number by her superiors. Though the exact reasons for the imposed restraints were never stated, Ignatia's increasingly high profile, and her outspoken concern for alcoholics, all seemed contrary to the humble, submissive behavior expected of a nun.

For a period after her transfer to Cleveland, Archbishop Edward F. Hoban and Mother Clementine, Ignatia's superior, suspended permission for her to speak outside the hospital. An effort was made to contain Ignatia's enthusiasm and thus limit her power. The most striking instance appears in the 1953 correspondence between Archbishop of Boston Richard J. Cushing (later a cardinal) and Archbishop Hoban.

Cushing wrote to Hoban, asking for his permission to invite Sister Ignatia to speak at the Sixth National Clergy Conference on Alcoholism (NCCA) "to some seventy-five or one hundred priests . . . because she was the unanimous choice of the committee."[13] Archbishop Hoban's response reveals a growing problem related to Ignatia's popularity and increasing notoriety. Apparently Hoban (and Mother Clementine?) felt the need to discipline Ignatia and perhaps even humble her:

> Your Excellency:
>
> We are complimented by the desire of the committee of the Sixth National Clergy Conference on Alcoholism, to have Sister Mary Ignatia of the Sisters of Charity of Saint Augustine, address the clergy at the Conference.
>
> There have been many similar requests in the past and the question of the advisability of accepting such invitations was discussed by the Sister, the Mother General and Bishop Begin, the Vicar for Religious. While the Sister is flattered by such invitations, she makes no pretense of being a speaker or at doing anything other than applying the principles of Christian Charity in her dealing with alcoholics. Accordingly, it was agreed that she would not accept invitations to speak on the subject of Alcoholism and, thus far, every invitation has been declined. As much as I would like to accede to your Excellency's gracious request, I believe that the policy which was established for Sister Mary Ignatia should be continued.

If she accepted the one invitation, she would feel obliged to accept the many other invitations, and this would not serve her personal or professional best interests. Sincerely regretting the necessity of discouraging the invitation, I am, with personal best wishes,

Faithfully yours in Christ,
The Most Reverend Edward F. Hoban
Archbishop-Bishop of Cleveland[14]

Hoban's response partially reflected the common attitude of his era. However, it also alluded to the male clergy's accustomed domination and disregard of women in the 1950s, pre-Vatican II Church mentality. The idea of a woman religious advising a convocation of priests about any spiritual matter no doubt appalled the reigning archbishop.

It could also pose questions related to his own episcopal credibility with his priests. How could a strong bishop control his local army of priests if he permitted a diocesan *nun* to travel the country as an invited spokesperson and teacher of priests outside his jurisdiction? What if her popularity with a national clergy grew to rival her general popularity in Cleveland and Akron? In the pre-Vatican II era, a nun addressing groups of priests severely threatened clerical power. Thus, the growing popularity of a simple nun with a significant following of laypeople and clergy worried the archbishop and the mother superior.

With these thoughts in mind, the archbishop reasoned that Ignatia had to be brought back into his line of authority. The answer was obvious: Keep her at home and call her to the practice of her vowed obedience. In other words, silence her.

However, this issue accounted for only a portion of Hoban's reluctance to permit Ignatia to address the National Clergy Conference on Alcoholism. A second concern subtly called into question the accepted drinking practices among Catholic clergy and hierarchy, as well as their set attitudes regarding the convivial use of alcohol.

Outside of recovering priest-alcoholics, most members of the clergy denied, first, that alcoholism was an illness and, second, that it existed within their own ranks. Thus, in 1953, if priests were drinking, they had a personal—and moral—problem, not a disease. And they could reform by simply practicing prayer and self-control. For more stubborn situations, a lengthy out-of-town retreat—usually in New Jersey or New Mexico—supplied a geographical "cure" while removing the problem from local view.

Against that background of rampant ignorance and denial, it was important to note Ignatia's differing opinion, based on her advanced knowledge and experience of alcoholism as a disease. Certainly, she joined the superiors of alcoholic priests in recommending the practice of prayer. The difference was that Ignatia did not limit alcoholic priests to the power of prayer alone. Before recommending any alcoholic—clerical or not—to prayer, Ignatia demanded a concurrent commitment to stop drinking permanently, to attend Alcoholics Anonymous meetings, and to practice the Twelve Steps. Only then would prayer help an alcoholic heal his spiritual sickness and maintain his sobriety. To AA's angel, priests were no different from laypeople in that regard.

Among the Church's other reasons for sidestepping the problem of alcoholism within the clergy was the closet mentality that kept family skeletons hidden from outsiders. According to the Catholic hierarchy, excessive drinking among the clergy concerned only the priestly fraternity or the bishop's chancellor and need not involve the laity or their treatment programs.

Given the Church's prevalent point of view that alcoholism was neither a disease nor a clerical problem, high-ranking Church officials saw no need for talks and conferences on the subject. Similarly, they envisioned no need for a training course on alcoholism in the seminary outside of some general remarks made in the context of moral and pastoral theology. Likewise, if a priest admitted he had a drinking problem, he was generally barred from ecclesiastical advancement and responsible assignments. That was the sum of pastoral strategy toward "problem" drinkers.

Nevertheless, other issues *were* present and, down the line, would be admitted grudgingly. One was that an honest recovery from alcoholism, as pursued in Sister Ignatia's ministry, questioned the social and recreational role of alcohol in the lives of more than a few priests and bishops. Even deeper, her emphasis on spiritual illness and spiritual recovery suggested that some part of the clergy had been overlooking important values in their own religious and personal development. In this vein, a physician at the 1953 Clergy Conference on Alcoholism was overheard chiding some priests:

> The trouble with you priests is, you all have "dignosclerosis," hardening of the dignity. If you weren't afraid to make a mistake, you'd be out curing people of these things.[15]

Early on, as the first few alcoholic priests courageously joined AA, their bishops began to ask the question, "Should a priest tarnish the Church's reputation by joining Alcoholics Anonymous?" At the 1953 Clergy Conference, nonalcoholic Father Edward Dowling, S.J., obviously distressed that more apostolic concern was leveled at preserving the good image of the Church than at saving the lives of its alcoholic priests, responded earnestly:

> Frankly, I don't think the Church needs saving nearly as much as this [alcoholic] man. God's cause is often hurt by people who are trying to save God.[16]

Unfortunately, Father Dowling's opinion was in the minority.

Most often, a priest's addiction and even his recovery were hidden from view. The Church's frank denial that alcoholism was a common enough problem among its priests created serious obstacles to prevention, education, and treatment efforts attempted on their behalf.

Clergy Conferences on Alcoholism Begin

Despite this strong opposition, the National Clergy Conference on Alcoholism germinated from the keen observation and honest discourse of a few well-informed priests who, for various reasons, concerned themselves with the Church's dire need for clergy education on alcoholism. The idea for a conference sprang from an informal discussion among four priests* eating hot-fudge sundaes at an Indiana soda shop in 1949.[17] The eventual organizer of the conference, Father Ralph Pfau, broke his anonymity and claimed himself to be the first Catholic priest to join Alcoholics Anonymous. In addition to organizing the NCCA in his home diocese of Indianapolis, Father Pfau authored a popular pamphlet series for alcoholics called The Golden Books. He also published an autobiographical account of his own alcoholism entitled *The Prodigal Shepherd.*

Thus, in 1949 the first NCCA convened amidst much secrecy in Rensselaer, Indiana. The participants recorded minutes from the proceedings in a special publication called The Blue Book. The foreword to the first Blue Book explains:

> Early in 1949 plans for a seminar for the Clergy who are active members of Alcoholics Anonymous were made by Fr. Ralph Pfau of the Archdiocese of Indianapolis and Fr. John Dillon of the Diocese of Lafayette, Indiana. After due reflection and further consultation with their Ordinaries, the Seminar was expanded into a general conference to include the Hierarchy, Rectors of Seminaries, Superiors of Religious Orders and interested members of the clergy.
>
> From Aug. 23 to 25, 1949, more than 100 priests gathered at St. Joseph's college, Rensselaer, Indiana. Their Excellencies, Archbishop Schulte, Bishop Bennett, and Bishop Cody (representing Archbishop Ritter) were in attendance.
>
> Many of those in attendance were active members of Alcoholics Anonymous. Others had been sent by their Ordinaries and Superiors to learn about alcoholism.
>
> Papers were read that presented alcoholism from a medical angle, from a psychiatric angle, from a moral angle, from an AA angle.
>
> These proceedings were privately published with ecclesi-

---

*The four priests responsible for initiating the NCCA were Fathers Ralph Pfau, John Dillon, Raymond Atkins, and John C. Ford

astical permission. Names of most of those who took part have been omitted. These have been identified by number and can be checked.

Copies of this book are being sent to all of the members of the Hierarchy in the United States, to Major Superiors of Religious Orders, to Rectors of Major Seminaries, diocesan and religious, and to those who attended. Recipients are asked to remember that this book is intended for a very restricted audience and information contained in it is not intended for public dissemination.[18]

The first clergy conference was a huge success. In fact, both the conference and publication of The Blue Book became annual events. Confronting the extent of clerical alcoholism as well as its treatment, Father Pfau told those gathered:

One opinion is that the priest alcoholic should not identify himself at the public level with the general Alcoholics Anonymous group, but should rather endeavor to merely participate in a closed priest discussion group formed of other priest alcoholics.

Now, suffice it to say that in all areas but a very few, such procedure is absolutely impossible. I believe that of the forty-nine priests active in AA today, forty-four of them would not be able to find another priest alcoholic, at least sober, within a hundred miles to discuss his problems [with].[19]

At this meeting, attendees attempted to determine statistically the number of priest-alcoholics in the United States. They estimated that approximately 12.5 percent, or five thousand, Catholic priests were then drinking at an alcoholic level—a figure projected to be considerably higher than the rate of alcoholism in the general population.

It was during the first clergy conference proceedings that Father John C. Ford, S.J., recalled hearing reports of Sister Ignatia's well-respected work through some of the recovering alcoholic priests who had been in contact with her prior to 1949. The priests spoke reverently about Sister Ignatia. They knew that many of their priestly brothers had escaped from the compulsion to drink because she had brought them the AA message and had committed herself to helping them find lasting sobriety.

However, it was well known that Sister Ignatia did not believe that alcoholism among clergy responded well to special treatment such as priests-only AA groups—and she was in a position to know. Because alcoholism was—and remained—the socially acceptable clerical sin, Ignatia felt that groups composed solely of priests tended to go easy on the dishonesty, rationalization, and ego pride that often impeded a priest's search for sobriety. But initially, when priests balked at discussing their alcoholism in the presence of laypeople at open AA meetings, a compromise was settled upon:

> Because of the fact that priests don't want to go in where laymen are, we have made sort of a compromise . . . we have a group meeting of only priests and doctors, professional men, medical men and dentists, because of the fact that . . . there is so much similarity in their position in the community.
>
> The doctors are finding that some of the men of their profession haven't the courage to enter [AA] because they don't want to let the neighborhood or their patrons know that they are alcoholic because it will affect them financially. And the idea of this group that we have—the exclusion group, you might call it—is more or less a stepping stone.[20]

The idea of a temporary arrangement that would serve as a stepping-stone to open AA membership had merit. However, many priests never graduated from the protective and enabling sanctuary that such exclusive groups offered and never became integrated into the healing fellowship of AA as a whole.

Without the influence of mainstream AA and the rigorous honesty and humility that such intermingling fostered, many leaders in alcoholism treatment—notably Sister Ignatia—viewed these special groups as vehicles for hiding and enabling the priest's alcoholism. After all, in recovery, attitudes that cried to be different, special, and disassociated from AA often signaled unhealthy exercise of ego. Like it or not, alcoholism's humanizing bond already linked the suffering priest to his alcoholic brothers and sisters.

Aside from the alcoholic priest's own problems in facing up to his alcoholism, there was the associated problem experienced by his superior, the bishop. Although the bishops were obviously concerned for the reputation of the priest and for the Church's own good name, they as yet lacked education and accurate information on alcoholism. In fact, to them the complexities of working with an alcoholic clergyman seemed a useless, expensive, and embarrassing pursuit.

Thus the clergy's easier practice of seeing excessive drinking in the simple framework of moral weakness, self-indulgence, and immaturity fell miles short of the mark. Another impediment to recovery arose from the universal viewing of God's wounded servant—the priest—in a different light from his other wounded children. It easily occurred that the alcoholic priest was condemned to remain sick and isolated, even in recovery. Often, a misdirected rush of sympathy from nonalcoholic peers and laypeople, frequently social drinkers themselves, created an unsupportive, even harmful, atmosphere that further indulged the alcoholic's natural appetite for self-pity and resentment and reinforced his reasons for drinking rather than positively supporting his efforts at sobriety.

From 1940 to almost 1970, it was common for a courageous priest to admit to his own alcoholism and then be refused permission by his bishop or superior to attend AA meetings. Instead, simple prayer and willpower were prescribed, although these rarely brought sobriety that endured. In some cases, bishops did allow priests to attend AA, provided that they did so in another diocese. In other cases, they were encouraged to attend meetings ostensibly as an "educational experience" without revealing their own alcoholism. All this led to a heartrending dilemma for priests seeking sobriety, many of whom drove as much as one hundred miles or more to attend an AA meeting on their one day off.

Fortunately, in an effort to address all of these issues, by 1953 the aims of the National Clergy Conference on Alcoholism had evolved to be the following:

1. rehabilitation of priest-alcoholics using the help offered by Alcoholics Anonymous coupled *with* the Sacraments of the Church
2. prevention of alcoholism among priests through the dissemination of information and through an educational program, especially in seminaries
3. cooperation with the most reverend ordinaries and religious superiors by placing at their disposal the knowledge and experience of the NCCA[21]

The Catholic Position Develops

Each year, the minutes and talks of the three-day seminar were edited, published, and mailed to every bishop and religious superior in the United States. These volumes were classic composites of Catholic thought and excellence. They offered Catholic leadership the opportunity for learning state-of-the-art information on alcoholism. But, similar to alcoholism, The Blue Books—for the most part—were ignored or hidden from view, never affecting their intended audience.

Forty years later, nearly all seminary libraries have on their shelves dust-covered copies of The Blue Book that contain some of the most thought-provoking and articulate Catholic writings on alcoholism to date. Unfortunately, because of the highly restricted circulation, the written proceedings were never made available to Catholic laypeople, nor were they encouraged for use by seminarians in formation programs. Had some of the better articles been widely distributed, the Catholic population would have been armed with valuable, theologically sanctioned information on the appropriate use of alcohol.

Among the early Blue Book articles was one written by Father John Ford. Emphasizing the practice of sobriety as a desirable virtue for Catholics to acquire was his way of suggesting that Catholics and their priests should seriously examine their consumption of alcohol. Father Ford's opinions as a ranking theologian in the U.S. Catholic Church were well respected by both Alcoholics Anonymous and Catholic Church leaders. Accordingly, he warned members of the clergy conference forty years ago, "There is good reason to believe that in some segments of our Catholic population the incidence of alcoholic excess and of alcoholism is disproportionately high."[22] Current statistics confirm Ford's warning. Today, alcoholism rates are higher among Catholics than those found in any other religious denomination.

Continuing his discourse, Ford discussed his concerns as a priest-theologian about the lack of alcohol education received by seminarians during their formative theological studies:

> It does not seem to be an exaggeration to say that the education and orientation of our seminarians in the fundamental problems of alcohol and alcoholism is frequently so meager that their frame of mind and general attitude is uninformed and immature. The sin of impurity is never funny to the newly ordained priest. But the sin of drunkenness is: and no one has calculated yet which of these sins causes the greater harm in our society or how much of the former is the result of the latter. An appreciation of the problems of alcohol as they exist among our own people would lead to a more mature and discerning attitude.[23]

Consequently Father Ford proposed that the Catholic Church's efforts in education and prevention should first begin in seminaries where priestly attitudes about alcohol use (and abuse) could be solidly and virtuously formed. If seminarians received accurate information, he reasoned, they would be better prepared to make healthy choices about the use of alcohol, first, in their own lives and, second, in their subsequent direction of troubled Catholics. He explained the problem of alcohol and the clergy as he saw and experienced it:

> I should like to mention at this point one idea in particular of which many younger seminarians need to be disabused: that is the idea that it is necessary for a priest to learn to drink like a man, either in order to be approachable and acceptable to the faithful, or in order to be socially at ease with his fellow priests.

The seminarian is just waiting for the day when he will be released from seminary restriction and take his place in the ranks of full-fledged priests. Drinking is a very common practice in the adult world and in the clerical world today. It is natural for young men to want to drink as the older men do. But here is the fallacy. *A great many of these elders drink because they have never really grown up. They have remained emotionally immature, and the way they drink is a sign of their emotional immaturity.* Amongst alcoholics, childishness in behavior and in reaction to unpleasant situations is characteristic of a very large percentage. But apart from them, the drinking of many others, including some priests, can only be called a childish manifestation of social inadequacy. Many adults drink because their personalities are so poverty-stricken that they do not know what else to do, socially.

Many more drink because they have a childish desire for excitement and thrills. They have never outgrown the child's eagerness to "have a party." And of course since ice cream and cake are no longer exciting, the party is no good unless there are drinks—plenty of them. These are the people who easily drink to excess in their search for release from boredom.

These are the priests who are always ready to insist that they were not *theologically* drunk. Truly virtuous moderation does not satisfy them because they are looking for a *kick* or a *jolt* in the drinking situation. And strangely enough, these are the very drinkers that many younger men are tempted to imitate when they start drinking. To become *one of the boys* is their aim; and the boys can *drink like men.*[24]

Sister Ignatia studied the forbidden Blue Books slipped to her by clergy members of the NCCA. She also devoured Father Ford's work and quoted from him often. Based on her own considerable experience with alcoholic priests, she found that Father Ford stated their problems accurately, artfully, and with unusual sensitivity and insight. Another gain was that his own prominence in the Catholic theological world had earned him episcopal credibility and ecclesial respect. As the 1950s progressed, Ignatia was gratified to see the Church addressing alcoholism, even though the message was limited to a small, hushed audience. And friends like Father Ford were a credit to the cause.

Although Ignatia had in fact pioneered the work that now made treating alcoholism an effective medical specialty, she had to leave the work of preventing alcoholism through Church-sponsored programs to others. Thus she minimized her own role in Church education efforts, leaving that work to Father Ford and other NCCA members. Although advised no longer to speak out publicly, Ignatia circumvented the archbishop and spoke privately to individual clergymen instead. In that way she remained obedient to the archbishop while faithful to her mission.

When a favorite young cousin entered the seminary, Sister Ignatia took him under her wing, hoping he could avoid some of the usual priestly pitfalls. That cousin, Father James O'Donnell of Cleveland, recalled his special relationship with Ignatia in loving terms:

> All throughout my childhood and young adult life, she was a kind and guiding light. I'd always go to Sister Ignatia, especially when I got into the seminary. She came to me and said: "I know the rhythm of the seminary and I know that on Thursday afternoons you have time off to go out and walk. So you come down here to Rosary Hall and sit in with these men for the afternoon. Listen to them.
>
> "I don't want you to think about the fact that you're going to be a priest or that you are now a seminarian. I don't want you to talk to the men, I don't want you to say anything, I just want you to listen to them."
>
> That was always a great bit of advice, and I think of it so often. In the days of the seminary, you might think that as a seminarian studying philosophy and theology, that you knew something, that you had something to share with the men. But she made it very clear: I wasn't there to teach. I was there to listen to the stories of life, and to the suffering of people's lives.

And then at the end of about a two-hour session she'd look at me and say, "Now why don't you take the men down to the chapel and lead them in the Rosary?" which I would do. I can always remember her talking to those men. She'd say: "Now Michael, remember: when you feel tempted, get on the phone. First of all, take out the Sacred Heart badge I've given you, and look at it. Before you take that drink, you call."

And the men always called her. That was always a special gift to see that, to see how the men came to really love her and respect her for what she was and what she called them to.

She was a gift to many families, because by bringing the men into sobriety she brought a lot of peace into those homes. She saved a lot of marriages that no one ever knew about. I'd say to the patients, "What is it about her that means so much to you?" And they'd get very quiet and say, "She loves us."[25]

Treating Members of the Clergy

Members of the clergy revered Sister Ignatia for her work among them. Sober priests greatly admired her methods; priests in denial occasionally blamed her unbending ways for their repeated downfalls. Yet these priests knew well in advance of their arrival at Rosary Hall that Sister Ignatia would show no partiality to clergymen where alcoholism was concerned. Especially during the Rosary Hall years, her efforts to help priests find their way back to sobriety were unrelenting. As her alcoholic priests recovered and returned to their assignments stronger in their commitments to sobriety, God, and their priesthood, Sister Ignatia gained the respect of many bishops and chancellors as well. The reason for the hierarchy's change of heart is clear:

> She was sending back to the dioceses priests whom she had successfully rehabilitated. All of a sudden, "problem priests" turned into the Church's outstanding contributors. Sober now, the priest was a fine pastor, doing a fine job.[26]

A trusted group of AA laypeople in Cleveland assisted Ignatia's efforts with the clergy. Although she still did not advocate special AA groups for priests, once she reluctantly saw the necessity of them, she was a leader in getting them started. Ultimately, she realized that it was sometimes necessary to provide a temporary bridge to the AA program. One of the Cleveland laymen involved with alcoholic priests recalled:

> Bishops did not encourage AA. They were sensitive to spreading scandal, and they simply did not want priests to attend AA.
>
> But Sister Ignatia *did* encourage priests to go to AA. She felt that alcoholism within the clergy should not be treated any differently than if the victim were a truck driver or banker.
>
> She argued that more scandal was inflicted on the Church by leaving a drinking priest out on the streets or in the parish. She made remarkable progress for the times because priests came to her from all over the country.[27]

The little Irish nun developed a special formula for rehabilitating priests. Selected laypeople sponsored priests and took them to open AA meetings while they were still patients in Rosary Hall. The same group of laypeople supported an outside group of AA priests and met with them weekly at the Cleveland Statler Hotel. Laymen were there to keep the focus of the priests' meeting on AA and off theological arguments and rationalizations.

Special clergy meetings were one of the few concessions she made in alcoholism treatment. Her dislike of this special priests/laypeople situation stemmed from her basic belief that only outright surrender and ego deflation would lead an alcoholic to the all-important spiritual anchors of gratitude and humility On her desk were Dr. Bob's favorite words, serving as a constant reminder of the humility that was needed for sobriety:

Humility

Humility is perpetual quietness of heart. It is to have no trouble. It is never to be fretted or vexed, irritable or sore; to wonder at nothing that is done to me, to feel nothing done against me. It

is to be at rest when nobody praises me, and when I am
blamed or despised, it is to have a blessed home in my self
where I can go in and shut the door and kneel to my Father in
secret and be at peace, as in a deep sea of calmness, when all
around and about is seeming trouble.[28]

Ignatia knew that alcoholics who did not admit their addiction had
very little chance of acquiring such humility. And without humility
and its strengthening peace of mind, alcoholics would always seek relief in the next round of drinks. Thus, because she well knew how in-
sidious the alcohol obsession really was, Ignatia treated all sufferers
alike, regardless of their vocation or position in life. For some, her de-
mand for the humility to admit alcoholism seemed *humiliating*. Perhaps that was precisely her point. Without the humility to admit to
alcoholism, could anyone acquire the honesty needed to change?

On one well-remembered occasion in the late 1950s, Sister Ursula
Stepsis, then Charity Hospital's administrator, summoned Sister
Ignatia to her office. Ignatia arrived to find an out-of-town bishop, intoxicated and pleading for help. Passing through town on his way to a
convention, he had indulged a little too freely and found himself now
under the weather. The bishop had heard of Sister Ignatia and Rosary
Hall through recovering priest graduates. He hoped that Sister
Ignatia could spare him a few days and help him overcome his "drinking problem," a more palatable term to him than alcoholism.

Unimpressed with his rank as well as his sincerity, Sister Ignatia
explained the Rosary Hall program, the AA outlook, and AA's rules.
She stressed that to become a patient, the inebriated bishop had to be
willing to do as directed and be treated like everyone else if he was serious about getting well. "I'm ready for the cure," he said.

However, Ignatia always tested preadmission sincerity. Before admitting him to the hall, she asked the quaking bishop for his Roman
collar and his breviary (prayer book) for safekeeping. When he balked
at her directives, she explained that he would wear the same pajamas
as the other patients and reminded him that Rosary Hall would provide reading materials that would adequately challenge his spiritual
skills. As he resisted her directives, Ignatia told him politely but firmly

that his bed was needed for an alcoholic who wanted to recover, not just dry out. When he refused to comply with the rules, Ignatia refused to admit him to Rosary Hall. Insulted, he left for a nearby hotel.

When the other sisters at the hospital later learned of the incident, many were incensed at Ignatia's "irreverence." Like most Catholics, they did not yet understand the serious implications of enabling alcoholism to continue unchallenged among the clergy. Ignatia's sisters in religion felt that she should have made allowances for the bishop's high ecclesiastical office that would have spared his dignity and prevented his humiliation. Others could not comprehend her audacity in presuming to dictate episcopal behavior. Most would have provided the bishop with comfortable overnight accommodations so that he could discreetly sleep off the drinking escapade and continue on his journey, retaining the secret of his alcoholism and, consequently, his right to drink. Ignatia, however, knew that such "Christian" charity had all too often cost priests and bishops their lives.

In spite of her peers' criticism, years of heartbreaking experience justified Sister Ignatia's actions. She knew that false respect for alcoholic priests and bishops did them and the whole Church immeasurable harm. In fact, such uninformed reactions only encouraged life-threatening alibis that further excused uncontrolled drinking behavior and intensified denial. Eventually, without honest help, priests most often died of their drinking habits. The chance that a priest-alcoholic could die under the abutment of a bridge as well as the canopy of an altar was incentive enough for Ignatia to enforce the same rules for the clergy that she expected of her other patients.

Ignatia held firm in her convictions, because she knew that the goodwill of the nonalcoholic laity and clergy toward the sick, alcoholic priests often dealt them a deadly blow. For example, brother priests tended to be loyal and sympathetic to one another's faults. Usually they protected and enabled alcoholic priests to continue on a death spiral of drinking rather than risk offending them with confrontation—and no member of the priestly fraternity wanted to be characterized by his brothers as a snitch. Often enough, though, the outcome of not intervening in the drinking of a fellow priest meant watching his career and possibly his life come to an end.

Likewise, well-meaning parishioners and friends often complicated the situation. Offering entertainment and relaxation to favorite
priests, they insisted that Father have "one more for the road," not
knowing that he may have already indulged in several "one for the
road" drinks at possibly two baptisms, one graduation, or three wedding receptions that same day. Or he would do so in the privacy of his
rooms when he returned to the rectory. The next day or the next
weekend would bring more rounds of the same indulgence until the
priest could barely function. It became a vicious circle for all concerned: Neither would risk offending the other by refusing to offer or
accept alcoholic drinks.

The Pitfall of Seminary Sobriety

For many priests, alcoholism and drunkenness resulted from ignorance and inexperience. During seminary days, priests in formation
were forbidden to drink. Before ordination, many dioceses required
new priests to take abstinence pledges for the first five years of their
priesthood. Thus, by the time they were permitted a social drink,
many men were in their early thirties and had rarely if ever experienced alcohol's mood- and mind-altering effects. Suddenly free to
drink, young priests were ill prepared for endless rounds of fraternal
celebrations and parish social events. In addition, from the time men
entered the seminary until several years after ordination, the hierarchy's messages regarding the priestly use of alcohol were inconsis-
tent, ranging from initial prohibition to unrestricted indulgence.
Lamentably, messages received from superiors and senior priests
were—at best—confusing. More often, clergy drinking practices were
condoned by silent approval. One alcoholic priest explained:

> As a young priest, I used to visit with some older priests.
> There was one old priest in particular who used to advise me
> when I was young. He used to warn me of the danger and the
> pitfalls that lie in the path of a young priest. One thing he used
> to warn me about particularly was the "Rhododendrons" as he
> used to say. That was his word for the female sex. He used to

be warning me all the time. "The biggest danger in the life of a young priest is the Rhododendron," he used to tell me. Then he would say, "Have a drink." Well, I went along with that program. I escaped the "Rhododendrons" but I got awfully scratched up from the Four Roses.[29]

Most of the priests whom Sister Ignatia treated at Rosary Hall came to her from other cities. Local priests were understandably reluctant to admit their alcoholism in a Cleveland hospital, but those who did were not reported to the local bishop. As long as they were sincerely making a new start in life, Sister Ignatia respected their confidential status. No records were kept on local priests unless the bishop himself referred them and required follow-up progress reports.

Still, nonalcoholic Cleveland priests were also affected by Sister Ignatia's way with alcoholics. One priest recalled an incident that involved Sister Ignatia not long after he was ordained:

One day a young man with a Dairyman's Milk insignia on his work clothes rang the front door bell of the rectory. He had scarcely stepped inside when he poured out his problem to me. Very recently he'd gotten a new job driving a milk truck. Moments ago, his vehicle hit a hidden chuck hole. The doors of the truck burst open, spilling and breaking milk bottles all over the street. Why had he stopped at the nearest church? Because he was fearful of losing his new job and he needed immediate help. But why was he showing me a Sacred Heart badge? Well, it turned out that he was an alcoholic and he'd promised to call Sister Ignatia and make arrangements to return the badge to her before he took a drink. Badly shaken and certain he would lose his job, he decided he would "hang one on." But, first, he had to keep his promise to this Sister Ignatia. As she had planned, that momentary pause before plunging into the bottle kept him from pushing the panic button. And it gave me an opportunity to calm him and help him. I called his employer and explained what had happened. I got our janitor to help clean up the mess.

And I called Sister Ignatia and made an appointment for the milkman and his Sacred Heart badge to touch home base with her.

As a young priest, I was most impressed that a very discouraged alcoholic man would keep a promise to call a nun, respecting his promise to her, before falling off the wagon. I decided to get some Sacred Heart badges myself and use them for the take-the-pledge penitents who for some reason were not ready for the AA program. Now I've come to understand better why they were not ready. As a priest I had to do more than tell them to go to AA: it was also my responsibility to *learn* about alcoholism and AA, to knowledgeably and compassionately *teach* the people who came to me for help.[30]

Not long afterward, another alcoholic touched the priest's life. This time the priest knew better what to do. He found the young man an AA sponsor and did what he could to support him:

He had a fear of crowds and needed a friend. I decided to attend the Monday night AA meeting with him. I think back on the testimonies given by the men and women in such a spirit of openness and humility. They said it like it was, the good news and the bad news.

At the AA meeting I witnessed hurting, confused adults questioning their own self-worth. I saw people who had learned to reach out in loving concern, not for just one moment in time, but for a commitment that has no time frame.

I saw why the AA program worked for those who accept it in fullness of mind and heart. I saw concerned people speaking and acting on a level of communication that few of us dare to enter. It is a risk to reveal who we are . . .

Three years later, I was reassigned to a preparatory seminary. No kind of alcohol was permitted for the student body, and possession was basis for expulsion. A decade later, after Vatican II, drinking rules relaxed. Beer was available in the student lounge; wine was served at meals for special celebrations. Looking back, I think, "If only we could have shared our strengths and weaknesses with one another as well as we learned to share our wine."

The Monday night AA sessions had brought me into a very real world of hurt, disappointment, and pain; but also, I saw a very real world of gratitude, serenity, humility, and rebirth that I'd not witnessed ever before. To be accepted by others for what I am and for me to love others for what they are is to love now as I hope to someday love in the Kingdom.

The AAs seemed to find that quality of life right here on earth, by helping each other. Looking at the mystery of their own darkness, I wondered, "How did they stumble so unknowingly into the Light?"[31]

This very question may explain why men and women trained in the sciences or in theology could miss the mark in trying to deal with alcoholism. Alcoholics did not "stumble unknowingly into the Light"; they had stumbled unknowingly into alcoholism. For Sister Ignatia, comprehension of that simple truth was where the problem for the clergy began as well as ended. The darkness alcoholics encountered was not a mystery of faith or religion; the darkness was their alcoholism! Until this simple truth was accepted, education and rehabilitation efforts would be wasted.

However, with the support of the AA fellowship and the comfort of a Higher Power combined, alcoholics recovered. As alcoholism's darkness faded, recovery's light glowed.

Allowing that God was the higher-powered light that dispelled the darkness of alcoholism, then Ignatia was the brilliant angel of AA who guided the tortuous return to sobriety. Sister Ignatia cast a brilliance over AA's horizon that illuminated the way for thousands of souls trapped in alcoholic darkness. The light of God spilled from her very being and directed her every movement. So resplendent was her mission that one priest said of her: "God was closer to her than the skin on her fingers."[32]

Like all guardian angels, however, Sister Ignatia had problem children—and none were more heartbreaking to her than the alcoholic priests who would not stop drinking. For these difficult cases she needed a deep feeling of compassion balanced with tough love, honesty balanced with humor. More than anything she wanted alcoholism eliminated from the clergy, knowing in her heart that when the Church has spiritually sick shepherds, it has spiritually sick flocks.

A Priest Remembers Rosary Hall

As the following witness of the little Irish nun's approach to the clergy demonstrates, Ignatia could be tough and hard-nosed one moment, then tender and humorous the next. Father P., a Cleveland priest who entered Rosary Hall under her determined direction, described her rapid-fire comments intended to challenge his motive for sobriety:

> They sat me down in a chair across the desk from her.
>
> "Oh, it's you!" she said. "I suppose you think that because your parents were good to our sisters many years ago, that will entitle you to a bed here at Rosary Hall."
>
> "I never really thought about it, Sister."
>
> "Well, it's a good thing you didn't, because that wouldn't get you in here. There's a lot I have to know about you, first. Do you want to quit drinking?"
>
> "I've got to." (A guy couldn't come up with a better answer than that, I thought.) "I've *got* to quit," I repeated.
>
> "That has nothing to do with it," she shot back to me.
>
> There was a window in her office and from it you could look down Twenty-second Street. She pointed and said, "You see that bar down there? If you were able, I'd like to walk you down to it. That bar is full. I'll bet if we walked in there, half of those men would say they've *got* to quit drinking. So that has nothing to do with it."
>
> "What did you ask me?" I said.
>
> And she replied, "I asked you if you *want* to quit drinking."[33]

This priest was one of the lucky ones. He did want to quit drinking, so he passed Ignatia's interrogation and was admitted to Rosary Hall. Next she offered some seasoned advice related to his priesthood:

"Because you're a priest, everybody's going to come to you with their troubles, and you've got more than anybody. I'll put down that you sell insurance."

"What?" I asked in disbelief.

"It's not a fib," she said with a wink. "When you're not drinking, you insure people's souls against hell, don't you?"

And so, only the nurses and two helpers named John and Ziggy knew that I was a priest. The other guys would ask me, "Are you married?"

"No."

"Well, what do you do?"

I knew she'd put down insurance, so I said, "I sell insurance," but I didn't say what kind, and nobody asked to buy any.[34]

At the time, the Rosary Hall program was just five days long. On that last day Sister Ignatia interviewed her patients before she discharged them and gave them their Sacred Heart badge. On his fifth day, as Father P. prepared to leave, she called him to her office:

She sat me down and said, "I suppose you think you're going home tomorrow?"

"Yes . . . the other two guys I came in with are leaving," was my answer.

She said, "Not you though. I've dealt with your kind before. I learned a long time ago that the hardest nuts to crack in this business were clergy and doctors. Whenever I get my hands on one, he stays here twice as long."[35]

Sister Ignatia kept Father P. hospitalized a full eleven days. On the day of his release she sent him with Ziggy to the priests' AA group:

Selected laymen helped us out. Guys like Tom M., Skid S., Joe M., Art D., Bob S., Warren C., so I attended that group for a while. That was the first group I went to as an admitted alcoholic.

One day she said, "I'm going to have Ziggy take you out tonight."

I thought she felt sorry for me being there so long and eating that hospital food. I thought Ziggy was taking me out to dinner! I got all dressed up, and he drove me to the flats; we went to the Angle AA group that night. I had a donut for dinner.[36]

Ziggy was Sister Ignatia's right-hand man at Rosary Hall. He attended to many of the things that Sister Ignatia as a woman and as a nun could not manage by herself. He took the priest to an AA meeting every night. For Father P., open AA meetings were initially unnerving, as he explained:

They couldn't get priests to go to AA meetings back then. They were afraid to go. Even today, they are reluctant to be seen at an AA group. Most won't put their collar on for fear of what people will say or think. But Sister Ignatia was adamant about that, too. She said to me:

"You wear that collar. Don't go there disguised. Go there as you are and be who you are. You are a priest. An alcoholic priest."

So, I did what she said. I wore my collar, and I went to open meetings. I'd even go early because I enjoyed sitting around and talking to the group. Then I'd stay around afterwards, too.

I remember there were three priests who came to the meeting at 8:29 P.M., and sat in the back; as soon as the meeting was over, they were gone. Sister Ignatia didn't go for that.

For a short time, I had a priest sponsor, but that didn't work out too well. He went to a few meetings with me but then he quit going so I went by myself. At that time I was scared to death to sit at home, because that's when I'd do all of my drinking.

When I finished my work, I drove to the hospital every night except Friday and attended a group meeting. Then I'd sit in the visitor's lounge, and stay there until I felt sleepy. Patients were still pretty intoxicated then; the detox methods were still in their infancy. They'd come wandering in and sometimes they'd go into these convulsions that we called, "gerry's." When you saw that, you didn't forget what alcohol could do if you drank it again.

When I visited Rosary Hall during the day, I'd often run into Sister Ignatia. She called me into her office one day. "I saw you talking to that patient over there. What do you think of him?" she asked.

"Oh, don't worry about him, he's dead serious about this program. He told me what he's going to do, and what could happen to him. He didn't even crack a smile," I told her.

She said, "I know. That's the problem. He hasn't smiled since he's been here; he's not getting out of here until he learns how to smile, because if you can't laugh at what you did while you were drinking, you don't view your drinking as insanity. When you see real insanity *as* insanity, you smile at it because it doesn't make any sense. That's what he's not doing."[37]

The Hard Road Back

An intuitive observer of human nature, Sister Ignatia evaluated her patients quickly, and readily got to the heart of their problems. As a result, the alcoholics' attraction to her was legendary. Many non-Catholics held her in higher esteem than those weaned on Catholicism. Citing an example of the way Ignatia affected alcoholics, Father P. told the following incident, a familiar one at Rosary Hall:

> One day we brought her a drunk, an old reprobate. He didn't want to go to "that Catholic place." We finally got him to go in, and Ignatia talked to him, all right. When she got finished, she asked him,
>
> "What's your religion?"
>
> And he said, after a pause, "Put me down for your kind."[38]

Sadly, priests like Father P. who followed Sister Ignatia's program and returned to help others at Rosary Hall were few and far between. Unlike the recovering priest, who has enjoyed many long years of uninterrupted sobriety, priests who followed their own program and associated only with other alcoholic priests who also resisted integration into AA had difficulty staying sober. For a priest, the price of sobriety may have seemed too dear. All too often, sobriety ostracized alcoholic priests from clergy fraternization. Priests who did not drink could become social outcasts at the hands of clergy whose recreational habits and self-images revolved around alcohol. What's more, priests who hosted social gatherings without serving alcohol soon found they had few guests.

It was indeed a fact that alcoholic priests found little affirmation from their peers for "going on the wagon." The recovering alcoholic priest, no longer one of the boys, became an island unto himself to safeguard his sobriety. He was simultaneously a threat and an anomaly to men who depended on alcohol for relaxation, sleep, recreation, and social acceptance. Many recovering priests simply could not cope with such alienation. Needing to retain the respect of their fellow priests because they lacked other meaningful friendships and stimulating interests, they returned to the familiar world of drinking. Interestingly enough, when these clergymen died premature, alcohol-related deaths, their funerals were well attended by clerical brothers—classmates who, for many years, had turned a blind eye to their overindulgence. Privately, they mourned that their friend could not control his drinking; collectively, they prayed that he would rest in peace, having died of it.

Although today's priests are somewhat better informed about the dangers of alcoholism in their profession, denial still exists in many quarters. Much education is still needed to convince priests and bishops that it is indeed charitable and lifesaving to professionally intervene when faced with a peer's alcohol or drug addiction.

Alcoholism and the Women Religious

Surprisingly, priests were not the Church's only casualties of alcoholism. Even more stigmatized and hidden from society's—and their community's—myopic view than priests, alcoholic nuns struggled with addiction problems too. And like alcoholic women in the general population, nuns who had problems were patronized by well-meaning physicians who dismissed revealing alcoholic symptoms as emotional distress or nerves. The simplest antidote available to the physician treating such problems consisted of prescription drugs: sedatives, tranquilizers, antidepressants, or pain pills. Before long, in addition to being undiagnosed practicing alcoholics, sisters became cross-addicted to a host of mood-altering drugs.

Recent research studies suggest that alcoholism among women religious is a relatively new phenomenon brought on by the change in community life following Vatican II. To be sure, the cultural upheaval and lifestyle transitions of the post-Vatican II era gave nuns new reasons for stress-related addictions. However, older sisters agree that alcoholism existed in their ranks long before the Second Vatican Council convened.

The truth is, a small percentage of nuns drank alcoholically before Vatican II's renewal opened the convents to the wider world and loosened their restrictive lifestyle. But statistics on nuns remain difficult to gather, for most women religious are still very reluctant to provide in-depth information about one of the most private convent matters—alcoholism. Among women religious living in convents, alcoholism was, and often still is, the most covert of spiritual problems. As with priests, the habit of denying alcoholism and other addictions has hampered educational and prevention efforts. Many superiors still rationalize that education is not needed for problems that simply do not exist in their communities. Nonetheless, in the case of women religious, other clues such as incidents of prescription drug abuse should have pointed to the presence of alcohol addiction as well.

Among her many credits, Sister Ignatia was also the first person to treat alcoholic nuns. In doing so, she was radical and progressive. But her methods must again be viewed within the context of a time when women habitually suffered from society's double standards, which were more binding and oppressive for women than for men. Consequently the stigma associated with alcoholism was undeniably the most devastating for nuns.

Unlike priests and brothers who received medical care to help them withdraw from alcohol, superiors of the earliest sisters involved in alcohol recovery did not permit them to be detoxified in hospitals where their affliction might spread scandal. Instead, alcoholic nuns endured withdrawal symptoms alone, isolated in their convent cells and unassisted by medical intervention. Only after the physical symptoms subsided was Sister Ignatia permitted to receive them at Rosary Hall.

However, once at Rosary Hall, the course of treatment for nuns differed radically from the norm. Alcoholic sisters, free of shakes and other telltale evidence of withdrawal symptoms, functioned ostensibly at the hall as "interested observers"—women sent by their communities to learn how to administer an AA hospital program. By pretending an interest in beginning treatment programs of their own, their presence went unnoticed. They remained as Sister Ignatia's "students" until they absorbed enough of the program, spirit, and atmosphere to remain sober on their own. Over the years, Ignatia had trained many interested sisters. Many returned to their communities healthy and recovered. Some, in fact, did pioneer programs in other cities to protect their own sobriety.

Unquestionably, of all the alcoholics whom Ignatia assisted to recovery, women religious suffered under the greatest stigma. However, nuns would not have been treated at all had Ignatia not agreed to protect their identities and hide their alcoholism. Although hiding their addiction chafed against her better judgment and certainly her professional knowledge of alcoholism treatment, the kindhearted nun had no other options. To resist a secretive approach to helping nuns meant gambling with their lives and squandering their only opportunity, such as it was, for sobriety. Thus, no one, including the other alcoholics on the ward, ever realized that some of the sisters they met at Rosary Hall were alcoholics too. Only Ignatia and the hospital administrator knew for certain when an alcoholic sister was visiting Rosary Hall.

Considering the pre-Vatican II conditions that restrained her, Ignatia's outreach to nuns was daring and compassionate. At Rosary Hall, Ignatia offered a safe refuge—and time—to alcoholic nuns who would otherwise have been offered nothing.

Fortunately since that time, alcoholism treatment and education opportunities have greatly increased for religious communities of

women. One important reason for the improvements is that many recovering sisters have made successful ministries of alcohol prevention, education, and outreach services to their own communities. Still
others educate society about alcoholic nuns, working to reduce preju-
dice and stigma through their lectures, writings, and personal recoveries. Illustrating the difficulties that alcoholic women religious must
face, one outspoken recovering sister wrote:

> Women religious engaged in the ministry of the Church
> and in its various forms of apostolates are no more immune to
> the illness of alcoholism than they are to other debilitating ill-
> nesses that afflict society. No longer should they close their
> eyes in denial or hide their heads in shame because this ill-
> ness is attacking their members.
>
> It is a fact that the problems that the alcoholic sister has
> are enlarged by the progression of the illness and become in-
> tensified by that progression. As the sister becomes depen-
> dent upon the alcohol, she becomes increasingly unable to
> experience the freedom to be the person she was intended to
> be. She is engaged in an unhealthy relationship, in a bondage
> to something that she does not want, that she did not intend,
> and that she does not understand. It is an extremely frustrat-
> ing, humiliating kind of experience when the minister to tan-
> gled lives finds herself tangled in alcoholism. As pertains to
> the realm of the spiritual, it can be said that the alcohol be-
> comes her "Higher Power." It takes over; it begins to dictate
> what happens. Her focal point shifts from God to that next
> drink. Unknowingly, she begins to organize her life around
> when she will drink again. . . .
>
> When the alcoholic is a sister, compassion usually takes a
> misdirected turn. Excuse or protection is offered under the
> guise of help. The alcoholic denies the reality of her situation,
> and family, community members, co-workers, friends refuse
> to accept the alcoholism despite its obvious visibility. Literally,
> this is "loving the alcoholic to death." Sisters are human be-
> ings and they are subject to the same limitations of human

nature as every child of God. Alcoholism, even for a woman religious, is closer to diabetes than it is to sin. We should keep in mind that when alcohol is ingested into the body of a woman religious, a sister, it does not know or care what she does for a living. If all systems are "go," she, too, can become an alcoholic.[39]

Successfully arresting the alcoholism of nuns and priests opened a challenging new treatment horizon to Ignatia. With her advancing knowledge of addiction and recovery based on Alcoholics Anonymous's spiritual principles, nuns and priests got well. Her student efforts in this unchartered area gave the Church its first recovered clergymen and women.

Like members of the Pioneers Total Abstinence Association of her native Ireland, Ignatia remained strong in her faith that a "widespread campaign of prayer and fasting could exorcise the demon of alcohol addiction from society."[40] But for those already addicted, prayer and fasting alone would not accomplish this great task. To these ideals, Ignatia added the powerful, synergistic ingredient of AA's action-oriented spiritual program. For the nuns and priests who followed her sage advice, sobriety could be restored. In a revealing letter to Ignatia, one of her recovering clergy members explained:

> I will never be able to be sufficiently grateful to you and Rosary Hall. Outside of the graces of the sacraments I consider my finding of Rosary Hall and AA the greatest grace granted to me in my priesthood. In my talks I sometimes mention that I am one of Sister Ignatia's graduates.
>
> In reference to the question and favor you asked, Sister, it is a tough one. God has been very good to me and I try to carry the message. I find the hardest ones to get through to are the priests. They will not go to meetings. I find out that the priests who make this program are the ones who attend meetings. United we stand, divided we fall, is not only true of nations, it is true of AAs—priests included. We need constantly to be reminded that we are alcoholics. There is good psychol-

ogy in the group therapy. I know that some say, "I will do it by prayer and the sacraments." Maybe some can. To me, it seems the same as a diabetic saying, "I will not take my insulin but will pray that God will arrest the diabetic condition." He had better make use of both the natural and supernatural means. The same with the alcoholic. Both means are to be used.

In this part of the country there are no priests' groups, so I attend the regular meetings, occasionally speaking. I spoke at the big meeting in San Diego at which there were four hundred present. The good that a priest can do is incalculable. I know we are but instruments but if God chooses us to be instruments, I think we should permit God to use us. It is an expression of our gratitude. As so often said, "Show me a grateful AA and I will show you a sober AA."

That's about all I can say, Sister. Every priest I know of out here who goes to meetings is living the program. Those who do not attend are kicking it around.

> Your grateful friend in Christ,
> Father X.[41]

Although saddened by such letters, Ignatia did not give up hope. Reinforced in her convictions and more determined than ever, she intensified her efforts to reach the clergy and held fast to her belief in God's and AA's partnership to heal them. Although outreach to the Catholic Church and clergy was not her mission to complete, there can be no question that it was hers alone to begin.

Seven

"Take Hope All Ye Who Leave Here"

Before I present Sister Ignatia to you, I should say that every so often you meet someone who is so dedicated to the cause of humanity that it is like a wonderful morning of the sun rising; you come across a beautiful personality. When I'm talking of beauty, I am not talking of eyelashes or cosmetics. I mean that inner beauty that shines through the face. When you are in the presence of it you have a certain feeling of reverence and humility. And this is the way I feel in presenting our guest, Sister Ignatia. Sister Ignatia is known to thousands as "The Little Angel." And if your life has been touched by what she has done, you will understand why she is called "The Little Angel."

—Dorothy Fuldheim
WEWS Radio Interview
Cleveland, Ohio, circa 1957[1]

The pioneer of alcoholism treatment crossed paths with another of Cleveland's legendary heroines during the radio days of the late 1950s, Dorothy Fuldheim. A nationally renowned pioneer of both radio and television, Fuldheim was loudly acclaimed for her bold, incisive interviewing style—one that had procured fascinating interviews with Adolf Hitler, Queen Elizabeth, and many other world leaders. Her great skill at scooping human interest stories from the heart of Cleveland's day-to-day events earned Fuldheim the city's largest audience and highest network ratings.

Part of the broadcast journalist's popularity emanated from her ability to extract and present the greatness buried in local success stories. The people and events that most reporters found unnewsworthy delighted Fuldheim and her audience. She entertained and taught her viewers what other Clevelanders were doing that had bearing on the wider world, thereby making her fans feel that they, in some small way, were important accomplices to history.

The program with Ignatia would be among the first of many such interviews for the shy, soft-spoken nun. It would also be Fuldheim's public introduction to the illness of alcoholism and Ohio's history in the founding of Alcoholics Anonymous. Independently, the two women had huge followings. Together, they dominated the airwaves when the reigning female impresario of radio and television invited the much-beloved angel of AA to be her noontime guest.

Ignatia drew out her interviewer's natural gusto for real-life stories and people. Fuldheim emerged as insightful, concerned, and sensitive in her discussion of alcoholism. The two pioneers fashioned a compelling drama of alcoholism, hope, and recovery for their listeners. Unashamed, Fuldheim exposed her own ignorance on the subject. Nervous, Ignatia offered simple, forthright explanations that informed her interviewer of alcoholism and its treatment. Their last few moments on the air displayed a mutual respect, quickly earned in this, the first of their encounters:

> Fuldheim: Sister Ignatia, you'll forgive me for saying it—you're so frail looking. You can't weigh more than ninety pounds! How did you ever start this most tortuous and difficult assignment?
>
> Ignatia: I wasn't selected, exactly—only by Our Lord Himself, I believe, because music was my life's work. I entered this community of the Sisters of Saint Augustine because I was interested in the type of work they did—taking care of the poor and the orphaned. I thought it would be wonderful. I was with the orphans for a while. But I find now that I have the *real* orphans because they have lost their homes, and sometimes their family doesn't know where they are.[2]

Without the help of videotape visually depicting the fragile nun confronting alcoholics at Rosary Hall, Dorothy Fuldheim's words alone projected the image of a frail, ninety-pound woman conquering both the disease and the diseased single-handedly. Ignatia seized control of the interview and made her role clear, showing the stark contrast between her appearance and her actions:

> Ignatia: Pardon me, I *do* want to say that I couldn't do this alone!
>
> Fuldheim: I know, but . . .
>
> Ignatia: Sometimes we're a bit overcrowded at Rosary Hall. We have only sixteen beds—fourteen for men and two for women—now how would I be able to take care of that group?
>
> Fuldheim: Well . . .
>
> Ignatia: I say that I turn the key, but it's these wonderful people who have dedicated their lives *and* their free time to come in and help others. We have a group visiting there *every* day.
>
> Fuldheim (recovering her composure): I'm perfectly willing to share the plaudits with them, but still my great feeling is for you, Sister, and I want you to *know* it! We are very much indebted to you . . .[3]

Representing one of the few times that Ignatia lost the battle for the last word, the interview with Fuldheim brought into view a new dimension of Ignatia's personality. No longer a shy, retiring nun known only to alcoholics, Ignatia's reputation as a miracle worker had reached the notice of the general public too. It seemed that as she aged, the contrast between her physical frailty and her indomitable spirit only intensified, making her more alluring to people than ever.

Something of the miraculous now penetrated her surroundings. As she grew older, the remarkably energetic woman sometimes stood by her window and mused out loud, "Time is running out and I must work while I can." A sense of urgency brought new courage to her work. All former signs of demureness passed from sight.

Now wise and more self-assured, she spoke her mind and minced no words. Many of the remarks she made to alcoholics at this time became legendary examples of her widening spirit, her easy humor, and her unyielding authority at Rosary Hall.

One day while admitting a tall, unruly patient, the petite nun shook her formidable index finger at him and said, "Listen big guy . . . you're going to hear what I have to say if I have to stand on a stepladder and talk to you."[4] Such down-to-earth language coming from an elderly nun put the meanest, toughest drunks in their place. From that point on, Ignatia held their undivided attention.

Her ways were exemplary and brought results. Some years later at Rosary Hall's twenty-fifth anniversary, former patients told of how they had visited the ward, studied her mannerisms, and mimicked her, often talking to new patients the same way she had spoken to them.

Les S. told those gathered of his first encounter with a well-trained old-timer named Skid S.—a favorite of Sister Ignatia's boys. In short order, Skid said Les had an inflated ego that might soon drive him back to drinking. Then, in typical Ignatia fashion, Skid told Les, "The ground is level at the foot of the Cross, you know. It's the same way here at Rosary Hall."[5]

Then Dick P. spoke of his first memory of Rosary Hall saying, "It was a haven when I needed a haven." His earliest encounters with Sister Ignatia show the pain and curative humor that filled their days in the hospital:

> I was in the defrosting room. The next day, Sister Ignatia came in. She cleared the room and took the time to make sure I understood every word, because then she said, "The men out in that Hall are busy people. And if you want to get sober, you go out there in that Hall and listen to what they have to say. And if you don't want to get sober, then you get your clothes and get out of here, and don't waste their time."
>
> We said the Rosary every day at three o'clock. One day I knelt in the Hall and really started to shake. Sister came over and knelt down next to me. I was so sick, I thought she was worried about me. But she turned and said, "Isn't this wonderful penance?"[6]

All Sister Ignatia's qualities represented essential traits for a counselor of alcoholics. It was true that each man and woman who went through Rosary Hall shared a common addiction to alcohol. But in addition, each patient also had a host of difficult situations and personal problems that demanded resolution too. For some, drinking had cost jobs and careers. For others, drinking had alienated families and loved ones. For all, the bottle that had once been a cure-all was now dry of hope.

Throughout Sister Ignatia's long experience, she found that most problems haunting alcoholics stemmed from troubled marriages, poor interpersonal relationships, and the lax application of spiritual principles to life. When she compiled the first Rosary Hall Solarium Association Report in May 1955, she emphasized the spiritual yields of Rosary Hall's work. The Rev. Mother Clementine could not deny the importance of a hospital ward that demonstrably concerned itself with the healing of its patients' bodies *and* souls. She was impressed when she read:

> It is the opinion of Reverend Lawrence J. Andes, Chaplain, that there is no other hospital ward more productive of conversions and general spiritual rehabilitation than Rosary Hall. The patients who are admitted are in dire need of spiritual as well as physical help if they are to achieve a lasting sobriety.
>
> At least sixty percent are definitely benefited and others are so impressed that they seek further religious guidance. Many have taken instructions to become Catholics and countless others have returned to the sacraments after years of negligence. Many invalid marriages have been validated. As a result entire families have entered the Church.
>
> . . . Many patients after leaving Rosary Hall have made retreats not only in the retreat houses in Greater Cleveland, but also with the Trappists in Kentucky.[7]

The mention of retreat houses illustrates another support system that Ignatia was first to use in fortifying spiritual recovery. In her view, retreat houses offered crucial reinforcement of the basic spiritual principles that alcoholic patients learned in their five-day hospital stay. Sister Ignatia rightly deemed spiritual recovery the most important aspect of an alcoholic's journey to sobriety. Accordingly, from 1940 onward she referred hundreds of patients each year to Cleveland's Jesuit Retreat House and to the Trappist Monastery in Gethsemane, Kentucky, for spiritual renewal and reinforcement of the Twelve Steps. The Rev. Henry Birkenhauer, S.J., assigned to Cleveland's Jesuit Retreat House in the late 1940s, vividly recalled how AA retreats overwhelmed their facility. Often the posting of a "No Showers" sign revealed a retreat that was filled beyond capacity; the priests assembled portable cots in the shower room to accommodate AA's overflowing crowd.

In addition to reinforcing Sister Ignatia's spiritual care, the retreat houses bought newly sober men extra time to recover—an aftercare, of sorts—not yet available in the short-term inpatient hospital setting. The Layman's Retreat League of Cleveland presented numerous awards and commendations to Ignatia for her clever use of retreat houses to facilitate the alcoholics' search for serenity.

The Birth of Cleveland Al-Anon

Another primary recovery issue that Ignatia was among the first to address concerned the alcoholic's reconciliation with spouse and family. At Rosary Hall she continued her practice of personally interviewing each alcoholic's spouse prior to the patient's discharge. In 1955, however, the caring nun realized that the Twelve Step group therapy for alcoholics could be carried one step further. Thus it was with her urging that Cleveland's first Al-Anon Family Group held its first meeting on January 14 of that year. Aware of the strong need for the nonalcoholic's support in alcoholic marriages, Ignatia pioneered as tirelessly and lovingly with Al-Anon as she had labored earlier with Alcoholics Anonymous itself.

One of Al-Anon's first Cleveland members was a nurse at Rosary Hall. Margaret H. first met Sister Ignatia in 1953 when, troubled over her husband's drinking, she joined the nursing staff. Of Al-Anon's Cleveland beginnings she recalled:

Sister found time to minister widely to the alcoholics and their families, and this fruitful part of her work became the prime inspiration to start the first Al-Anon group in Cleveland in January 1955. And her inspiration is still with us today.

Lois Wilson had talked to Sister about such a group—which was by this time active in many other parts of the country. And as Lois told us at one of the early Al-Anon meetings, we might have trouble starting a group in this area since members of AA did not feel the need for such a group. But thanks to Sister Ignatia and the help and understanding of the fine people in AA, Al-Anon has flourished.[8]

Indeed, Al-Anon did flourish at Rosary Hall. Soon, Sister Ignatia stressed Al-Anon's merits and publicized its cause in an article written for her by Charity Hospital's public relations director, Adalyn B. Ross:

The rehabilitation of the person is not complete until he is fully reinstated in his family life, and a successful program for aiding the alcoholic *must* include this continuity after hospital dismissal. One attempt to do this is with the Al-Anon program, a group of wives of alcoholics. . . .

The primary purpose of Al-Anon is to help the wives of alcoholics. Guided by the 12 Steps of the A.A. program, each member tries to uncover her own shortcomings—not those of her husband.[9]

To the Twelve Steps advocated by Al-Anon, Sister Ignatia added four guidelines extracted from her own experience with Rosary Hall's Al-Anon Group members:

1. Draw a curtain on the past.
2. Look only for the good in your spouse.
3. Shut out comparison.
4. Tolerance is slow in growth, but with it comes the fine quality of patience.[10]

Ross's article continues:

> This case history reveals the slow but steady progress made
> by Al-Anon: "First, because of Al-Anon and A.A. I grew to
> know that Our Lord is both loving and merciful, and I have
> learned to grow closer to Him. Secondly, through this group I
> soon found that all the faults in our marriage were not solely
> my husband's. My own thinking became irrational and con-
> fused, which resulted in my creating more problems."[11]

From Al-Anon's inception, Sister Ignatia always attended the
Friday night meetings. Relating her part in Cleveland Al-Anon, Ross
insightfully wrote:

> She offers hope, encouragement, guidance, and always—
> confidence that God will help. She reminds them too of two
> wives, Lois and Anne. If they had given up hope during a try-
> ing 20 years, there would have been no A.A. today; for they
> were married to the founders of this great cause and were the
> angels of their awakening.[12]

Initially, Ignatia's viewpoint in the Al-Anon meetings seemed to
favor the male alcoholic spouse and tended to criticize the wife. Early
on, it seemed to the women that she blamed them for their husbands'
drinking problem. But Ignatia was feeling her way through the un-
defined maze of codependency, learning as the meetings progressed.
Soon enough, she came to realize the coalcoholics were troubled and
needed as much help as, if not more than, their husbands. During this
time, she leaned on Lois Wilson for advice and direction in working
with the wives.

Rosary Hall's first Al-Anon wives said that it took time for Sister
Ignatia to understand how deeply a husband's alcoholism could affect
the well-being of his family. Because the women also suffered from
character defects of anger and resentment, they needed the same
kind of compassionate understanding that the alcoholic received. In

some instances, they needed even more, as the coalcoholic's problems were less visible and therefore more resistant to detection and change. Edna C., a pioneering Al-Anon member, reflected:

> After she sat with us for a while she began to see our side, too. She would stick up for the men at first, and then one night this little Irish gal got angry and said, "Well, Sister, *you* didn't have to *live* with him."[13]

The exasperation in the remark made a deep impression on Ignatia, shocking her into a new consciousness of the far-reaching effects of alcoholism. With a sharpened awareness, she saw and heard the coalcoholics' collective pain and determined to do something about it. Things changed. The angel of alcoholics thrust herself wholeheartedly into the Al-Anon endeavor, befriending every wife while attending the Friday night meetings for the better part of ten years.

During Al-Anon's Cleveland infancy, Sister Ignatia offered a list of "Ten Rules for a Wife" that, in turn, provided topics for the first group discussions. As in the first years of AA, Al-Anon literature was scarce. Margaret H. and Edna C. recalled a "little brown book printed in Arizona" that contained a few stories of nonalcoholic wives, the Twelve Steps, some inspirational verses, and the Serenity Prayer. Another popular aid to the Al-Anon women was an early pamphlet, *So You Love an Alcoholic.*

Other activities of the weekly meetings varied. Sometimes discussion groups focused on how the Al-Anon member could apply AA's Twelve Steps to her own life. Other times, Sister Ignatia held education sessions to teach the women about alcohol's triple effects on the body, mind, and soul. Often she scheduled a knowledgeable speaker—usually a physician, a priest, or an AA member—to address the Al-Anon group. And sometimes she spoke to the women herself, mostly in simple spiritual parables and inspirational verse. A favorite poem of the women was one that Sister Ignatia often recited to them:

I Didn't Have Time

I got up early one morning
and rushed right into the day
I had so much to accomplish
that I didn't have time to pray.

Problems just tumbled about me
And heavier came each task
"Why doesn't God help me?" I wondered
He answered, "You didn't ask."

I tried to come into God's presence
I used all my keys at the lock
God gently and lovingly chided,
"My child, you didn't knock."

I wanted to see joy and beauty
But the day toiled on gray and bleak
I wondered why God didn't show me
He said, "But you didn't seek."

I woke up early this morning
And paused before entering the day
I had so much to accomplish
That I had to take time to pray.

Anonymous[14]

Continuing to talk about Al-Anon, Edna said:

That was her favorite poem for us. She used it all the time. When she would talk, her voice was so very little. You could hear a pin drop in that room, and you could hear every word she said. Al-Anon meetings usually close with the Lord's Prayer. But we closed our Rosary Hall Al-Anon Meeting with the Prayer of St. Francis. "Lord, make me an instrument of your peace."[15]

Family Recovery, Family Conversion

Edna and her husband Ed's story reflects the cases where Ignatia's miracles shine through. They show, too, Ignatia's deepening spiritual impact on her patients, which was especially evident during the last ten years of her life. Remarkably, their accounts do not stand alone. One familiar with the lifelong trend of Ignatia's work can detect a subtle shift in spiritual tone and emphasis that occurred during her Rosary Hall days at about the time Ed met her. Even nonbelievers could not deny that true miracles, "extraordinary events manifesting divine intervention in human affairs,"[16] followed Sister Ignatia as she made her way through the alcoholism ward of Charity Hospital.

Ed and Edna's story tells how the strength of Sister Ignatia's prayers defied human understanding, making suffering, alcoholic hearts vulnerable to the proddings of their personal Higher Power and suddenly aware of his presence in their lives. Eddie C. began the remarkable story of his journey to God and sobriety with Sister Ignatia's help:

> I came into AA in 1955. A good friend of mine, Bill, got me into Rosary Hall. For the previous two years, he had been in and out of AA himself, never quite putting it all together. He knew I had a problem and would tell me so.
>
> Finally my day came. Bill's wife, Margaret, worked at Rosary Hall. So he called her and asked if they had a bed.
>
> "Yes. If you get a sponsor you can come in," Margaret replied. "The bed's not for me," Bill protested, "it's for Eddie."
>
> Margaret wasn't certain what to do because Bill did not have the prerequisite year of uninterrupted sobriety needed to act as Ed's sponsor. She asked Sister Ignatia. "Child, put him to bed, and make your husband Bill his sponsor. It will do him a lot of good."
>
> Bill took me into Rosary Hall, and then Sister found sponsors for both of us. Neither of us ever drank again.
>
> My five days in pajamas, with Bill visiting every day, were

beautiful. Towards the end of my stay, my wife got the usual call to come down and talk to Sister Ignatia.[17]

Edna continued the story, sharing her own impressions of Sister Ignatia and the surprising things she learned about her husband of twenty-two years:

> Sister Ignatia was so sweet. I was in awe of this woman who had done so much with her life. While talking about AA, she remarked that when Ed signed into Rosary, he'd put down Roman Catholic as his faith. I didn't even *know* he was a Catholic. He hadn't been to Church in all the years that I'd been married to him.
>
> Sister told me that she felt if Ed could get back to his Church, it would help keep him sober. That sounded good to me. For Ed to be a Catholic in good standing, all we had to do was have the marriage validated by a priest.
>
> She never said a word to *me* about becoming a Catholic; she never pushed religion on anyone. But I would have become a Communist if I thought it would sober Ed up.[18]

Edna knew the future held hope only if Ed could get his life organized and make his peace with his God. Ed continued the story of his startling rebirth:

> A priest came around to see me. I told him I couldn't go to confession because I'd been married outside of the Church. So he wrote "N.P." on my card for "nonpracticing." I was off the hook!
>
> Next, Sister called me into her office. She said that all I had to do to get back to my faith was to have my marriage blessed by a priest.
>
> In my heart, I really think this problem was a contributing factor to my drinking. When I got married by a non-Catholic minister, I really felt that I had excommunicated myself. Edna

knew nothing about all those feelings. She didn't even know I had once been Catholic.

When I got out of Rosary, I knew what I had to do. I went over to St. Tim's parish and told the priest my troubles. "No problem," he said. "All we need to do is get your records and find two people who will vouch for the fact that you were a practicing Catholic before your marriage."

I told Sister Ignatia all of this and she said, "You're all set now."

"What do you mean I'm all set? What do you want me to do? Go home and tell Edna, 'Hey, there's something I forgot to tell you—when we married twenty-two years ago, I was a Catholic and the ceremony was supposed to have been done by a priest!'

"I have two kids, twenty-one and fifteen, who were never baptized in *any* church! What do I tell kids that age? Start taking instructions?"

"First things first," she replied. "First, let's get *you* straightened out."

So I went to confession for the first time in thirty years. That evening Edna and I had our marriage blessed. The following morning I received Holy Communion for the first time since I was sixteen; something I thought could never happen, happened!

Sister Ignatia said to me, "We're doing all right now. What happens to any one else now will be the result of your example."

She was so right. Soon my son came to me and told me he was going to get married. The girl was Catholic, and he'd planned on having a mixed marriage.

"But," he said, "now that you're back in the Church I think I want to take instructions on becoming a Catholic." A few days later my daughter came to me and said she wanted to take instructions with her brother.

Lastly, my wife said, "I think I'm interested too." Soon all four of us were taking instructions.

On Holy Saturday, Edna was baptized. I was in the front row of the Church watching her. When everything was over, Edna walked towards me. I stood up to greet her but she kept on walking.

I turned around and there was Sister Ignatia! No one knew she was coming. She had my buddy, Bill, bring her so she could share in our blessing.

The next morning, Easter Sunday, my whole family, all four of us, received Holy Communion together. To me, it's still unbelievable. All of this happened during the forty days of Lent, a few months after I stopped drinking.

Sister Ignatia explained that it was like a big jigsaw puzzle. When one piece, my sobriety, was put together, everything began to fall into place.

She said to me, "Ed, take one step in God's direction and He will take two in yours."

It's all true. Later she told a friend of mine that when I finally took that first step towards God, "the Lord made a one-hundred yard dash towards Ed."

I figured there was a ledger sheet up in heaven, and for thirty years I hadn't put a single check mark behind my name. So during that Lent I went to Mass every day. I thought I could at least do that much to make up for lost time.

On the Monday following Easter, I woke up and said, "Oh boy, I don't have to go to Church today." I laid there for a minute, then got up and went to Mass. I kept going for many, many years and served Mass until a few years ago.[19]

As they told this story of Sister Ignatia's influence on their lives, unmistakable gratitude and love illuminated their faces. Softly, Edna concluded:

I really thought Ed was hopeless. I was thinking divorce and had even written to my mother telling her I was coming out to California with the children.

But the night that Eddie was leaving Rosary Hall, he

invited me into a little chapel. I think it's now the Sister Ignatia Reading Room. It was such a sweet chapel! We went in and knelt down together.

In twenty-two years of marriage we had *never* knelt together and prayed; we did that night, though. Looking back, that was the turning point in our lives. Nothing was ever the same from that time on. Miracles can happen.

Since then, I haven't missed a single night of saying a prayer for Sister Ignatia.[20]

Ed continued to mature in the fellowship of AA. When he spoke at meetings and shared his sobriety and spirituality with others, he felt that the Lord continued to work through him. He became a kind of dual sponsor to new people, offering sobriety as well as helping to rekindle some members' lost faith. At first as AA sponsor carrying the message of sobriety, Ed, by returning to a practice of his faith, often also served as a baptismal sponsor.

But Ed and Edna C. were just two of the people whose lives Sister Ignatia radically transformed at Rosary Hall. Margaret H., the Al-Anon nurse who admitted Ed, said of Sister Ignatia, "She saved my life. I've never been the same since I met her."[21] In witness to the daily wonders occurring at her workplace, Margaret often remarked to Ignatia:

> "Oh, I wish we could remember and record every good and beautiful thing that happens here."
>
> And Sister Ignatia would reply, "Child, they are for God to record and they will be remembered and not forgotten. The Lord Himself takes notes of names and events and people and relationships."[22]

Margaret observed that extraordinary occurrences happened routinely. As a staff nurse, Margaret met the alcoholic patients when they were the sickest. Many were still experiencing the acute stages of withdrawal. Sometimes all the medical intervention known to Rosary

Hall's staff had no effect on thrashing, hallucinating patients. But Sister Ignatia could quiet them almost instantly by her prayers and presence at their bedside. Though most alcoholics never realized it, Sister Ignatia placed her hands on their heads and prayed over them. Usually she would call upon Jesus Christ and the Blessed Virgin for assistance, placing the distressed alcoholic wholly in their care. Time after time, Margaret watched contorted patients lapse into immediate, restorative sleep after Sister Ignatia prayed over them. A sense of calmness and peace traveled from Ignatia's hands into the patient and then flowed out into the ward. As Margaret described:

> Sister had the gift of empathy—the ability to project herself into the sensory or emotional dimension of another human being. And she wasn't afraid to talk about God.
>
> Early in the morning before the other nuns were up, she called the floor to get the night's report. Sometimes, if a patient was bad, she would call during the night or come down herself and sit with him. She passed through the emergency room on her way to work in the morning. If she found an alcoholic who was in bad condition, she'd send him to Rosary Hall and have him admitted. Then she'd find someone to pay for his stay and sponsor him into the program. Many came in that way.
>
> As long as she was able, Sister Ignatia came over early in the morning to pray with the patients in Rosary Hall's chapel. Often she recited a poem called "No One Needs Thee More Than I." At 3:00 P.M. she and the patients and their visitors recited the Rosary for alcoholics still suffering throughout the world. As she advanced in years and illness, the men wondered what would happen to Rosary Hall when she was gone. And she assured them that Rosary Hall's spirit and miracles would continue until they stopped saying the three o'clock Rosary.[23]

The great power of prayer in calming the alcoholic's emotional upheavals during treatment received emphasis in the Dorothy Fuldheim interview. When asked about the persuasive effect of prayer—individual and group—Ignatia replied: "Prayer is the finest sedative that anyone can administer because it brings peace of soul. They realize through prayer that their present help is God Himself and that He still loves them."

Ignatia's Great Healing Power

Perhaps because of her prayerful spirit, Ignatia seemed at times to sense the future. One time while discharging a healthy patient who had completed his length of stay, Sister Ignatia suddenly stopped and said, "Please stay here one more night." The patient returned to his room and changed back into pajamas. Late that evening, he nearly died in the throes of a sudden and violent convulsion. Had he been at home, doctors said there would not have been time to summon help.

On another occasion a young man was brought to Rosary Hall one night by his parents and brother. He had been on some medication, but family members could not identify it by name. They told Sister Ignatia that they would find the label and let her know the next day. "Tomorrow may be too late," she told them. And it was. During the night, the boy died.

Remarkably, alcoholics and their families were not the only people whom Ignatia influenced and worked with. Many nonalcoholics spoke with her, learned from her, and sought her spiritual help. Prayer requests came to her from all over the world. One such request came from a Canadian man in Toronto who first sought her prayers when he learned that he had an inoperable throat cancer. Joseph, as he identified himself, first approached her while she was still in Akron. He had just learned of his grim diagnosis and asked her to pray for him. More than ten years later, he wrote to tell her of his gratitude; the malignancy had completely and mysteriously disappeared.

Many unexplainable things occurred through the power of Ignatia's intercessory prayer. People learned of "the nun in Cleveland who was healing alcoholics" and wrote to her from distant parts of the world. A few letters sent from Canada, Ireland, Australia, England, and the

Philippines survive. She answered all her mail and prayed passionately for all who sought her invocations.

From Ireland, a recovering alcoholic who visited her at Rosary Hall wrote:

> I am looking forward one of these days to walking into your office again and being gently bullied into doing more work in one day than I normally do in a week. Meanwhile, you may be glad to know that AA is catching fire slowly in the West of Ireland.[24]

And from the Philippines, correspondence with a lifelong leper named Remarcelito fueled some of Sister Ignatia's more inspirational messages to the patients at Rosary Hall:

> I am a leper patient, Catholic in religion, living on this island of the living dead, surrounded by waters, mountains, and rocky places. I inherited leprosy from my beloved parents when I was born twenty-two years ago. We are separated far from civilization because of the stigma and affliction of Hansens Disease, which is called leprosy. I have enclosed my picture, and you can see how miserable it is to be a leper. But God loves me very much because of my hardship in life. Sister Ignatia, please send me a rosary and a Sunday Missal, because I have no prayer book. If you have a second hand dictionary I'd like to have one because English is not my native tongue. I shall pray for you at my communions and include you and your patients in the Holy Rosary as my sacrifice in life. You know my disease is only a trial given by God to serve Him.[25]

Further letters from the leper in the Philippines confirm that Sister Ignatia did indeed forward letters, packages of religious articles, and badly needed medicines to the "island of the living dead."

Some striking parallels between Hansen's disease and alcoholism are evident in Remarcelito's heartbreaking letters. At some point, he had read of Sister Ignatia's work and learned about the disease of alcoholism. It seemed to him that alcoholism was a leprosy of the soul that stigmatized, isolated, and destroyed its victims in much the same manner as his own disfiguring malady attacked the human body. He felt empathy for the victims and rejoiced that they could recover, for unlike leprosy, alcoholism could be arrested.

Sister Ignatia was sensitive to his plight and awed by his exemplary acceptance of such a fatal, devastating illness. She was also familiar with Hansen's disease. Early in her career at Rosary Hall, one of her own patients recovered from his alcoholism only to fall gravely and mysteriously ill soon after. Many tests later, doctors at Charity Hospital diagnosed his illness as leprosy. Fearing contagion and hysteria, physicians discharged him immediately and referred him to a leper hospital. After enduring many long months of isolation, he returned to his hometown in Pennsylvania with both his alcoholism and Hansen's disease healed. During the long dark months of recovery, Sister Ignatia had sustained his spirits with her supportive letters and many, many prayers.

Most ordinary people would have collapsed under the weight of misery and unrelenting suffering that often filled Ignatia's days. Great grace befell Ignatia and empowered her to carry many burdens, but she had, after all, a secret recourse: prayer. The strength she gained through praying enabled her to carry ever-increasing responsibilities, because she had learned to share them with her God. Thus prayer was a powerful example of her deepening humility. Without preaching to her patients, Ignatia awakened them to a universal concept of God's providential care. Doug McD., a physician and former Rosary Hall patient, described how this worked:

> When she addressed the patients she always did so on the basis of spirituality as opposed to the person's religion. She was much more intent that we find spiritual peace than debating how to find it. I recall that her sheer small size and apparently boundless energy was on the one hand intimidating and on the other, encouraging. I suspect it would have been im-

possible to lie to this little woman. She extended to me a rare privilege in those days. It was an extra day in treatment. Back then Blue Cross would only pay for five days but I got to stay a sixth because she didn't like what she saw in my eyes on the fifth day. Despite the good Sister's work those were tough days in which to be alcoholic. The only sympathy, understanding, or support one ever got was through the ward or through A.A.[26]

Soon Sister Ignatia's reach extended well beyond the immediate range of alcoholism out into the wider world of hospital administration. During Rosary Hall's zenith years in the 1950s, large metropolitan hospitals like St. Vincent Charity served also as early training sites for interning professionals in hospital administration. Naturally, Sister Ignatia took advantage of every local opportunity to further alcoholism's cause in the world at large. New graduate students offered a fresh audience in which to sow the seeds of alcoholism's treatability.

Richard D. O'Hallaron earned his master's degree in hospital administration and then accepted his first job at Charity Hospital in 1957. Hospital orientation brought him in touch with Sister Ignatia:

I was impressed with Sister Ignatia. I recall her as being very small and very quiet. You almost had to strain to hear her talk.

Her personal characteristics were hard to describe. She had a charisma that immediately made you feel at ease and want to listen to what she had to say. Her stature was small and she appeared to be up in years and frail. Her attitude toward others was that of a very loving and wise person.[27]

Sister Ignatia's winning ways with this young administrator and with others outside her world of alcoholism treatment point to an enticing inner quality that somehow lured people into following in her footsteps. Ignatia's personable demeanor balanced propriety with informality. Possibly a well-practiced Irish charm, the resulting blend of personal traits and professional decorum drew people into her life and attracted them to her work. Dick O'Hallaron's description of their encounter continues:

> She offered me many opportunities to learn about the treatment of alcoholism within the hospital setting as well as outside of it. She invited me to A.A. meetings, she invited me to conferences which she conducted on the unit, she allowed me to visit on the unit, *and* she allowed me to visit on my own to see what was going on. She answered a lot of questions I had about various aspects of the program. I was very impressed with the importance of this program and the great good it did. It salvaged human beings in a very effective way.
>
> One of the things that Sister Ignatia taught me was to have faith in the program of alcohol recovery. After visiting with her and knowing her, there never was any doubt in my mind that a good program in alcohol rehabilitation was a legitimate form of health care treatment. With that conviction, I was able to support those efforts in the hospitals I have managed and in the community as well. My learning experience from her came from listening and from watching and some personal conversations.
>
> It was almost as if she had been placed in her position by the stroke of God. As I understand it, Sister Ignatia was a music teacher and worked at St. Thomas Hospital because she was frail and ill. I assumed her role in the admitting department was an opportunity to give her something to do during her convalescence. For her to become so intimately involved in the development of this new program was certainly a plan of the Almighty.
>
> My recollection of Sister Ignatia's spiritual effect was that she loved everybody, and although she wore the habit of a Catholic sister, that didn't turn people off who were not Catholic or were not practicing Catholics. She seemed to be promoting the belief in one's self and the mercy and interest of a higher power. She let you know though, that her religion was important to her by the fact that she gave a Sacred Heart

badge to each of her graduates with instructions that before they take their first drink, they bring it back to her personally. This gave her patients the realization that this scapular with the picture of Jesus and the Sacred Heart was important to her and that she was asking Jesus to watch out for the person to whom she gave it.[28]

Nearly thirty years elapsed between the time when Dick met Sister Ignatia and then wrote down his memories and impressions of her. It is noteworthy to mention that he is not a recovering alcoholic. Now a busy hospital administrator in Richmond, Virginia, he is one of many nonalcoholics whose lives were influenced by Sister Ignatia. His testimony of her continues:

> I would have to say that Sister Ignatia made a big impression on me. She taught me something new. She gave me an insight into the importance of addressing the rehabilitation of this desperately needing population, and the confidence to promote this effort wherever I went.
>
> If I were describing her to someone I didn't know, I would say she was a holy person with a good sense of humor whom you had to respect and enjoy meeting from the very first occasion.
>
> I believe Sister Ignatia had a great impact on the development of alcohol rehabilitation programs in other parts of the country, particularly in the area of Catholic hospitals. Alcohol rehabilitation is very prominent today because it has become profitable. In prior years it was *not* profitable and those who picked up the project did so because they wanted to help people. That is also true today, but profitability has a lot to do with the efforts we see. I find that wherever I visit alcohol treatment programs, people seem to know Sister Ignatia or know of her, and she is revered by them. So, her influence in A.A. history and programs is outstanding.
>
> In retrospect, looking at Sister Ignatia, I would have to say that she was one of the most outstanding people that I have

met in my career, and perhaps the very highest achiever. In
the context of my environment, I saw many sisters like her
who, in an unassuming way, went about their work on a daily
basis doing the very best they could to help their fellow man.
So, in working with Sister Ignatia, although she had a great
charisma, she didn't act any different than any of the other sisters. She was looked upon as part of the community and another sister at the hospital just doing her job. I suppose I
never really appreciated how famous she was until perhaps
ten to fifteen years after I left Charity Hospital. But I can tell
you today, there are few people whom I know or have met or
shaken hands with who have more friends or are known more
widely than Sister Ignatia.[29]

Just how widely did her influence reach? And what kind of people
besides alcoholics and hospital administrators were attracted by
Ignatia?

Certainly, her relatives in Ireland were proud of her ministry to
one of their own country's most devastating problems. Though her
philosophy and teachings represented orthodox Alcoholics Anonymous thinking, many of the practices and customs that were second
nature to Sister Ignatia reveal her own strong Irish origins and thus
the influence of the Pioneers Total Abstinence Association of the
Sacred Heart. It is likely from her native knowledge of the Irish
Pioneers that Sister Ignatia encouraged their alcohol prevention strategy of abstaining from alcohol because to do so is "a good thing for a
good reason."[30] She had in fact quoted that very strategy in a number
of her speeches.

Sometimes her great success at Rosary Hall forced her into a spot-
light that made it difficult for her to reconcile with her spirit of humility and her vow of obedience. Media exposure was then new to
everyone, but for a Catholic nun living in the 1950s, publicity was a
rarity. Even so, fame pursued her despite her loud and frequent
protestations and her personal distaste for it.

The public cry for information about Ignatia surged to another
high after she received the Catherine of Siena Medal in 1954. The following year, a flurry of telegrams and correspondence transpired be-

tween a Cleveland couple and motion picture actress Loretta Young regarding the Cleveland nun's life and work. On January 14, 1955, Mr. and Mrs. Lawrence McDonough wired the following message to Miss Young, which reads in part:

> We have seldom missed one of your excellent "Loretta Young Shows" on Sunday evenings, and are grateful for several fine bits of philosophy which you have given us. Three weeks ago we were astounded to hear you sign off with the prayer which has become the "credo" of Alcoholics Anonymous. Last Sunday you gave the finely sympathetic story of a troubled alcoholic. Thank you.
>
> Here in Cleveland at St. Vincent Charity Hospital we have a little saint in the making, Sister M. Ignatia of the Sisters of Charity of Saint Augustine. . . .
>
> Since coming to Cleveland she receives about twenty-two men and women into her care every five days. Although past seventy years of age and weighing about one hundred pounds, she is on duty eighteen to twenty hours every day—a little dynamo of understanding, faith, and spiritual grace. Men and women of all religions or no religion who come to her in despair leave her gentle care with confidence, with humility, and with a deeply rooted faith in God's Love. May we suggest that you portray some phase of the life of this extraordinary woman on your program?[31]

The letter piqued Miss Young's interest, for she herself had been a recipient of the Catherine of Siena Medal. Three days later, Loretta Young's story editor, J. Frank O'Neill, replied:

> Miss Young expressed interest in the life of Sister Ignatia . . . and she would like very much to see a more detailed resume of her life.[32]

However, O'Neill's letter never reached Sister Ignatia's Cleveland admirers. After receiving it back unopened, he forwarded it to the superior at Charity Hospital on the chance that she could locate the senders. Along with his message, he also forwarded the original wire explaining Loretta Young's interest in Sister Ignatia. The Charity Hospital superior apparently received the correspondence but never acknowledged it. Two weeks later, O'Neill traced the McDonoughs' address through the original wire service and managed to reestablish communications. Excerpts from their next letters read:

Feb. 14, 1955

Dear Mr. and Mrs. McDonough:

Miss Young was very much interested in the contents of your wire and would like additional information about Sister Ignatia if you can supply it.[33]

The McDonoughs replied:

Feb. 19, 1955

Dear Mr. O'Neill:

Since we ourselves are not story writers we can only suggest to Miss Young's writers that here is a wealth of material—either in Sister Ignatia herself or in the lives of some of the men and women who have been so powerfully influenced by this unusual woman.

She is a tremendous force. Without leaving her little world in the second floor of her hospital this woman in spotless white robes returns to the world each year a thousand whole men and women—people who had come to her hopeless, their lives ruined, useless to themselves and to society. It would be interesting to know how many children of these people will have a better chance in life because of the days their mother or father spent in Rosary Hall.[34]

The sincere exchange of hopeful letters stimulated Hollywood interest in portraying the story of Sister Ignatia, Alcoholics Anonymous, and Rosary Hall to television viewers. But then, abruptly on March 3, O'Neill received this urgent message:

SISTER IGNATIA OPPOSED TO ANY TYPE OF PUBLICITY. PLEASE FORGET ENTIRE MATTER. SORRY. PLEASE ACKNOWLEDGE.

LAWRENCE MCDONOUGH[35]

Five days later the Cleveland couple's acknowledgment arrived, their disappointment evidently matched in feeling by O'Neill and Miss Young:

March 8, 1955

Dear Mr. and Mrs. McDonough:

I received your wire and of course am very sorry that we cannot continue with the research and the story idea on the life of Sister Ignatia. The more information we received, the more interested we became, for she is truly a wonderful person.

However, I do want to thank you both very much for your cooperation and assistance. I know that you must be as regretful as we are that her life and experiences cannot be brought to the attention of the public.[36]

When Ignatia had learned of the matter, she had brought it to a swift conclusion. Though national publicity for the cause of alcoholism offered a tempting opportunity to promote both hospital treatment and Alcoholics Anonymous, the highly principled nun rejected the proposal. She had many sound reasons to do so.

In 1955, living nuns were not the usual subjects of television drama. In pre-Vatican II times it would have been unspeakably inappropriate of Ignatia or any woman religious to glorify her own life in such a public manner.

So even though much potential good might have arisen from free and widespread publicity of the cause, harmful criticism might have resulted as well. Although AA's tradition of anonymity at the level of the press did not bind the nonalcoholic nun, it was she who had long ago fostered it. Led by her conscience and the habit of providing a good example to others, Ignatia declined to expose her life, her work, her community, and Alcoholics Anonymous to the world at large.

President John F. Kennedy's Tribute

Despite Ignatia's efforts to lead a private life, the growing legacy of her work among alcoholics continued to heap acclaim on her door-step. Most tributes had little emotional impact on her. The diligent, prayerful woman took her accolades in stride, accepted them in the name of Rosary Hall, the hospital, or her community, and proceeded with her usual business.

One exception to her disregard of public honors occurred in 1961 when the Irish Catholic U.S. President John F. Kennedy wrote to her of his pride in her stalwart efforts to resolve alcoholism in America. Bashful, childlike pleasure overwhelmed Ignatia. She nearly burst with pride when she received this correspondence from the White House:

March 1, 1961

Dear Sister Mary Ignatia:

Through an admirer of yours, the President has learned of the fine work you have done in the past at St. Thomas Hospital in Akron, and, more recently, at St. Vincent's in Cleveland.

He has been informed that a large number of citizens have been restored to useful citizenship as a result of your efforts. As you have been a strong influence for the good to many people, you have added strength to your community and nation.

With all good wishes.

Sincerely yours,
Frederick L. Holborn
Administrative Assistant to the President[37]

This was one glorious occasion when she could not help sharing her intense delight with Bill Wilson and a few close friends. Sincerely pleased that Sister Ignatia had been recognized by the president, they encouraged her to answer the White House letter. After deliberating for two weeks, she wrote back:

> My dear Mr. President:
>
> I feel highly honored to have received this message from your office.
>
> I prayed for you during your campaign, and frequently since you have assumed your duties. I know the decisions which you must make are tremendous, and need God's Light and Grace.
>
> I shall continue to remember you in my prayers and trust that some day I may have the honor and privilege of meeting you and your lovely wife.
>
> Respectfully yours,
> Sister M. Ignatia, C.S.A.[38]

Ignatia's correspondence with the White House provided a great measure of joy during her later years as health problems and old age slowed her energy. Until President Kennedy's assassination, she corresponded regularly with him, and her letters were always answered. By then, her regular correspondence ranged in scope from friends in the workhouse to friends in the White House.

From about 1958 onward, Sister Ignatia's delicate constitution began showing the effects of twenty years of hard labor, fasting, and little sleep. Bouts of pneumonia, ulcer attacks, high blood pressure, occasional irascibility, and general physical weakness characterized her days. After celebrating one of Rosary Hall's exhausting anniversaries, she quipped to Bill Wilson: "I was in bed for two days as a result of too much publicity."[39]

Her physical condition deeply concerned her superiors, though no amount of human reasoning could induce her to leave Rosary Hall. Ignatia was not temperamentally suited to enjoy a graceful retirement. She valued life and meant to live hers out by helping others. Even the need for canes, walkers, and wheelchairs did little to slow her pace. Her answer to those who expressed concern for her well-being was a quick retort, "Time is running out and I must work while I can."

Further complicating things for the superiors who wished her to retire was the fact that growing infirmity had increased the alcoholics' love and devotion to the aging angel. Regardless of age and frailty, Ignatia was still very much a woman to be reckoned with. She held patients and co-workers spellbound when they met her during her final years at Rosary Hall, much as she had done at the start of her ministry in Akron. An eighteen-year old student working at Charity Hospital in 1959 sensed the atmosphere around her:

> While working at the Information Desk in the evenings I became acquainted with Sister Ignatia. The sisters would pass by the desk on their way to the chapel for evening prayers.
>
> I remember Sister Ignatia peering over the top of the counter one evening and asking me what I was studying. She asked me about alcohol and when she found out I was attending John Carroll University, her interest was piqued. She peered over the counter at me and asked how I was doing almost every evening. My relationship with her grew. She was not well even at that time. We kept a wheelchair by the side of the desk. It was difficult for her to navigate the long walk to Rosary Hall. There were a couple of us whom she allowed to take her up to Rosary Hall. (She didn't want her fellow sisters to help her, but if we coaxed her into the chair, she accepted our assistance.)
>
> It was quite an experience to witness the love and joy that greeted her when I took her into Rosary Hall.
>
> It was probably two or three years after I began working there when I discovered what a remarkable person she was. And I was not to recognize this fully for another twenty years.
>
> One day I was working in the mail room and I saw her coming toward me. She was walking a little faster than usual. She walked up to me and said in a tone of voice I had not heard before, "Do you drink?"

I was taken aback. I said "Yes, but just a bit of fun drinking on the weekend." She asked me more questions. This was not the sweet little nun I knew!

Finally, she wound up the whole business by coming very close under me, jabbing that finger under my chin and saying, "You better watch it!" She turned on her heel and left.

I finished school and got on with my life. I forgot her and continued my "occasional" drinking for the next twenty years. I finally arrived back at Rosary Hall and to Father John a total mess.

He worked closely with me and at one point told me I was one of those whom he called an "alpha alcoholic"—an alcoholic from the first drink. But she saw that twenty years earlier and tried to tell me.

This woman was far ahead of her time and I believe she had the spiritual gift of discernment. I came into A.A. in 1978 and have been sober since. I am now forty-six years old and I think of Sister Ignatia so often.[40]

Last Years at Rosary Hall

Even in declining health, Ignatia's commitment to alcoholism and her alcoholic patients never wavered. When her health permitted, she was as active as ever. Like the sisters, Bill Wilson realized that Sister Ignatia was getting on in years. He feared that newer members to the organization might never know the magic inspired by AA's angel. He also knew that wherever Cleveland AAs traveled in this world, they were met by eager strangers whose first request was, "Tell us about Sister Ignatia." Thus Bill felt it was important to preserve her memory in the fellowship—and possibly to prevent later myth-making— by making her a key presenter at Alcoholics Anonymous's Silver Anniversary.

In 1960 the seventy-one-year-old nun traveled to Long Beach, California, where she spoke to an audience of seventeen thousand AA members who had gathered to celebrate Alcoholics Anonymous's first twenty-five years of service and fellowship. She regaled and charmed the huge audience with understated stories and quips from AA's earliest days and her pioneering hospital effort with Dr. Bob, concluding the address with her work at Rosary Hall.

Not long after her return to Cleveland, financial problems—her lifelong albatross—surfaced once more. With all the free care for the destitute that Ignatia permitted, Rosary Hall annually operated thousands of dollars in debt to the hospital. Though Ignatia was capable of raising $60,000 overnight to pay her bills, the hospital administrator and treasurer had had enough of the hall's lax business practices.

Now that Ignatia was becoming older and occasionally seemed even feeble in her judgment, Sister Ursula Stepsis pressed hard for a resolution to Rosary Hall's financial woes. She traveled to Washington, D.C., where she learned that financial assistance in the form of government grants could offset the cost of caring for the alcoholism unit's medically indigent patients.

Needless to say, Ignatia adamantly opposed the idea of government funds to support Rosary Hall. She strongly believed that the receipt of public money would obligate Rosary Hall to introduce experimental techniques that would dilute the simple, spiritual effectiveness of Rosary Hall's program. Discouraged and alarmed, on May 23, 1963, she wrote to Bill Wilson:

> The National Conference of Social Workers is taking place in Cleveland this week. On Tuesday, three social workers came to Rosary Hall to discuss our methods and treatment. It seems that a great many agencies in different states are obtaining funds from the state governments to open alcoholic hospitals, and are paying for the salaries of doctors, nurses, and social workers.
>
> This worries me as the hospitals are associated with the government rather than with A.A. They are treating the patients as mental patients and using antabuse and tranquilizers. Our hospital administrator, Sister Ursula, went to Washington to talk with Mr. Anthony Celebrezze, head of the department of Health, Education and Welfare about using government appropriated funds for our hospital.

I hope there aren't many changes in Rosary Hall due to this. God willing, I intend to stick to the standards and principles of A.A. which have worked so well over the years.

P.S. All is in God's Hands and I shall do His Holy Will. I'll let you know the outcome.[41]

Soon after, President Kennedy selected forty-one alcoholism leaders to attend a historic meeting in Washington, D.C., on July 9, 1963. This marked the first such conference convened since the days preceding Prohibition. Headed by Health, Education, and Welfare (HEW) Secretary Anthony J. Celebrezze, a Clevelander, the committee was to discuss how HEW could mobilize its agencies to address the national epidemic of alcoholism. Sister Ignatia headed the list of honored invitees. Afterward, the president invited Sister Ignatia to have tea with him at the White House, but she respectfully declined out of consideration for the dignity and importance of his office—a great sacrifice for such an adoring admirer.

After the Washington trip, Ignatia summarized her impressions of the conference work in a personal letter to President Kennedy. Special Assistant to the President, Ralph A. Dungan, replied for him on August 6:

Dear Sister Ignatia:

The President asked me to thank you for your thoughtful letter. He is indeed pleased to learn that you found the recent conference of much interest, and at his request your comments are being made available to Secretary Celebrezze.[42]

On August 12, Sister Ignatia submitted a detailed report, this time to Secretary Celebrezze, entitled "Recommendations to the Secretary of the Department of Health, Education, and Welfare on Methods of Combating the Rising Alcoholism Problem." Highlights of her report urged the secretary to closely scrutinize government planning and policy-making efforts concerning alcoholism. Ignatia, sensing the inevitability of future government involvement, sought to ensure the preservation of AA's abstinence philosophy, treatment integrity, and future needs. She outlined her objectives succinctly, advising the secretary to provide for the following in public policy:

1. Financial assistance for treating the destitute and the indigent alcoholic
2. Evaluation of divergent methods presented by various agencies, organizations, and individuals influenced more by diverse professional disciplines and backgrounds than by alcoholism
3. The necessity of a total abstinence philosophy in treating alcoholism
4. Close teamwork with Alcoholics Anonymous for the necessary lifetime maintenance of total sobriety
5. The importance of voluntary and one-time only hospital admissions to avoid the syndrome of getting the practicing alcoholic well so that he or she can drink again
6. Research into the causes and treatment of alcoholism
7. Establishment of separate alcoholism wards in general hospitals
8. Alcohol education at all levels of society[43]

These represent the brilliant but simple viewpoints that were Ignatia's wise directives, left to her successors in "the age of sedation." As such, they amplify her intensity and wisdom, leaving a warning for professionals to come. Her greatest fear, like Dr. Bob's, was that professionalism would one day override and destroy the basic philosophy of abstinence and replace a simple treatment approach with complicated psychiatric practices that would only dilute AA's spiritual medicine for recovery.

After this conference, Sister Ignatia's health rapidly deteriorated. Her presence in the hall was sporadic, dictated mostly by day-to-day health crises. Sometimes she was hospitalized, and other times she was merely ordered to rest in her room. Oftentimes, she appeared to be near death's door. Still, AA's ardent angel fought to stay alive and struggled to remain visible at her beloved Rosary Hall. She labored to reconcile the conflict of once more accepting the inevitable will of God in her twilight years. For Ignatia, the final temptation was to deny aging, illness, and even mortality. Her life was still full and, relatively speaking, productive. Rosary Hall bulged at the seams with patients who were recovering, and a women's ward had recently opened.

Yet not even with advancing age and declining vitality had she lost her special gift for healing alcoholics. During the year when Ignatia's ability to direct Rosary Hall was under close administrative scrutiny, Art S. relapsed after six years of sobriety. Perhaps organizational matters were slightly askew. Perhaps Rosary Hall's bills remained unpaid for long periods. However, to this patient's way of thinking, those were trivial matters. The work of Rosary Hall—healing alcoholics—went on undaunted by administrative details. But Art regained his sobriety during this upheaval, and he praised Sister Ignatia's unwavering abilities to solve her patients' problems—if not the administration's:

> About the fifth day* I was interviewed by Sister Ignatia about my history, attitudes, and plans. She gave me a great deal of hope and encouragement, and at the close of the interview she shook hands with me. Some power that came from her made my hair feel like it was standing on end, as if electricity was flowing through my scalp and the back of my neck. In the next few days I experienced two very clear demonstrations of Sister Ignatia's spiritual power.
>
> There was a young man in D.T.s who broke loose from his bed ties and started down the hall, headed for the open door to the rest of the hospital. Sister was in her office and heard the commotion. She wheeled her chair out in front of the fleeing patient and asked him where he was going. "To get a newspaper," he said.
>
> She looked him in the eye, pointed back toward his room, and told him to get back in bed. He meekly returned to his room.
>
> It was awesome to see a little old lady of perhaps eighty-five pounds and in a wheelchair exert such control over a large man in such a serious mental state.
>
> The second incident concerned a man in my room who

---

*Length of stay increased to ten days at this time.

was in violent D.T.s for at least three days of constant physical struggle and conversation with an imaginary companion.

He was given many injections of paraldehyde; the room reeked of it, but nothing quieted him down. I overheard the staff discussing that they feared for his life because of exhaustion or heart failure.

Late in the afternoon Sister Ignatia wheeled into the room. The door was closed and I was asked to remain out of the room. She must have been in there for two hours. I went in shortly after she left and the patient was quiet and sleeping.

The next morning he awakened with all of his faculties and ate breakfast.

I am convinced that Sister Ignatia had a direct line to God and that she was praying for the patient's recovery while she was secluded with him.

I left Rosary Hall after ten days and was again interviewed by Sister. She gave me a Sacred Heart amulet and a little black book, "Confidence in God," in which she wrote a blessing for me and a request to pray for her. The final handshake had the same electrifying effect on me as the first one I described. I truly believe that Sister Mary Ignatia should be sainted.[44]

The new Mother Roberta, and the Sisters of Charity found themselves in a terrible bind at this point. If they removed Sister Ignatia from Rosary Hall for her health's sake, the public would have thought them cruel for uprooting a beloved, elderly nun from her life's mission. On the other hand, if they allowed her to stay in place, they stood to be equally criticized and accused of, in effect, draining Sister Ignatia's last drops of blood. The solution lay in finding her an assistant, someone who could help her. But no one met Ignatia's expectations—that is, until the lovable Father John came along. Sister Ignatia had always longed to have a priest in residence at Rosary Hall. It seemed that finally God answered her prayers.

Transition into Retirement

During Sister Ignatia's declining days, a new personality claimed his place in Rosary Hall's history. Father John McCarthy, S.T., was a Trinitarian priest. When he arrived in Rosary Hall, he had only one year earlier begun his own recovery from alcoholism. In March 1963 his superior, Father Girard, sent the affable Irish priest to Cleveland from Mt. Clemens, Michigan, because "Cleveland was a good AA town,"[45] which Father Girard hoped would reinforce Father John's elusive sobriety. "Perhaps you can be of some help to Sister Ignatia. Go and see her when you reach Cleveland," he told the young priest. "More likely, she'll be a great help to you!"[46] Father John recalled the day that he first walked into Rosary Hall and "reported for duty":

> In spite of having been to various other treatment facilities, I was overawed by Sister Ignatia, though she was a tiny little thing. I stood in awe—that's the only word I can think of . . . and I knew that Rosary Hall had the benediction, if you will, of Bill Wilson, and a fellow by the name of John Fitzgerald Kennedy, and it carried Dr. Bob's name, so this was uptown stuff as far as I was concerned. Even though I'd been to some pretty classy facilities, I figured that these people had the golden coffee pot and I'd be lucky if I could just visit there now and then and just listen to them.[47]

When Father John arrived and introduced himself to Sister Ignatia, she recognized his name from among her mental list of recovery-resistant alcoholic priests—stragglers whom she had learned of over the years. Indeed, she had been on the lookout for Father John Baptist Dillon McCarthy! As a greeting, she offered him a bed and some clean pajamas. Finally convincing Ignatia that he was sober, Father John got her permission to spend some time in Rosary Hall's visiting lounge. How he became acquainted with Sister Ignatia is another story:

I went down there almost every day, and I sat in a corner of her office. I just sat there. I didn't dare talk. She treated me as though I were a statue in the corner.

Patients came in, and she talked to them. She'd scold some, and commend others. She talked about the early days of AA and how the patient should find God, clean house, and help others. I was part of the furniture in her office, unless I'd miss a day. Then she'd say, "Where were you yesterday?"

Little by little, I started hearing confessions for her. She allowed me to do that because the patients needed a priest and I was right there. She used to give the patients a morning talk, and sometimes she would sort of doze off right in the middle of it. That was one of the most astounding displays of respect I have ever seen. The patients would just politely sit there and not make a move. They'd try not to talk or sneeze or cough while she slept. Then she would wake up and say, "Now, where was I?"

One particular morning I was sitting next to her when she dozed off again. Then she woke up, touched my arm, and said, "Father John, *you* talk to the men."

Well, I was afraid to talk to them, and I was afraid not to, so I started to talk. I have no idea what I said, but she closed her eyes again. Then, every morning she had me talk to them.

Sister Ignatia was prayerful, forthright, and almost blunt. She didn't bandy words. For a time, I thought my name was Yougo . . . "You go get this, you go do that" and I would always answer back, "Yes M'am, Sister!"

Finally around 1964, Sister Victorine returned to Charity Hospital and volunteered to help Sister Ignatia run Rosary Hall. She'd worked with some alcoholics back in the 1940s, but she'd be the first to tell you that it was Sister Ignatia, not she, who founded Rosary Hall.[48]

The capable and sensitive assistance of trustworthy "volunteers" like Father John and Sister Victorine Keller who understood AA and alcoholism lightened Sister Ignatia's workload and allowed her an easier transition into retirement when it came about the following spring. Father John pointed out that Sister Victorine was a very capable nurse and administrator, one who could have easily intervened to smooth out the operation of Rosary Hall. But more to her credit, she respected the many years of Sister Ignatia's hard work and devotion. Victorine made it clear to everyone that she was there only to assist Ignatia, not replace her. Her deep thoughtfulness left Ignatia's dignity, program, and reputation intact, despite the fact that Ignatia could no longer manage her duties alone.

As he had done when Dr. Bob was dying, Bill Wilson once more made frequent trips to Ohio. He supported Sister Ignatia very lovingly in her growing infirmity and helped her to maintain the integrity of the Rosary Hall program. At the same time, he began his fruitful relationship with Sister Victorine, knowing that one day soon she would be Rosary Hall's director.

Conscious, too, of Sister Ignatia's monumental contributions to the AA movement, Bill decided that some kind of personal recognition from Alcoholics Anonymous was now timely. Sister Ignatia celebrated her golden jubilee, fifty years of service to the Sisters of Charity of Saint Augustine, in March 1964. Bill chose that occasion to arrange a small surprise gathering of Cleveland's AA leaders. He telephoned Sister Ignatia and asked her to arrange a dinner party for an unannounced visit he was planning to make to Cleveland. He gave her the guest list, and she coordinated the arrangements and invitations, not realizing the party was intended for her. John B.'s recollections of the evening follow:

> I think there were about a dozen of us. We had a good meal and very stimulating conversation. Then Bill pulled a surprise. He felt that Ignatia had worked for twenty-five years, tirelessly, on behalf of us drunks, and it was time she got some recognition for it. And he pulled out a big parchment, beautifully printed with Old English lettering, testifying to this good woman's dedication and just about embarrassed poor Sister Ignatia to tears. That was quite an evening![49]

Bill wrote the words printed on the parchment and planned the surprise himself. He would have enjoyed making it a huge occasion but realized that Sister Ignatia would not have been comfortable in a large, ostentatious setting. More than anything, he wanted to express in a memorable, intimate way AA's gratitude to their pioneering angel. The parchment read:

IN GRATITUDE FOR SISTER MARY IGNATIA
ON THE OCCASION OF HER GOLDEN JUBILEE

Dear Sister,

We, of Alcoholics Anonymous look upon you as the finest friend and the greatest spirit we have ever known.

We remember your tender ministration to us in the days when A.A. was very young. Your partnership with Doctor Bob in that early time has created for us a spiritual heritage of incomparable worth.

In all the years since, we have watched you at the bedside of thousands. So watching, we have perceived ourselves to be the beneficiaries of that wondrous light which God has always sent through you to illuminate our darkness. You have tirelessly attended our wounds; you have nourished us with your unique understanding and your matchless love. No greater gift of grace than this shall we ever have.

Speaking for A.A. members throughout the world, I say, "May God abundantly reward you according to your blessed works—now and forever."

In Devotion,
Bill W.
March 25, 1964[50]

Sister Ignatia's health problems finally forced her to retire to Mount Augustine, the Richfield motherhouse, in May 1965. Father John continued his recollections of that difficult transition:

About a year later, Sister Ignatia retired to the Mother House and Sister Victorine and I stayed on to watch the store. I went out to visit Sister Ignatia about twice a week to tell her the news and ask her advice about things. It was sad to see her out there because she missed the work so much.

She was fearful of professionalism in this field as was my sponsor, Lynn Carroll, who founded Hazelden. She didn't want the spiritual part of the program destroyed. Things in the hospital program that weren't strict AA deeply distressed her. She felt they were watering it down.

We were hesitant to change anything in Rosary Hall that Sister Ignatia started. But we both knew that we couldn't operate as she did. We didn't have that charisma, that charm. We decided to put more program and order into it, so I sent Sister Victorine up to Hazelden to learn from Lynn Carroll.

We didn't dare talk to Sister Ignatia about that because to her mind that wouldn't be old-time AA. Now, as I get older, I agree with her. The most important thing in treatment really is just AA.[51]

Sister Ignatia rested in the infirmary and struggled to regain her health. Bill wrote and visited her frequently, often suggesting remedies she might try to help ease her health problems and to buoy up her spirits. AAs visited her whenever allowed and wrote constant notes of cheer, good wishes, and gratitude. Les W., a longtime AA member, was the mailman at the motherhouse. So each day when he delivered the convent's mail, he stopped to chat with Sister Ignatia, cheering her to better health and delivering the latest news of Rosary Hall.

Ignatia described her retirement in a last recorded letter to Bill. It was dated May 18, 1965. She wrote:

My Dear Bill:

Since I have come to this lovely place to rest and regain my strength those who take care of me have tried many forms of

T.L.C. to bring me to my former zest and vigor. But I personally feel that the greatest and most effective form of therapy
applied to me has been your personal visit and the wonderful
letter which came so soon after I had visited with you. You
have done much for my morale and you have made me more
eager to return to the beloved apostolate than I have ever been
before. Heaven bless you for taking time out to come to inspire
me for greater things. Needless to add that I spend all my
time counting the days till June 18 when we will again treat of
many things and plan our future ventures in new living . . .[52]

Bill's eyes must have moistened when he read on:

Spring came to Mount Augustine three weeks ago and you
should see the glories of nature as revealed in the surrounding countryside. Such sheer beauty will be in evidence when
you come in June. How I would love to have you see it now.
You are going to be astonished at the vast improvement in my
general condition. It is just incredible. Of course, there are a
few other features, such as legs that don't shake and fold, left
to be desired. But for now I'm stoutly praising the dear Lord
for keeping me in mind and sending me blessings galore! I
look better, that I know. I've lost that tired, way-in-the-future
look which sometimes frightens my best friends and makes
them say new and more fervent prayers for me . . .[53]

And Ignatia's final words to Bill express her deep concern for him
and the ongoing work of AA. Even as she approached her time of final
surrender, Ignatia offered Bill and AA all that remained hers to give:
time, prayers, and gratitude for sharing in their work:

Bill, you must have been aware that you and "all your favorite things" have always occupied a place well near the beginning of my special-people prayer list. Well, I have some
good news for you. Since I now enjoy that rare and precious
thing called leisure time, I have many more and much better

chances to talk to God about you, your hopes and desires, your plans for the fellowship, and whatever is nearest and dearest to your heart. So you can count on these special prayers.

Don't be fearful of telling all of your plans to the Divine Healer who knows you well and is aware of your mighty efforts to carry on the work which He began more than 1900 years ago.

Now I must close and prepare my lunch. Thank you once more for all of the inspiration and joy I've fallen heir to because you've shared with me your mighty effort to bring men to Christ and Christ to men. God love and bless you, Bill. May He grant you your every wish and prosper your smallest project. May He send you good health, happiness, success, and complete peace of soul, now and always.

Devotedly yours,
Sister M. Ignatia[54]

Sister Ignatia lapsed into deep illness during the last two weeks of the following March. But even as death approached, the light of her spirit filled the heart of one of her treasured AA lambs. As she lay dying during the long night of March 31, love for her life spilled from the pen of one of her grateful patients and was on its way to her when her great spirit left Earth the next morning. Never was a more coincidental or appropriate message sent to AA's angel:

My very dear Sister Ignatia:

God has been good to me and thru His goodness, patience, and understanding I am privileged on this eve of my fifth anniversary [of sobriety] to express my gratitude for the many thousands of men and women who, in their many and varied ways, founded and have maintained the Program that has given me my life and my sanity and have helped me in the maintenance of my sobriety for these last five wonderful years.

To you, who offered me and helped me find peace that night five years ago, I am grateful. You are in my thoughts many times, particularly each morning when God and I plan for the day ahead. With His help the days are no longer difficult. I simply "GO WITH GOD." Saturday evening I am privileged to tell my story at the Lorain St. Mary's Saturday night [AA] group. Be with me in your prayers. I pray that I may say or do something that will help someone even as I have been helped.

GO WITH GOD, Lovely Angel!
Arthur O'H.[55]

Shortly after nine o'clock on the morning of April 1, 1966, a soft breeze stirred the air at Mount Augustine. The glorious wings of gentle, sober angels carried Sister Ignatia's spirit home.

Appendixes

Appendix A

A Note on Sources

Research for this work was collected from a variety of sources, including but not limited to news stories, letters, journals, awards, citations, speeches, articles, tape recordings, radio interviews, and eulogies. Personal interviews were conducted and recorded by the author throughout the midwestern and northeastern United States with Alcoholics Anonymous's pioneering members, as well as pioneering professionals in the field of alcohol and drug addiction treatment. In addition, surviving members of Sister Ignatia's religious community (the Sisters of Charity of Saint Augustine), distant family members, AA members, nurses, physicians, counselors, hospital administrators, clergy, community leaders, and personal friends contributed greatly to the authenticity of this work.

The following archives also provided extensive primary source materials: Alcoholics Anonymous, New York; the Sisters of Charity of Saint Augustine, Richfield, Ohio; Catholic Diocese of Cleveland, Cleveland, Ohio; Summit and Cuyahoga County Archives, Ohio; Rosary Hall Archives, Cleveland, Ohio; St. Thomas Medical Center (Ignatia Hall), Akron, Ohio; Archives of the Society of Jesus, Missouri and Detroit Provinces; and the *Akron Beacon Journal* Archives, Akron, Ohio.

Appendix B

Regarding Anonymity and Confidentiality

In most references made to or by recovering alcoholics, the AA tradition of anonymity has been respected with the obvious exception of the use of the full names of AA's cofounders and their wives. The same confidentiality has been extended to nonalcoholics at their request or when to reveal full names would cause unnecessary distress or hardship for such individuals, their surviving relatives and friends, or both.

Although AA members' anonymity can be broken after death, I elected not to do so out of respect for the traditions by which most AA pioneers lived. One exception occurs in the foreword of this book. The Rev. John C. Ford, S.J., elected to break his anonymity if publication of this work occurred after his death. Father Ford died on January 14, 1989, a few months after writing the foreword to the first draft of the manuscript.

Appendix C

The Twelve Steps of Alcoholics Anonymous*

1. We admitted we were powerless over alcohol—that our lives had become unmanageable.
2. Came to believe that a Power greater than ourselves could restore us to sanity.
3. Made a decision to turn our will and our lives over to the care of God *as we understood Him.*
4. Made a searching and fearless moral inventory of ourselves.
5. Admitted to God, to ourselves, and to another human being the exact nature of our wrongs.
6. Were entirely ready to have God remove all these defects of character.
7. Humbly asked Him to remove our shortcomings.
8. Made a list of all persons we had harmed, and became willing to make amends to them all.
9. Made direct amends to such people wherever possible, except when to do so would injure them or others.
10. Continued to take personal inventory and when we were wrong promptly admitted it.
11. Sought through prayer and meditation to improve our conscious contact with God *as we understood Him,* praying only for knowledge of His will for us and the power to carry that out.
12. Having had a spiritual awakening as the result of these steps, we tried to carry this message to alcoholics, and to practice these principles in all our affairs.

---

* The Twelve Steps of AA are reprinted from *Alcoholics Anonymous,* 3d ed., published by AA World Services, Inc., New York, N.Y., 59–60. Reprinted with permission of AA World Services, Inc. (See editor's note on copyright page.)

Appendix D

The Twelve Traditions of Alcoholics Anonymous*

1. Our common welfare should come first; personal recovery depends upon A.A. unity.
2. For our group purpose there is but one ultimate authority—a loving God as He may express Himself in our group conscience. Our leaders are but trusted servants; they do not govern.
3. The only requirement for A.A. membership is a desire to stop drinking.
4. Each group should be autonomous except in matters affecting other groups or A.A. as a whole.
5. Each group has but one primary purpose—to carry its message to the alcoholic who still suffers.
6. An A.A. group ought never endorse, finance, or lend the A.A. name to any related facility or outside enterprise, lest problems of money, property, and prestige divert us from our primary purpose.
7. Every A.A. group ought to be fully self-supporting, declining outside contributions.
8. Alcoholics Anonymous should remain forever nonprofessional, but our service centers may employ special workers.
9. A.A., as such, ought never be organized; but we may create service boards or committees directly responsible to those they serve.
10. Alcoholics Anonymous has no opinion on outside issues; hence the A.A. name ought never be drawn into public controversy.
11. Our public relations policy is based on attraction rather than promotion; we need always maintain personal anonymity at the level of press, radio, and films.
12. Anonymity is the spiritual foundation of all our traditions, ever reminding us to place principles before personalities.

---

* The Twelve Traditions of AA are taken from *Twelve Steps and Twelve Traditions,* published by AA World Services, Inc., New York, N.Y., 129–87. Reprinted with permission of AA World Services, Inc. (See editor's note on copyright page.)

Appendix E

The Ideal Alcoholism Counselor

The ideal alcoholism counselor constantly strives to be a living witness to the Four Absolutes and Twelve Steps of Alcoholics Anonymous. Within the framework of these values he avails himself of a working knowledge of human behavior and brings both to bear when confronted with a person in distress.

If he has anything distinctive to offer it is his serene sobriety. Without this abiding reference he is as sounding brass: "What you are speaks so loudly I can't hear what you say."

Father John B. McCarthy, S.T.
Rosary Hall
St. Vincent Charity Hospital
Cleveland, Ohio 1972

Appendix F

How Do We Choose a Substance Care Program?*

In Greater Cleveland, there appears to be an adequate number of alcoholism/drug treatment programs for the insured population. Inpatient programs of various lengths of stay, daylong treatment programs which allow clients to remain at home after the treatment day, and evening treatment outpatient programs are the main examples of programs available in the community. Nearly all health insurances pay for some form of treatment.

The question becomes, "How does one choose a facility that can be counted on to help an alcoholic or cocaine addict?"

As an employer, parent, spouse or friend, we may find ourselves involved in getting someone to a treatment program. If we have the luxury of time, the following are some guidelines as to what constitutes a quality treatment program. Asking questions is a good idea, no matter what we are buying, so be willing to get answers in formulating an opinion.

First, the counseling staff represents the soul of a program. Find out how long the counseling staff has been employed. A high turnover rate may indicate counselors are overworked (most are already underpaid).

An ideal counselor-to-patient ratio is 1-to-6. Also, how long have counselors been employed in chemical dependence counseling? If they have only one or two years of direct counseling experience, they may not have an extensive enough background. How many counselors are themselves recovering from chemical dependency? Many people feel that at least 50 percent of the staff should be recovering, preferably for five years. Are para-professionals part of the counseling staff? It is often effective to have non-professionals working along with degreed individuals in order to give patients different perspectives on recovery issues.

Second, clinical expertise. While good chemical dependency treatment keeps a focus on alcohol and drugs, a program should also be able to identify significant emotional or psychiatric issues needing to be ad-

---

* John Finnegan, "How Do We Choose a Substance Care Program?" *Healthsense* (May 1990).

dressed. These issues may only be evident in a minority of patients, but not to diagnose a mental disorder may eventually result in a relapse.

Third, family treatment. Chemical dependency is often called the family disease. Everyone in the family system may be hurt to some degree by another's addiction. Family members (or friends or employers) need to become aware of what chemical dependency is, how they have been affected, and what they need to do to help the family system recover. Al-Anon and Alateen are especially useful self-help groups for the spouse and children of chemically dependent people.

Fourth, continuing care after treatment. Normally called "aftercare," these counseling sessions are designed to keep the chemically dependent person involved in recovery after primary treatment. Recovery is an ongoing "day-at-a-time" phenomenon, not simply a "treatment."

Fifth, twelve-step orientation. Long-term recovery, plus an improved quality of life, is best found in programs such as Alcoholics Anonymous, Cocaine Anonymous, or Narcotics Anonymous.

Sixth and last, "vibes." This intangible may be just a good feeling you get in talking to the program representatives. Above everything else, good treatment is a good feeling one has about the program.

Appendix G *

Sister Ignatia
The Third AA International Convention
Long Beach, California
July 1960

Master of Ceremonies: I looked forward to this opportunity of chairing the meeting because it would give me an opportunity to meet her. And I'm very happy that she has been able to come to the Coast and be with us this afternoon so that you may feel and come to know the sweetness of her spirit, the depth of her concern, and the effectiveness of her service to suffering alcoholics. Sister Ignatia.

Mr. Chairman and many of my good friends—in fact, I feel Alcoholics Anonymous is part of my family—I know that God works in mysterious ways. How little did I know, when I entered the convent, that I would spend my days, as many of them as I have, in caring for alcoholics. But God works in mysterious ways, and certainly His Divine Providence has directed all this. I feel He can use very weak instruments to carry out His designs, but from His vantage point, as I know Colonel Towns would say, you see many wonderful results, nothing short of miracles. We are not given to a lot of imaginary things, but certainly, God is extremely kind to the alcoholic, because He'll never refuse to help.

I feel that it's a privilege to work in this field. I owe it to my community. When Bill Wilson called me about this, I certainly could hardly think of appearing on a program like this. And as I said, well, it's something like the AA Third Step—we turn our life and our will over to God, under the direction of our superior. My superior might have sent word at any time that I was to take no more. It came nearly to that point in a few cases. But thank God and the fervent prayers of, well, I suppose many of the Sisters

---

* This appendix contains several historical inaccuracies, but it has been reprinted as it was transcribed.

who were interested, and our beloved Dr. Bob, and Bill himself. Somehow we weathered it through.

Bill W. asked me to say a few words about how we got started in Akron. I hardly know myself. I was sent there in 1928, just as a—well, my doctor recommended occupational therapy. A change of occupation for a while. I was in the field of music and as you know that's rather nerve-wracking. They thought a change might be good for me. So I was sent to St. Thomas, which was just opened in 1928, and it was there I met Dr. Bob Smith. We had an open staff the first year because we didn't know the men, nor did they know us. Dr. Bob operated at our hospital and other hospitals. I didn't know that he had a drinking problem, and in fact I wouldn't have known it had he not told me so because he didn't come to the hospital when he was drinking.

Oh, I can recall sometimes his voice was rather reverberating. I could hear him when he came in the back door. He had a decided New England accent. But somehow I liked him because he was so straightforward. Those of us working around hospitals know that some doctors make everything an emergency, a matter of life or death. Others will tell you the exact truth about the case, or if they can't, then you know that you take them for what they say. However, Doctor was so straightforward, I enjoyed working with him.

One day he looked rather down—we often had little chats, and this morning he looked rather down. I said, "Doctor, what's the trouble this morning?" "Well," he said, "I might as well tell you that I came in contact with a New York broker. I've had a drinking problem for a long time and somehow we got together and tried to work out something that will help these drunks." "Well," he said, "we've tried a few rest homes, and he had some in the other hospitals." He said, "Sister, would you consider taking one?" Well, I hesitated because sometime before, probably two months before, I took a man in who looked—I didn't know much about this drinking. I knew some could drink and handle it well, and others couldn't. So they called me to the emergency and I went down and talked with him. I said, "Just lie down a little while." He worked at the city garage and looked like a very respectable person. He said, "I've been drinking a little too much and I want to get straightened out," which I thought was a good thing.

Well, the only bed we had at the time was a bed in a four-bed room.

Then we knew nothing about special treatment, and I assigned him to the man on medical service and registered him and put him to bed. And I said, "You won't cause any trouble." Oh no—he'd be an angel!

Well, I forgot about him. When I came over early the next morning, the night supervisor, who was a tall sister—we always teased her about her big feet—well, she was standing at the door waiting for me. She said, "The next time you take a DT in this place, please stay and run around after him as we had to!" I decided then that was enough. I often felt sorry to see them turned away, but I was not the last word in the hospital.

So when Dr. Bob proposed my taking in a real alcoholic, well, you can imagine my misgivings. I thought, Oh dear me. I told him, "Doctor, not only will I be put out, but the patients and everything else—I don't think they want alcoholics." He said, "Sister, this patient won't give you a bit of trouble because I will medicate him. I assure you."

Well, I had much confidence in him because he never said anything that wasn't so. Well, very carefully, I said, "Well, Doctor, I shall take him then," and put him in a two-bed room. I thought I was doing pretty well because we were so crowded in those days and beds were at rather a premium. So I took him to this two-bed room. Dr. Bob went up and medicated him and everything, and I figured I wouldn't hear much until the next morning anyway. So there wasn't a word about it. Dr. Bob then came to the admitting office. He said, "Sister, would you mind putting my patient in a private room?" I thought I had done pretty good to put him in a two-bed room! He said, "You know, there will be some men come to visit him and they'd like to talk to him privately." Well, I said, "I'll do what I can, Doctor."

After he left, I went up and looked the situation over. Right across the hall, we had a flower room where we used to prepare the patients' flowers. And I thought, Well, they can fix their flowers somewhere else for today; and I figured I could push the bed in there. That's what we did. His visitors came, and we kept a close eye on them! And I thought, My, they're respectable-looking men—they don't look as if they ever took a drink!

I thought, Now, the next time I won't have this trouble. I'll put them in a private room. So the next one that came along I put in a private room. And I didn't know much about these alcoholics—I was not an expert;

surely the Lord picked out a weakling when He picked out me, I know. However, I took him down to the room as I would any patient, and then was taking the chart to the desk to explain to the nurse a little about it. I couldn't tell her too much, but I said Dr. Bob would give her the orders.

And wouldn't you know, he was out of his room and after me! Well, he had on his shorts and nothing else. I nearly went through the floor because the nurses all looked. And I said, "You go right back to the room and we'll be right down." So the nurse came down with me and here he was under the bed. Well, I thought, this will never work. I don't believe this will go at all. I'd better put two together the next time. I didn't want to give up . . . at once . . . I don't know just exactly what I did, if I had someone stay with him, or what I did. But I know after that, I put two together and then finally we took a four-bed room, and it seemed to go pretty good. One would help the other. Usually one or two would be coming out of it pretty well before a new patient came.

And so then we took another two beds across the hall. And it was hard to say no when they really wanted to do something about their drinking. And by that time the men were coming in quite often, so much so that some of the sisters said, "Who are these fine-looking men who come in so often and seem so interested in the patients?" And I didn't say much at first, but later I said, "Well, that is AA." "What is AA?" "Would you like to know something about it?" "Why, yes." "Well, I'll bring some literature then."

But of course before that, a committee from Alcoholics Anonymous talked with Sister Superior. She was one who had a lot of experience in the old days of Charity and all, and she knew what we were doing. And she said to these men, "Well, we had them at Charity—they'd be running around the halls and getting in a lot of trouble. But since Dr. Bob has been treating them, we don't know that they're in the house." So she said, "There's no problem as far as I can see. Just go right along."

Well, that was wonderful. But that wasn't all, of course. Later other patients complained because they didn't have visitors like the alcoholics; and to them, these AAs—they seemed like such privileged characters. So finally they decided to move the alcoholics to a small accident ward we had—it was sort of off from the rest of the hospital—and there we put in a coffee bar and Dr. Bob set up the program.

I must tell you this. The first opportunity he had, he brought Bill

Wilson over. And of course I couldn't imagine who this wonderful Bill was, but I soon learned that God had chosen two great men. What one didn't have, the other supplemented, and together they worked perfect. I often say to our boys, "Had the Lord picked out two great religious leaders, no one would have come near them," because the alcoholic doesn't want anything about religion, nor do we try to preach religion to them. But they aren't in there very long until they're asking or telling us what experience they've had and what they'd like to do. They know they haven't been living right, and I feel that, as many of our nurses have said, the best sedative is peace of mind. If once they can be relieved of their anxieties and worries, and treated properly, there should be no trouble.

When they first came in and Dr. Bob set up the program, no televisions, no radios, no newspapers. Only literature pertaining to AA or something that would have a building of their morals and that kind of thing. They have all the reading they can take care of, and then their visitors, too.

But anyway, during Dr. Bob's time, I think we treated between four and five thousand. And he treated them—he came in every day unless he was out of town or something like that—and without any charge. He said, "That's my contribution to AA." Of course, in those days, they didn't have too much either, to start with. And you couldn't mention money very well, or how much it would cost, because if we'd just get them sober, it meant a great deal. But that was taken care of later on. Thank God. It worked out very well, and there are no problems. Oh, many times, whether they have it or don't, we take them in because God certainly provides, and the man who has this program is everlastingly grateful.

Sometimes Dr. Bob would make rounds, and he'd come down and he'd say, "Sister, let that man go home. He doesn't want this program." "Oh, but Doctor, he has a big family and he has this and that and the other." "He doesn't want the program, Sister. He isn't ready." So, he was always right. Many times they'd frighten us, they'd have heart attacks, or they'd tell me they had a bad heart or something. And I hated to bother Doctor too much. Often I'd call his wife, Anne. I think members of this group or any alcoholics should often say a prayer for Anne, because she was the backbone of this. In her calm, quiet way she was really an angel. I would call her and say, "Oh, Anne, I'm so worried about this fellow." She knew most of them from either reputation or Dr. Bob telling her about them. And she would get the Doctor if it was anything serious, but otherwise she'd say, "Now don't worry about him, because . . . they're all alibiologists in other words." And I learned they were—they'd do anything to promote another drink or treatment of some kind.

So, we take them but once. That was Dr. Bob's plan—and I said, "Oh, my, that's kind of strict, isn't it?" But, oh, I see the wisdom of it. Because if there is a merry-go-round, when that temptation comes, they think, "Oh, I can get back in there for five or six days and that would be all right. Sister's good—she'll take me back." And I'd only be encouraging their drinking. They know that it's a one-way trip. The AA sponsors are tremendously cooperative. Any hospital who tries to just take them in on their own is very foolish because they need this sponsorship. I often say it's something like learning the technique of golf. You may know all the angles and all the rules, but unless you get out there in the field and do some footwork and practice, you won't be much of a golfer.

So we tried. Dr. Bob felt if they could be taken out of their environment, at first it was just five days because people were pretty depleted after the Depression and all—financially—and the sooner we got them back to their families, the better. Although many of those first AAs would take them into their own homes and try to help indoctrinate them. They worked in groups, and it was marvelous what they did. But, however, we certainly have found that it was very wise because a sponsor will not bring them until they are ready. And he screens them carefully and goes over it. We want to be sure the sponsor is not just a person they met in a bar somewhere. We usually ask them what group they're attending. Of course, now, I know most of them well—know who are good sponsors and who are not. But it's a tremendous help.

So, finally, the time came—well, Anne of course died in '49. And that was very hard for Dr. Bob. He called from the Cleveland airport; they had just gotten in from Texas and the plane was grounded—Bill knows more about this than I. Anyway, they brought her directly to the hospital, and we kept Doctor there, too, because he was pretty well shaken up with all this. And Anne died of pneumonia.

So it went on from there. Dr. Bob then died in 1950, about a year and a half later. We knew then, I believe, that he had a malignancy. He talked with Bill, well, I think several times a week, if not every other day. He'd give me a little message. And I felt as though I knew Bill and his guiding spirit, because there wasn't very much done that they didn't consult together on, especially anything affecting the foundation of AA.

Then one day I got word—we're just like people in the army, you know. We go to where we're sent. I often wondered whether I was off the mailing list or whether I was forgotten! I was there twenty-four years, one week short of twenty-four years. And finally the word came that I was going to Charity Hospital and work with AA there. They had had AA at Charity and fine workers there, but they just had a small department. And Sister Victorine, a very fine sister who everybody loved, was there, too. And she came down and we told her everything, and Dr. Bob talked with her, and she really did a good job. But they decided to build a new wing and all the extras. I don't know if they thought Alcoholics Anonymous was a frill then or not, but everything discontinued. They didn't think it was a matter of life and death, so they just kind of forgot about AA.

But Reverend Mother didn't—she saw much good in it, I know. I went there in August and I didn't hear a word about—other than on my Obedience it said that I was to take care of this floor, visit with patients, and work with AA. Well, I knew someday maybe we'd have them. But anyway, I just observed and went along day by day. Finally, one day I got a call—I was in surgery checking on a patient to find out the condition—the family was worried about this patient. And the bell rang furiously and said, "Superior wants you. She's on your floor." And I came down, and the architect of the new building was there, and a few nurses, the director of our nursing service was there.

And Superior said, "What kind of a setup would you like for this AA?" Well, you can imagine me standing in the middle of the floor and feeling rather strange, and really didn't feel at home yet. And I couldn't think very fast. So this nurse said, "Well, Sister, are they violent?" I said, "No, they're not violent." "Oh, they're not intoxicated?" "Yes, they are intoxicated, but they're clean enough to be screened because we must make sure that they want the program." "Well," she said to the architect, "you won't need those cages then." Well, I said, "Would you mind—give me a few days and we'll draw up a little plan of what we'd like?" "Fine."

Well, the day that they came was on the Feast of Our Lady of the

Rosary—that's how we came to call it Rosary Hall. When I was moved there, I thought, Oh, I'd love to have this in memory of Dr. Bob. Well, I thought, if I got permission, rather than call it the alcoholic ward, we'll call it Rosary Hall. And I was thinking of marking their robes monogrammed R.H. And I thought, All I need is an *S* and I have Doctor's initials—Robert Holbrook Smith. So we called it Rosary Hall Solarium! The insignia on the door is R.H.S. This was granted by the hospital authorities on October the 7, 1952, Feast of the Most Holy Rosary.

I feel that people—whether they're in the church or out, whatever their denomination—when you see a rosary you know it means prayer. People get their rosary out and you think they're praying somehow. So I think this is all the result of someone's prayers. The grace of God comes through someone's prayer and penance, that's for sure. The insignia ultimately expresses the efforts of the Sisters of Charity of Saint Augustine, a Catholic religious order, as they joined forces with the members of AA, a strictly nonsectarian movement, in an attempt to rescue men and women of all creeds from the bottomless pit of alcoholism.

To be admitted to this ward, you must be sponsored by a member of AA in good standing. You must also evidence the desire not just to get sober but also to preserve and perpetuate your sobriety on a day-by-day basis. Unless you yourself are willing to admit that you are an alcoholic, you are advised to seek help elsewhere. The physical therapy is the most modern known to medical science. The patient's entire stay is a retirement from the outside world and the habits which have caused their collapse.

There are not radios, televisions, newspapers, or magazines. Nothing but AA literature and other literature in keeping with the program are available. The patient may have no visitors except members of Alcoholics Anonymous who are welcome between 9:00 A.M. and 9:00 P.M. The conversation turns to alcoholism and its ravages. Every evening a member of AA comes to the hospital to conduct a brief AA meeting with the patients. An attractive coffee bar stands in the center of the hall where AA members and the patients often gather to discuss their common problems and solutions. A little oratory is open at all times—just if they want to do some prayerful thinking, it's there.

The remodeling and construction for the solarium were done by members of AA who contributed their time and money. Members who belonged to the building trade worked day and night during their spare hours to complete the lovely quarters, at no cost to the hospital.

Rosary Hall accepted its first patient one year ago, and since that day, one thousand men and women have been hospitalized therein. We haven't much room for women; we're hoping to get more. Oh, we have three usually, sometimes four, and even a stretch to five, but that isn't good. However, Rosary Hall accepted its first patient one year ago, and since that day, one thousand men and women have been hospitalized therein.

They have been offered not only the key to sobriety but also the key to a happy sobriety. The Sisters of Charity and the members of Alcoholics Anonymous who had assisted them decline any individual credit. They are aware that it is in giving that we receive. Well, God bless you all, and I wish you a continued happy sobriety and may God's grace be with you always, and bless every one of you.

Appendix H

Care and Treatment of Alcoholics

An Interview by Sister M. Ignatia, C.S.A. of St. Thomas Hospital, Akron, Ohio

Delivered in Panel Discussion during the Convention of

Catholic Hospital Association of the United States and Canada

Philadelphia
June 2–5, 1951

Reverend Fathers, Sisters, Doctors, and Dear Friends:

Before going into our hospital procedures, I thought it best to tell you how we became interested in this work.

Nearly twelve years ago, one of the cofounders of Alcoholics Anonymous, Dr. Bob, was on our staff. (Doctor died November 19, 1950. May his dear soul rest in peace). Doctor was a skilled proctologist. He was on our staff five years before we knew that he had a drinking problem. We would not have known it then had he not volunteered the information.

Dr. Bob often discussed the problem of alcoholism with us, with regard to auto accidents and other tragedies caused by excessive drinking. Many of these cases had to be admitted to the hospital, even though they were intoxicated. After talking with members of the families of these compulsive drinkers and realizing the misery, suffering, and sorrow brought into the homes and lives of these afflicted ones because of drink, we became deeply interested as Dr. Bob unfolded his plan to us.

This was in 1939, just about the time we were trying to pull out of the Depression. Hospital beds were at a premium, without any prospect of adding to our bed capacity. There was very little enthusiasm around the hospital about admitting people who were imbibing too freely in those days.

However, prompted by the grace of God, we very cautiously admitted one patient, with the diagnosis of acute gastritis, under the care of Dr. Bob. The patient was placed in a two-bed room. The next morning Dr. Bob came to the admitting office and very timidly requested that the patient be moved to a spot where the men who came to visit him might talk with him privately. The only available space we could think of was a small room across the hall called the "flower room," where patients' flowers were changed and arranged. We pushed the alcoholic's bed into this room. It was there that he received his first AA visitors. The men who came to visit him were such respectable, dignified-appearing men that we could hardly believe they had ever been addicted to alcohol.

We then set aside a two-bed room, then a four-, and later a six-bed room. Today our AA ward has eight beds, adjoining a corridor which serves as a lounge. The corridor opens into the gallery of our chapel.

Our alcoholic ward is not a great problem. It is simply a large room with accommodations in one end for eight beds. The other end of the room is a small lounge with comfortable chairs, a davenport, a "bar," a coffee urn, and an icebox. To the rear of this ward-lounge is a room with a lavatory and shower into which the new man is brought for admission to the ward.

An important point is that he is helped out of his street clothes and into hospital attire *by other patients in the ward.* The advantage for the *new patient* is that, from the first, he is in the care of understanding friends. The advantage for the older patients who perform this duty is that they are thus able to see *themselves* again as they were upon admission. Administratively, an economy is effected by thus eliminating the need for hard-to-get employees.

Directly across the hall from our ward-lounge is the choir loft of our chapel, which permits AA patients to hear Mass every day if they wish and to make visits in hospital attire when they so desire—all in complete seclusion. Bearing in mind always that the alcoholic is a person who is sick *spiritually* as well as *physically,* the ready access he is thus given to the source of spiritual healing is a powerful factor in his recovery.

To return to the mechanical operation of the ward, it can be stated that it is almost wholly self-operating. A nurse's aide, it is true, comes in to make the beds and an AA employee does the heavier cleaning. The cleaning of ashtrays, the making of coffee (the coffee urn is in operation twenty-four hours each day), the washing of coffee cups—these are all done by the patients themselves. Usually they welcome these small opportunities to busy themselves and thus keep their minds off their problems. Activity eliminates brooding, and the volume of such work is never great at any time.

The function of the lounge is to provide a place where the patient can chat with AA visitors and listen to informal talks. A secondary value, but a most important one to the *former* patient, is that by visiting current AA patients, the former patient helps to perpetuate his own sobriety. It is axiomatic that the alcoholic is never "cured"; his ailment is simply arrested, but it is *positively* arrested if he perseveres in the program. The visitors lounge, which is supplemented by chairs in the hallway that divides the ward from the choir loft, helps not only to aid the current patient to sobriety but also to preserve and perpetuate the sobriety of former patients.

The icebox is kept stocked with food and particularly with milk and citrus juices, for the alcoholic is frequently an undernourished person. The patients are encouraged to eat at will. The coffee urn and bar are the AA equivalent for the brass rail and bottles of the drinking days.

The AA visitors perform a multitude of chores for the current patients. Sometimes they secure a job or effect a family reconciliation or pacify a creditor pressing for payment of a bill. These and other services are done by AAs for the dual purpose of showing true Christian brotherhood and as a means of perpetuating and ensuring their own sobriety.

Hospital Procedure

We begin *where reality begins* for the alcoholic. *Reality* for the alcoholic is drinking. It is most important that the approach be made through another alcoholic, namely, a sponsor. The sponsor speaks the language of the alcoholic. He knows "all the tricks of the trade" because of personal experience.

Those of us who have anything to do with admitting these patients would do well to have the humility to rely upon the judgment of the sponsor. Let him decide when the patient is ready for the program. We do not accept *repeaters!!* Sponsors know this; hence, they are very careful to properly qualify the person before bringing him into the hospital. Above all, he must have a *sincere desire to stop drinking.* Wives, relatives, friends, and well-meaning employers may try to *high-pressure the alcoholic* into accepting the program. Someone may even persuade the family doctor to use his influence with the hospital so that the prospect may be admitted into the alcoholic ward.

The role of the sponsor is not an easy one. He leaves nothing undone to clear away all the ill feeling, indignation, and resentment that have accumulated in the path of his patient. The sponsor acts as a catalytic agent (to use a chemical term) in combating all adverse forces. He tries to appease an exasperated wife, talks with the employer, landlord, creditors, and others. He explains the program, tells them that this is not simply another "sobering up process." This time he is being treated not only physically but morally and mentally as well. The sponsor assures them that with God's grace, their cooperation, and the help of his fellow AAs, his charge will be given a real opportunity to make a complete recovery.

The Patient Admitted to the Hospital

After registration the sponsor escorts his patient to the AA ward.

The ward is virtually self-governing. Two or three of the senior patients in the ward take over and welcome the new patient. They check his clothes and prepare him for bed. (Many of these patients are in such good condition that they sit in the lounge and join in the conversation.) Nothing is left undone to make the new man feel at home. This reception inspires hope in his heart. It also gives the AA patients a splendid opportunity of doing Twelfth Step work, namely, helping others.

The alcoholic is ill—in body, mind, and soul—hence, we begin with the physical care.

Second Day: The Day of Realization

The physical condition of the patient is usually much improved on the second day. His mind is beginning to clear. He feels encouraged because everyone seems interested in him. Visitors call on him, telling him, "This is how I made it." Some of the visitors may be men with whom he used to drink. The power of example is a great incentive to the patient. He begins to say to himself, "If he can do it, so can I. But how am I going to make it?" At this point, he generally has a "heart-to-heart talk" with his sponsor.

He acknowledges his utter *powerlessness* over alcohol. He honestly admits that he has tried innumerable times to drink normally and has always failed. He is finally ready, honestly and humbly, to admit defeat. His sponsor is delighted to know that his patient is really honest about his drinking. The sponsor says, "Good! We can help you since you are humble and honest."

This is the grace of God at work in the soul of the patient: to admit helplessness and to seek help outside of self. This may be the first time the patient has admitted the fact that he is powerless to help himself.

The next step is to humbly turn to God. "Ask and you shall receive." Patients have often said that this is the first time they sincerely prayed. The "Our Father" takes on a new meaning at this point. They feel that they really *belong*.

The Day of Moral Inventory

The patient makes a searching and fearless moral inventory. He faces the past honestly; admits to God, to himself, and to another human being the exact nature of his wrongs. He is finished with alibis and reservations. "I am an alcoholic. What a joy to be honest! The truth will make you free." Now he is sincerely asking God's help and the help of his fellow man.

Fourth Day: The Day of Resolution

"Give us this day our daily bread." This is interpreted by the alcoholics to mean "I can surely stay sober today." This is usually followed by an act of complete surrender to God. The past is finished. "I am heartily sorry." "I'll try to make amends." This means confession, repentance, and firm purpose of amendment. Many Catholics return to the sacraments after years of negligence. Scripture says, "There is more joy in heaven over one sinner doing penance than ninety-nine just who need no penance." He used to drink because he felt like it. He permitted his emotions to run away with him. Now, with God's help and the help of his fellow AAs, with his clear thinking, he can control his feelings and emotions. Reason now governs his life. Strong convictions are given him as to why he cannot take that *first drink*. He has learned from his fellow alcoholics that it is more blessed to give than to receive, and that it is a privilege to help others. What a joy, too! He is kept so busy helping others that he does not have time to even think about a drink. What a transformation takes place in the lives of these men!

Fifth Day: Plans for the Future

As he leaves the hospital, he must now face his problems. The way has been paved by the sponsor. The future is in God's hands. He has learned to say, "O God, grant me the serenity to accept the things I cannot change, courage to change the things I can, and wisdom to know the difference." He is urged to guard against pride, self-pity, resentment, intolerance, and criticism; to attend meetings; to do Twelfth Step work; and to visit the hospital.

Before leaving the hospital, the patient is given a "Following of Christ" by Thomas à Kempis. During his stay in the hospital, he learns the significance of the little Sacred Heart badge. He requests one, with a thorough understanding of conditions implied: "That it must be returned *before he takes the first drink*."

We have hospitalized well over four thousand AA patients at St. Thomas. They have come to Akron from Alabama, South Carolina, Michigan, Maryland, Texas, and many other distant parts. They would not have had to travel so far if their *local* hospitals made it possible for them to receive the program nearer home.

Time and finances prohibit many from making such a long trip. Many may be forced to accept treatment under less favorable circumstances. Our policy is not to accept alcoholics for rehospitalization. We've learned from experience that in institutions where the majority of the inmates are repeaters the program is defeated for the new man because it creates an atmosphere of pessimism and discouragement. The patient often gives up in despair. It might have been quite different had he been given the proper exposure to the program in a spiritual atmosphere as provided in a local Catholic hospital.

A priest once told me that the AA program is the most fruitful source of conversions. It is perhaps the best means by which the work of the hospital can be interpreted to the community. It gives the hospital a good name, not only with the reformed drunkard, his family, friends, and neighbors, but the whole community can point to something constructive which the hospital has done. These people are seeking truth; in other words, they are thirsting for God.

This is a tremendous movement. According to figures from the New York office, new members are registered at the rate of about 1,500 per month. At present there are about 112,000 active members and some 4,000 chapters scattered throughout the United States, Canada, Latin America, and thirty-six other countries.

In conclusion, may God's grace give to my weak words influence and strength that they may *penetrate* the *hearts* of those who have it within their power to urge the establishment of this *great apostolate* in their respective hospitals.

Appendix I*

Eulogy of Sister M. Ignatia
by Reverend Thomas L. Coonan
April 5, 1966

*"Greater love than this no man hath than that he lay
down his life for his friend." (John 15:13)*

As we gather here today in this beautiful cathedral to celebrate the last, sad obsequies of the dedicated and heroic little lady, who was at once the apostle of Alcoholics Anonymous and the angel of deliverance to tens of thousands of men and women afflicted with the grim, rampant, and fatal malady of alcoholism, it is fitting that we begin by contrasting the Christian with the pagan concept of death. To the pagan mind, death was the end of life. "Oh Pale Death," wrote the Roman poet Horace, "which knocks impartially at the palaces of the rich and the cabins of the poor." To the Christian mind, however, death is the beginning of a new and more perfect life. As stated by the early Christian poet Fortunatus, "There is no death. What seems so is transition. This place of mortal breath is but the pathway to the land Elysium, whose portals we call death."

"I am the Resurrection and the Life," said the Lord. "He who believes in Me, although he be dead shall live, and everyone who believes in Me shall not perish but shall possess life everlasting."

In attempting to eulogize the life of Sister Ignatia, we are reminded of the opening lines of Marc Antony's oration, "I come to bury Caesar, not to praise him." She sought neither honor nor glory in life, but honor and glory sought her. In the words of the Apostle to the Gentiles, "The life she lived, she lived for men. The death she died, she died to God."

Sister Ignatia was born in Ireland in 1889. Her birthplace, Shanvilly in County Mayo, is a wild moorland interspersed with silver lakes, blue mountains, golden gorse, and purple heather, where in summertime one

---

* This appendix contains several historical inaccuracies, but it has been reprinted as it was transcribed.

hears the skylarks warble and the ceruleus cry. Her people were hospitable Irishmen and women imbued with deep faith, Christlike charity, and a love of liberty. The great poet Yeats, who was raised close by, considered the setting one especially fitted to produce poets, artists, saints, and heroes. And in her frail, delicate, and starched composure, Sister Ignatia possessed, in an eminently practical way, all of these priceless qualities.

Rich in the wisdom of the Emerald Isle, she had the soul of a poet and the genius of an artist. And whatever she touched turned to gold. The more, in her supreme modesty, she tried to conceal her holiness, the more it became known to all men. As long as "memory holds a seat in this distracted globe," history will point to her as one of earth's sublime heroines.

At the age of six, Sister Ignatia immigrated to America with her parents and her brother Pat and took up residence here in Cleveland. She specialized in music in various American schools, and before entering the convent, instructed pupils in her parents' home. In September 1914, she received the habit of the Sisters of Charity of Saint Augustine and served the community as a teacher of music until she was incapacitated by a physical breakdown in 1933. She cheerfully accepted the doctor's directive "Better a live sister than a dead musician," and in 1934 she was appointed to St. Thomas Hospital in Akron, Ohio, as registrar.

The following year, 1935, Divine Providence drew together two alcoholic laymen, Bill, a Wall Street broker, and Dr. Bob, a surgeon attached to the staff of St. Thomas Hospital in Dr. Bob's hometown, Akron, Ohio. Had these two men been great religious reformers they might have failed to attract a following, but although both were men of genius, they were neither reformers nor exhibitionists. They were rather two humble, open-minded American gentlemen, conscious only of their failure in their respective professions because of alcoholic overindulgence. They were far too wise and honest to think that they had discovered a cure for alcoholism, a disease which continues to baffle the collective resources of medical science, psychiatry, and denominational religion. On the contrary, they prefaced the findings of their experience with the humble acknowledgement "We admitted that we were powerless over alcohol."

Neither did they claim to have discovered a unique way of release and recovery from alcoholism. They made no claim at all other than the modest profession that through the grace of God "as they understood Him" they had devised a set of principles based on the spiritual and moral nature of man, a program of spiritual kindergarten, which, if practiced by the alcoholic on a day-to-day basis, would restore him to a serene and permanent sobriety.

In the nature of things, there had to be a catalytic agent to get their program into action, and Dr. Bob approached a third person of genius, Sister Ignatia, the registrar of St. Thomas Hospital. He told her that he and a friend had been working on a new method of rehabilitating alcoholics, and he requested her, as registrar, to provide a private hospital room for an alcoholic patient.

Apart from the fact that no such room was available, and that alcoholics, as such, were refused admittance to any place other than jails and workhouses at that time, Sister Ignatia understood the import of Dr. Bob's request. Her heart welled with pity for the poor alcoholic children of this world. So, in her wisdom and charity, she quietly prepared a bed in the hospital flower room and admitted Dr. Bob's alcoholic patient. Her mother superior approved of her improvisation and assigned her to the task of adopting a permanent hospital plan for alcoholics in cooperation with the cofounders of Alcoholics Anonymous, Bill and Dr. Bob. St. Thomas Hospital in Akron thus became the first institution in the world to cater to alcoholic patients, as such.

Meanwhile, in order to gain insight into the alcoholic mind and heart, Sister Ignatia chose to identify herself with the alcoholic and continued to direct the work of alcoholic rehabilitation as an undertaking of the Sisters of Charity until her final incapacitation, a few months before her death last Friday morning.

Despite the fact that progress was initially slow, that complaints were heard on every side, that people were skeptical, and that many professed to regard AA as an ephemeral curiosity, if not a racket, Sister Ignatia, with the aid and guidance of the AA founders, surmounted every obstacle. She dedicated the last twenty-eight golden years of her religious life as one incessant heroic sacrifice to the rehabilitation of alcoholics, irrespective of race, color, creed, or condition. After the manner of Christ's injunction in the Sermon on the Mount "What you have freely received, freely give," she unreservedly put her piety, her wisdom, her experience, her mercy, her compassion, her purity, her love, and her very life at the service of every alcoholic disposed to accept her help, however hopeless, abandoned, or degraded. "Greater love than this no man hath than that he lay down his life for his friend."

Throughout it all, her marvelous sense of humor never failed her. A few examples will suffice. One of the rehabilitated who had prayed the rosary with her daily for many years approached her one day with the remark: "Sister, this is the tenth anniversary of my restoration to sobriety." "That's wonderful, Marty," she replied, "but don't forget that should you ever need our services again, we still have your size in pajamas."

Another, who had been what the AAs call a "slipper," returned to her disconsolate and in tears with the request: "Please pray for me, Sister." "I will, indeed, Jim," she replied, "but you also must do a little praying. There is nothing God likes to hear so much as a strange voice."

It was characteristic of Sister Ignatia's self-effacing thoughtfulness that when she opened a second alcoholic ward in St. Vincent Charity Hospital, Cleveland, in 1952, she had it dedicated as Rosary Hall Solarium. It was intended as a memorial to Dr. Bob, who had died in Akron in 1950, and the insignia on the door—"R.H.S."—coincided with his initials as Robert Holbrook Smith.

Sister Ignatia's career, as the angel of deliverance to alcoholics, reads like a fabulous success story. In Rosary Hall alone, she treated more than ten thousand alcoholic patients, and of those, 65 percent were immediately restored to a happy and permanent sobriety. Of the remainder, although many struggled for a time, they ultimately ended their suffering by accepting the AA program. Her method was eminently practical. Her aim was to restore the alcoholic victim to a happy sobriety. In accordance with AA principles, in combination with the latest medical therapy, alcohol was slowly withdrawn from the patient. His mind was gradually defogged and his distorted thinking was then replaced by a new philosophy of life, which was inculcated through persuasive group therapy. The whole person was treated. The spiritual and moral character was reintegrated, and the rehabilitated alcoholic was restored to his family and society as a valuable member of the community. In due time, he in turn began to sponsor other alcoholics, and in this manner, the beneficent therapy of Rosary Hall was diffused throughout the nation.

Today, Rosary Hall—Sister Ignatia's creation—administers to alcoholic patients from all over the United States and Canada. And since the

AA fellowship has become worldwide, Rosary Hall also engages in an extensive correspondence, answering appeals for advice from AA groups in the British Isles, France, Germany, Switzerland, and Italy. In addition, Rosary Hall functions as a training center and as a hospitable clearinghouse for rehabilitated alcoholics and their friends, not only from Cleveland but from all over America and the free world.

Cleveland has, therefore, good reason to mourn the passing of Sister Ignatia, the abiding genius of Rosary Hall, the institution which has lent the city such a unique civic, social, and humanitarian distinction. This was precisely the point emphasized by President Kennedy in his letter of March 1, 1961, congratulating Sister Ignatia on the success of Rosary Hall in restoring an increasingly large number of citizens to useful citizenship, and in adding moral and spiritual strength to the American community and nation.

And yet, as Sister Ignatia's fame became known throughout the land, as men spoke of her charismatic power of rehabilitating helpless alcoholics, and as her name became a legend from coast to coast, she expressed her distress lest anyone might think that she had any other aspiration than to be a humble, dedicated, and anonymous Sister of Charity. Of her greatness and her fame, she was utterly unconscious. To her, the AA movement was inspired and God-given, a mystery in the sense that it was the medium through which God ordinarily imparts the gift of sobriety to alcoholics. As for herself, she was but a poor, weak, and imperfect instrument in the hands of Almighty God. She loved to cite the divine paradox posed by the Apostle to the Gentiles.

> For the foolish things of the world, has God chosen to put to shame the wise, and the weak things of the world has God chosen to confound the strong, and the base things of the world and the despised has God chosen, and the things that are not, to bring to naught the things that are, lest any flesh should glory in His sight. (1 Cor. 1:27–30)

In rehabilitating alcoholics who had lapsed from their religion, Sister Ignatia was always careful to urge them to return to their church. She was as ecumenical in spirit as Pope John, whom she revered, and to whom she bore a significant comparison. Like him, she thoroughly understood the human equation, and like him also, she thought of the Catholic Church in terms of its Christian and evangelical moorings. To an alcoholic who had expressed concern about Pope John's approach to our separated brethren, she replied: "The importance of our religion lies in making it heavenly to all around us. In its essentials, Catholicism is not as far apart as you suppose from the beliefs of our separated brethren. Under the guidance of good Pope John, love can surmount every obstacle."

It is a small mead of praise to Sister Ignatia to say that in her sublime vocation, she lent tone, dignity, and distinction to the saving AA fellowship, to her community, the Sisters of Charity of Saint Augustine, to the city of Cleveland, and to the American nation.

To comprehend her life-giving sanctity, it is helpful to recall Milton's outpouring of the spirit, when as a blind man he returned to Christ Church, Cambridge, the scene of his youthful inspiration.

> But let my sure feet never fail to walk the studious cloister pale,
> And love the high embowered roof, with antic pillars massy proof,
> And storied windows richly dight, casting a dim religious light.
> There let the pealing organ blow, to the full voiced choir below,
> In service high and anthems clear, as may with sweetness through
> mine ear, dissolve me into ecstasies and bring all heaven before
>   mine eyes.

Sister Ignatia's lofty moral stature had as many beautiful facets as Milton's heavenly vision in the venerable edifice of Christ Church, Cambridge. Her life was an incessant labor of love for afflicted humanity. Her success was truly miraculous. If in life, this charming, radiant little lady was such a powerful force for good, may not the tens of thousands to whom she brought salvation and who are so liberally represented here today, rest assured that in death she will remain the inspiration, the burning and the shining light, and the sacred symbol of the cause of Alcoholics Anonymous. May we not be sure in our faith, hope, and love that, like the woman of the Apocalypse clothed in the sun with the moon at her feet, God has already raised up His good and faithful servant, Sister Ignatia, above the highest hills to a pinnacle of immortal glory.

Appendix J

Sources for Information on Alcoholism

Al-Anon Family Group Headquarters, Inc.
1600 Corporate Landing Parkway
Virginia Beach, VA 23454-5617
1-888-4AL-ANON (1-888-425-2666)
www.al-anon-alateen.org

Alcoholics Anonymous World Services, Inc.
Box 459
New York, NY 10163
1-212-870-3400
www.alcoholics-anonymous.org

National Association of Addiction Treatment Providers (NAATP)
501 Randolph Drive
Lititz, PA 17543-9049
www.naatp.org

National Association of Alcoholism and Drug Abuse Counselors
    (NAADAC)
901 North Washington Street, Suite 600
Alexandria, VA 22314-1535
1-800-548-0497
www.naadac.org

National Council on Alcoholism and Drug Dependence, Inc. (NCADD)
20 Exchange Place, Suite 2902
New York, NY 10005
1-212-269-7797
www.ncadd.org

National Institute on Alcohol Abuse and Alcoholism (NIAAA)
6000 Executive Boulevard
Willco Building
Bethesda, MD 20892-7003
www.niaaa.nih.gov

Notes

Preface to the First Edition: The Messenger and the Message

1. *Alcoholics Anonymous Comes of Age,* 147.

Chapter 1: Legend and Lore of Sister Ignatia

1. Correspondence to Mother M. Roberta, C.S.A., mother superior of the Sisters of Charity of Saint Augustine at the time of Sister M. Ignatia's death on April 1, 1966. Courtesy of Mount Augustine Archives, Richfield, Ohio, and Catholic Diocese of Cleveland Archives, Cleveland, Ohio.

2. Quoted with permission from Alcoholics Anonymous Archives, file 18.8, 145, New York, N.Y.

3. Personal interview recorded October 15, 1985, Sister M. Beatrice Brennan, C.S.A., and the author at Mount Augustine Convent, Richfield, Ohio.

4. Tape-recorded oral history of Sister M. Ignatia, C.S.A., 1954. Interview with Bill Wilson. Alcoholics Anonymous Archives, New York, N.Y., from a transcription. Also see *In All Things Charity* (Gavin), 117–18.

5. Tape-recorded oral history of Sister M. Ignatia, C.S.A., 1954. Interview with Bill Wilson. Alcoholics Anonymous Archives, New York, N.Y., from a transcription.

6. Personal interview recorded October 15, 1985, Sister Mary John Halter, C.S.A., and the author at Mount Augustine Convent, Richfield, Ohio.

7. Personal interview recorded January 28, 1986, Sister Ruth Kerrigan, C.S.A., and the author at Saint Augustine Convent, Lakewood, Ohio.

8. Ibid.

9. Ibid.

10. Ibid.

11. See note 5 above.

12. See note 6 above.

13. See note 5 above.

14. Personal interview recorded September 26, 1985, at the home of Thomas P. Scuderi, M.D., in Akron, Ohio. Present were Dr. Scuderi, Mrs. Dorothy Scuderi, and the author.

15. Ibid. Dr. Scuderi vividly recalled feeling that Sister Ignatia's prayers were the crucial part of the recovery process at that time. He felt that on many occasions, Sister Ignatia's prayers were the only "medicine" that removed an alcoholic from the danger of death by convulsion.

16. See note 14 above.

17. Dark Karo syrup was thought to both restore a chemical balance and calm the nerves of the alcoholic by a rapid restoration of blood sugar levels. Also, a distinction was made between light syrup and dark syrup; dark Karo was preferred because it was thought to have a high vitamin B content, and most alcoholics were thought to have vitamin B deficiencies.

18. Tape-recorded oral history of Bill V., 1954. Interview with Bill W. in Akron, Ohio, Alcoholics Anonymous Archives, New York, N.Y.

19. See note 7 above. Sister Ruth was the night nursing supervisor at St. Thomas Hospital, 1943–48.

20. Ibid.

21. Ibid.

22. Ibid.

23. Ibid. As an innovative night supervisor herself, Sister Ruth often took the alcoholics on nighttime rounds with her when they were restless and unable to sleep. She also took them to early morning Mass in the hospital's chapel. She remembers feeling sympathetic (she thought most of the sisters were) to the alcoholics, provided Sister Ignatia did not steal her medical beds for them.

24. See note 5 above.

25. Notes from a speech delivered by Sister M. Ignatia at the Twenty-fifth Anniversary Convention of Alcoholics Anonymous on July 1, 1960, Long Beach, California. Alcoholics Anonymous Archives, New York, N.Y.; Mount Augustine Archives, Richfield, Ohio; Rosary Hall Archives, Cleveland, Ohio.

26. Ibid. Also see note 5 above.

27. Ibid.

28. Personal interview recorded May 9, 1985, Margaret H. and the author at Margaret's home in Cleveland, Ohio. When it was later suggested that Ignatia write down the history of her AA activities, she retorted that there was no need to do so because "God keeps all the records."

29. Confirmed in a letter from Nell Wing, secretary to Bill Wilson and former AA archivist, New York, N.Y., to Sister Ignatia, dated March 31, 1958, in response to Ignatia's letter of request dated March 21, 1958. Originals in Alcoholics Anonymous Archives, New York, N.Y.

30. See note 5 above.

31. From a transcript of memoirs recorded by Henrietta Seiberling, 1971, Alcoholics Anonymous Archives, New York, N.Y. Also, courtesy of the Hon. John F. Seiberling, Akron, Ohio.

32. Tape-recorded speech delivered by Dr. Robert H. Smith, labeled, "Dr. Bob Smith, 45 minutes at Detroit, Michigan in 1948." Courtesy of Sister M. George, C.S.A., from the Rosary Hall Archives, Cleveland, Ohio.

33. Ibid.

34. See note 31 above.

35. *Alcoholics Anonymous Comes of Age,* 71.

36. See note 5 above.

37. *Alcoholics Anonymous,* 2d ed., 1955, 25.

38. Ibid., 46.

39. Ibid., 44–45.

40. Ibid., Step 2, 59.

41. Ibid., 49–50.

42. *Contemporary American Authors: Personal Statements* (Adams and Montague), 97.

43. Ibid.

44. See note 37 above, 59.

45. From a speech known as the "Three Legacies of AA," delivered by Bill Wilson at the 1955 convention of Alcoholics Anonymous, St. Louis, Mo. Courtesy of Sister M. George, C.S.A., Rosary Hall Archives, St. Vincent Charity Hospital, Cleveland, Ohio, 1985.

46. *Not-God: A History of Alcoholics Anonymous* (Kurtz), 79.

47. Tape-recorded memorial commemoration delivered by Bill Wilson in New York on the occasion of the first anniversary of Dr. Bob Smith's death, November 1951. Courtesy of John F. Finnegan, Cleveland, Ohio. Also, from a transcript of memoirs recorded by Henrietta Seiberling, 1971, Alcoholics Anonymous Archives, New York, N.Y., and "Origins of Alcoholics Anonymous" by the Hon. John F. Seiberling, Akron, Ohio.

48. *Alcoholics Anonymous Comes of Age,* 164.

49. See note 33 above.

50. Ibid.

51. From a letter from Bill Wilson to Dick S., February 18, 1946, given to the author by Father John B. McCarthy, S.T.

52. See note 25 above.

53. See note 45 above.

54. See note 25 above.

55. Informal interview recorded Founders' Day, June 10, 1985, Johnny R., John F. Finnegan, and the author at the home of the late Dr. Robert H. Smith, Akron, Ohio.

56. *Evangelical Dictionary of Theology,* "Moral Rearmament," 733–34; the Oxford Group, later known as Moral Rearmament, was founded by Frank Buchman (1878–1961).

57. In the years 1935–39, the Oxford Group meetings provided a group experience for the early alcoholics. AA did not meet as a separate group officially *named* Alcoholics Anonymous until May 1939 at the home of Abby G. in Cleveland.

58. Personal interview recorded June 1985, Robert R. Smith and Sue Windows (surviving children of Dr. Bob and Anne Smith) and the author at the former Smith residence on Ardmore Avenue, Akron, Ohio.

59. *Alcoholics Anonymous Comes of Age,* 74–75.

60. For additional background, see *Alcoholics Anonymous Comes of Age,* 74–77; *Not-God: A History of Alcoholics Anonymous* (Kurtz), 50–51; *Alcoholism: A Source Book for the Priest, an Anthology,* 394–401; minutes from the proceedings of the National Clergy Conference on Alcoholism, i.e., The Blue Book, "Moral Re-armament and Alcoholics Anonymous" (Ford), 1960.

61. Personal interview recorded July 31, 1985, John C. Ford, S.J., and the author at Campion Center, Weston, Massachusetts. See also *Alcohol-*

ism: A Source Book for the Priest, an Anthology, 394–401; minutes from the proceedings of the National Clergy Conference on Alcoholism, i.e., The Blue Book, "Moral Re-armament and Alcoholics Anonymous" (Ford), 1960.

62. See note 5 above.

63. Ibid. See also *Not-God: A History of Alcoholics Anonymous,* (Kurtz), 50–52, 78.

64. See note 57 above.

65. From an attendance sheet recorded at the first AA meeting at the home of Abby G., May 18, 1939, Cleveland, Ohio. Courtesy of Warren C., Jr. See also *Not-God: A History of Alcoholics Anonymous* (Kurtz), 78.

66. See note 57 above.

67. *Alcoholism: A Source Book for the Priest, an Anthology,* i.e., The Blue Book, minutes from the proceedings of the National Clergy Conference on Alcoholism (Ford), 395, 1960.

68. *Alcoholics Anonymous Comes of Age,* 148–50.

69. Ibid., 143.

70. Ibid., 7.

71. For additional information, see *Alcoholics Anonymous Comes of Age,* appendix v., 253–61, from a talk delivered by the Rev. Edward ("Puggy") Dowling, S.J., 1955.

72. From a personal journal kept by Sister M. Ignatia, C.S.A., courtesy of Mount Augustine Archives, Richfield, Ohio.

73. *A Thought from Saint Ignatius for Each Day of the Year,* translated from the French by Margaret A. Colton (New York, Cincinnati, St. Louis: Benziger Brothers, 1887). In the early days of alcoholism treatment at St. Thomas, Sister Ignatia sometimes gave a copy of this book to patients leaving treatment. Because of the copies' age and scarcity, she more often distributed copies of *The Imitation of Christ* by Thomas à Kempis.

74. Courtesy of an Akron AA member's signed copy of *The Imitation of Christ.*

75. These words from the parable of the Good Samaritan (Luke 10:25–27) can still be seen above the altar in the original chapel at St. Thomas Hospital.

76. Known by Catholics as the "corporal works of mercy," these are the separate inscriptions on each of the six stained-glass windows of St.

Thomas Hospital's chapel. They remain unchanged from the day when Sister Ignatia lived and worked there (1928–52).

Chapter 2: Beginnings of History

1. *Irish Saints* (Reilly), 129.

2. Ibid.

3. Ibid., 131.

4. Ibid., 137.

5. Ibid.

6. Tape-recorded oral history of Sister M. Ignatia, C.S.A., 1954. Interview with Bill Wilson, Alcoholics Anonymous Archives, New York, N.Y., from a transcription.

7. From an interview with John C. Ford, S.J., April 5, 1986. *Two-boaters* was a depreciating term used by Irish Americans for Irish immigrants who could not afford to cross the Atlantic Ocean nonstop; though often prudent, those who bought a frugal passage were regarded as pennypinching. When entire families immigrated, they often had to travel the less expensive way. "They didn't have enough money to come on one boat" was another of the term's disdainful implications.

8. From the previous research notes of Thomas J. Coonan, S.J. Courtesy of the Sisters of Charity of Saint Augustine, Mount Augustine Archives, Richfield, Ohio, 1966.

9. *City of Cleveland Directory,* 1896.

10. See note 6 above.

11. Ibid.

12. Ibid.

13. Ibid.

14. *Erin's Daughters in America* (Diner), 47–49.

15. See note 6 above.

16. See note 8 above.

17. Personal interview May 27, 1985. Margaret Bernhardy, John Finnegan, and the author, regarding Margaret Bernhardy's recollections of growing up Irish Catholic in Cleveland during the early 1900s at Immaculate Conception Church.

18. "Recollections of Those Who Knew Sister Ignatia," Mount Augustine Archives, Richfield, Ohio, unsigned.

19. Personal interview October 22, 1985. Sister Adele Hart, C.S.A., David Simpson, and the author taped at Mount Augustine, Richfield, Ohio.

20. See note 18 above.

21. As required by the Third Part of *The Constitutions for the Government of the Congregation,* chap. XII, p. 114, rule 3 (1909); Sisters of Charity of Saint Augustine, Mount Augustine Archives, Richfield, Ohio.

22. *The Rule of Saint Augustine and the Constitutions for the Congregation of the Sisters of Charity of Saint Augustine,* Second Part of the Constitutions, "Vows, Virtues, and Spiritual Exercises," chap. XXV, 75–76; Cleveland, 1909. Courtesy, Sisters of Charity of Saint Augustine, Mount Augustine Archives, Richfield, Ohio.

23. Ibid., chap. 1, 1.

24. See note 19 above.

25. See note 18 above, Sister Paul Johnston, C.S.A.

26. Ibid., Sister Jane Frances, C.S.A.

27. Ibid., Sister Marie Estelle, C.S.A.

28. Even later in life, Sister Ignatia was known to be in the chapel each day by 4:00 or 4:30 A.M.

29. *In All Things Charity* (Gavin), 100.

30. Telephone interview, December 17, 1985, Theodore J. Van de Motter and the author.

31. See note 6 above.

32. See note 18 above, Sister Therese Marie, C.S.A.

33. Personal interview recorded July 31, 1985, John C. Ford, S.J., and the author at Campion Center, Weston, Massachusetts.

34. See note 32 above.

35. See note 29 above, 101.

36. As documented in personal interviews with numerous Cleveland diocesan priests by the Rev. Msgr. R. C. Wolff, 1985–86.

37. Personal interview recorded July 7, 1986, between the Rev. Francis Zwilling, the Rev. Msgr. R. C. Wolff, and the author in Cleveland, Ohio.

38. Ibid.

39. Personal interview recorded on June 18, 1986, Sister Agnes Therese, C.S.J., the Rev. Msgr. R. C. Wolff, and the author. Taped in Cleveland, Ohio. Also, St. Joseph Academy school records, 1920.

40. From *A History of Saint Rose of Lima Church,* James A. Skelly, 1974, Cleveland, Ohio. Also, telephone interview with the author, August 1987.

41. Documents from the Society of Jesus' Missouri Province Archives confirm that Father Wilwerding performed an exorcism in the Diocese of Cleveland at the time in question. Contrary to Cleveland diocesan records, which, as told to the author, state that Father Wilwerding left Cleveland in 1923, official Jesuit records confirm Cleveland as Father Wilwerding's officially assigned residence until his death in 1926.

42. See note 29 above, 101.

43. Personal interview recorded August 27, 1987, Sister Marie Estelle, C.S.A., and the author. Mount Augustine, Richfield, Ohio.

44. See notes 36 and 37 above.

45. Ibid.

46. The Catholic Diocese of Cleveland, per the Rev. Ralph E. Wiatrowski, diocesan chancellor, could not provide needed documentation of this well-remembered event, despite the author's repeated efforts to verify pertinent information. On separate occasions the chancellor offered conflicting testimony to explain an apparent lack of diocesan records on this historic case. First, in a letter to the author dated April 1, 1986, Father Wiatrowski wrote: "Given the constraints of both canon law and confidentiality, nothing would have been put down on paper." However, canon lawyers assert that canon law requires the documentation of cases of exorcism.

A few months later, in a private discussion with the author and the Rev. Msgr. R. C. Wolff, Father Wiatrowski suggested that all records of this case (which in his previous assertion would not have been written down on paper) seemed hopelessly lost. Although other Cleveland historians verified that they had read the diocesan records of this case, and in spite of the diocesan-requested written permission of Sister Joan Gallagher (major superior of the Sisters of Charity of Saint Augustine) to release the material in question to the author or a designee, all efforts to examine needed documentation failed.

47. See note 36 above.

48. Personal interview recorded October 16, 1986, Sister M. Beatrice

Brennan, C.S.A., and the author at Mount Augustine Convent, Richfield, Ohio.

49. Personal interviews recorded April, June, and August 1986 and June 1987, the Rev. John Brady (then the oldest living priest in the Cleveland diocese), the author, and the Rev. Msgr. R. C. Wolff, Cleveland, Ohio.

50. Ibid.

51. See note 42 above.

52. From numerous informal interviews with members of the Sisters of Charity of Saint Augustine and the author.

53. Personal interview recorded July 1985 with a former Sister of Charity of Saint Augustine who wished to remain anonymous, the author, and John F. Finnegan, Akron, Ohio.

54. Telephone interview, February 1986, the Rev. Henry Birkenhauer, S.J., former vicar for religious, diocese of Cleveland, and the author.

55. See note 52 above.

56. From notes compiled for the author by Sister Cheryl Keehner, archivist for the Sisters of Charity of Saint Augustine.

57. A possible explanation suggested by Sister Joan Gallagher, major superior of the Sisters of Charity of Saint Augustine, regarding Sister Ignatia's undocumented whereabouts during the time in question.

58. Personal interview recorded October 16, 1986, Sister Mary John Halter, C.S.A., and the author at Mount Augustine, Richfield, Ohio.

59. See note 48 above.

60. See note 29 above, 110.

61. See note 48 above.

62. Ibid.

63. See note 6 above.

64. As discussed in consultations with psychiatrist James Fry, M.D., and psychologist Richard Halas, both of Cleveland, Ohio.

65. *Encyclopedia of Human Behavior,* vol. 1, under the words *conversion reaction.*

66. See note 8 above. Also, Sister Ignatia kept a carefully folded copy of Dr. Francis Doran's obituary, found by the author, in her daily prayer book.

67. Personal interview recorded June 9, 1986, Mrs. Carl F. (Helen) Mayer, and the author. A former patient of Dr. Doran's, Mrs. Mayer provided many key insights into the type of medical care and the professional manner of Dr. Doran during the 1920s.

68. See note 8 above.

Chapter 3: Spiritual Connections

1. *The Silence Behind the Music from Akron* (Ciccolini), author's note.

2. Bill Wilson, "In Memory of Sister Ignatia." *AA Grapevine* (August 1966).

3. Personal interview recorded June 17, 1985, Robert R. Smith, Sue Windows, John Finnegan, and the author at the Smiths' former home on Ardmore Avenue, Akron, Ohio.

4. Personal interview recorded January 17, 1986, Sister Ruth Kerrigan, C.S.A., and the author. Taped in Cleveland, Ohio. In a separate interview on September 15, 1985, Sister Victorine Keller, C.S.A., related that Sister Cornelia, C.S.A., also provided discreet care for alcoholic priests at Charity Hospital.

5. From a letter written by Sister Ignatia to Bill Wilson, April 3, 1957, Alcoholics Anonymous Archives, New York, N.Y., and Mount Augustine Archives, Richfield, Ohio.

6. Tape-recorded oral history of Sister Ignatia, C.S.A., 1954. Interview with Bill Wilson, Alcoholics Anonymous Archives, New York, N.Y., from a transcription.

7. Ibid.

8. Ibid.

9. Ibid.

10. Sister Ignatia, C.S.A., "The Operation of the AA Ward," p. II; "The Admitting Policy of the AA Ward," Mount Augustine Archives, Richfield, Ohio (circa 1953; draft copy).

11. Ibid.

12. Ibid.

13. Ibid.

14. Ibid.

15. Ibid., p. I, "Historical Background."

16. Ibid., p. III, "The Cost of Treatment in the AA Ward and Payment."

17. Ibid.

18. Ibid.

19. There were no exceptions (per numerous interviews) to these important questions. Sister Ignatia was adamant on this point.

20. Personal interview recorded July 22, 1986, Pat R., Chuck N., and the author in Bath, Ohio.

21. See note 10 above, p. VIII, "Indoctrination in Principles of A.A."

22. See note 20 above.

23. See note 6 above.

24. Ibid.

25. Ibid.

26. From the previous research notes of Thomas J. Coonan, S.J. Courtesy of the Sisters of Charity of Saint Augustine, Mount Augustine Archives, Richfield, Ohio, 1966.

27. See note 6 above.

28. Personal interview recorded September 19, 1985, Dr. Thomas P. Scuderi and the author in Akron, Ohio.

29. Personal interview recorded January 28, 1986, Sister Ruth Kerrigan, C.S.A., and the author in Cleveland, Ohio.

30. *But for the Grace of God* (Reese), 46.

31. Ibid., 42.

32. Ibid., 51.

33. From the text of Sister Ignatia's speech to the Catholic Hospital Association, Philadelphia, 1951.

34. Ibid.

35. Ibid.

36. Ibid.

37. Ibid.

38. Ibid.

39. Ibid.

40. Ibid.

41. Ibid.

42. *Alcoholics Anonymous Comes of Age,* 8–9.

43. See note 2 above.

Chapter 4: Akron's Magic Blend

1. *Alcoholics Anonymous Comes of Age,* 9.

2. From a memorial speech for Dr. Bob, November 16, 1952, by William G. Wilson.

3. From Anne Ripley Smith's Oxford Group notebook. Alcoholics Anonymous Archives, New York, N.Y., 9 (Anne Ripley Smith Archives, Box 33A).

4. Ibid.

5. Ibid.

6. From a letter of Henrietta Dotson to Dr. Bob Smith following Anne's death in 1949, Alcoholics Anonymous Archives, New York, N.Y. (Anne Ripley Smith Archives, Box 33A).

7. Ibid.

8. Personal interview recorded June 1985, Robert R. Smith, Sue Smith Windows, John F. Finnegan, and the author at the Smith family home, 855 Ardmore Avenue, Akron, Ohio.

9. Ibid.

10. Tape-recorded oral history of Sister M. Ignatia, C.S.A., 1954. Interview with Bill Wilson. Alcoholics Anonymous Archives, New York, N.Y., from a transcription.

11. Ibid.

12. Ibid.

13. See note 3 above, 42.

14. From a letter written by Wilson to Smith in 1938, Alcoholics Anonymous Archives, New York, N.Y. (Box 33), 4.

15. *Pass It On,* 200.

16. Tape-recorded oral history of Anne C., 1954. Interview with Bill Wilson in Akron, Ohio, Alcoholics Anonymous Archives, New York, N.Y.

17. Tape-recorded oral history of Ethel M., 1954. Interview with Bill Wilson in Akron, Ohio, Alcoholics Anonymous Archives, New York, N.Y.

18. Ibid.

19. Ibid.

20. Ibid.

21. Ibid.

22. Ibid.

23. Ibid.

24. Ibid.

25. From a letter dated December 15, 1949, Alcoholics Anonymous Archives, New York, N.Y.

26. Words to the formula of Catholic Baptism.

27. *Akron Beacon Journal* news service, June 1, 1949.

28. Ibid., editorial page.

29. A letter from Bill Wilson to the fellowship of Alcoholics Anonymous, following the death of Anne Smith. Wilson felt that Anne's service to the fellowship was crucial to the success of the pioneering days in Akron and sought to preserve her memory for history by collecting personal remembrances of her, Alcoholics Anonymous Archives, New York, N.Y.

30. From a letter dated December 15, 1949, in memory of Anne Smith, Alcoholics Anonymous Archives, New York, N.Y.

31. See note 1 above, 143.

32. From the previous research notes of Thomas J. Coonan, S.J. Courtesy of the Sisters of Charity of Saint Augustine, Mount Augustine Archives, Richfield, Ohio, 1966.

33. Letter from Bill Wilson to the fellowship, October 1949, Rosary Hall Archives. Courtesy of Sister M. George, C.S.A., St. Vincent Charity Hospital, Cleveland, Ohio.

34. From a letter written by Helen G. Brown, corresponding secretary, to Sister Ignatia, October 19, 1949, Alcoholics Anonymous Archives, New York, N.Y.

35. Tape-recorded oral history of Dan K., Alcoholics Anonymous Archives, New York, N.Y.

36. Ibid.

37. From one of the few remaining pages of personal notes in Sister Ignatia's spiritual journal. Courtesy of the Sisters of Charity of Saint Augustine, Mount Augustine Archives, Richfield, Ohio.

38. See note 1 above, 4.

39. Ibid., appendix D, 301.

40. The inscription on the Poverello Medal. Courtesy of the Sisters of Charity of Saint Augustine, Mount Augustine Archives, Richfield, Ohio.

41. From a letter dated December 3, 1949. Courtesy of the Sisters of Charity of Saint Augustine, Mount Augustine Archives, Richfield, Ohio.

42. "The Drunkard's Best Friend" (Alexander), 76.

43. "Dr. Bob's Last Talk," Alcoholics Anonymous Archives, New York, N.Y.

44. Personal interview recorded July 30, 1985, John C. Ford, S.J., and the author at Campion Center, Weston, Massachusetts. Wilson also called Dr. Bob and Sister Ignatia "benign conspirators" in his August 1966 *AA Grapevine* tribute to Sister Ignatia, "In Memory of Sister Ignatia."

45. An important treatment of alcoholism, John Ford's writings were well studied and commended by Bill Wilson.

46. Personal interview recorded July 30, 1985, John C. Ford, S.J., and the author at Campion Center, Weston, Massachusetts.

47. *Man Takes a Drink* (Ford), 1.

48. *Alcoholics Anonymous Comes of Age,* 209–14, for additional information.

49. Ibid., 214.

50. Cleveland and Akron AA members still maintain adherence to the four absolutes, a regional AA peculiarity in the Midwest. AA does not officially consider these a part of the AA program. A testament to the orthodoxy of AA's birthplace, these cardinal rules (or four absolutes) remain a throwback to the Oxford Group days in Ohio.

51. From a talk entitled "Care and Treatment of Alcoholics," presented by Sister Ignatia to the Catholic Hospital Association of the United States and Canada, Philadelphia, June 1951.

52. Letter dated July 18, 1951, from Mount Augustine Archives, Richfield, Ohio.

53. Letter dated January 24, 1952, from Mount Augustine Archives, Richfield, Ohio.

54. Ibid.

55. Ibid.

56. Ibid.

57. Ibid.

58. Letter dated February 13, 1952, from Mount Augustine Archives, Richfield, Ohio, and Alcoholics Anonymous Archives, New York, N.Y.

59. Ibid.

60. Letter dated March 6, 1952, from Mount Augustine Archives, Richfield, Ohio, and Alcoholics Anonymous Archives, New York, N.Y.

61. From a speech made by Sister Ignatia at the Twenty-fifth Anniversary Convention of Alcoholics Anonymous, Long Beach, California, July 1, 1960, Mount Augustine Archives, Richfield, Ohio.

62. Tape-recorded oral history of Sister M. Ignatia, C.S.A., 1954. Interview with Bill Wilson, Alcoholics Anonymous Archives, New York, N.Y., from a transcription.

63. *Akron Beacon Journal,* by Oscar Smith, August 6, 1952.

64. See note 62 above.

Chapter 5: The Cleveland Frontier

1. Letter to Bill Wilson, Alcoholics Anonymous Archives, New York, N.Y., and Mount Augustine Archives, Richfield, Ohio.

2. *Alcoholics Anonymous Comes of Age,* 20.

3. Ibid.

4. *Dr. Bob and the Good Oldtimers,* 211.

5. The original of this document courtesy of John L., Interval Brotherhood Home, Akron, Ohio.

6. Ibid.

7. Remarks of Eddie G., tape-recorded for the Rosary Hall anniversary meeting, October 7, 1970, Cleveland, Ohio. Courtesy of Vic M., Cleveland, Ohio.

8. From a letter dated September 1, 1952, Mount Augustine Archives, Richfield, Ohio.

9. Ibid.

10. Ibid.

11. Ibid.

12. Ibid.

13. Ibid.

14. Ibid.

15. Ibid.

16. Ibid.

17. Personal interview recorded October 11, 1985, Victor D. Ippolito, M.D., the Rev. Msgr. R. C. Wolff, and the author at Dr. Ippolito's medical offices, Cleveland, Ohio.

18. From one of several undated histories of Rosary Hall. Courtesy of Sister M. George, C.S.A., St. Vincent Charity Hospital, Rosary Hall Archives, Cleveland, Ohio.

19. From a paper entitled "The History of AA Activities," St. Vincent Charity Hospital, Rosary Hall Archives, Cleveland, Ohio, 1953, anonymous.

20. From personal interview notes September 16, 1985, Sister M. Victorine, C.S.A., the Rev. Msgr. R. C. Wolff, and the author, Mount Augustine, Richfield, Ohio.

21. See note 19 above.

22. See note 20 above. Also conducted on October 1, 1985.

23. Ibid.

24. See notes 19 and 21 above.

25. Ibid.

26. See note 20 above.

27. Per Sister Victorine, from another drafted history of Rosary Hall, St. Vincent Charity Hospital, Cleveland, Ohio, 1971.

28. From the previous research notes of Thomas J. Coonan, S.J. Courtesy of the Sisters of Charity of Saint Augustine, Mount Augustine Archives, Richfield, Ohio, 1966.

29. Ibid.

30. Ibid.

31. Ibid.

32. Ibid.

33. Ibid.

34. From a speech given by Sister Ignatia at the Twenty-fifth Anniversary Convention of Alcoholics Anonymous, Long Beach, California, July 1, 1960, Mount Augustine Archives, Richfield, Ohio.

35. See note 27 above.

36. Cleveland *Plain Dealer,* December 5, 1952.

37. See note 27 above.

38. Preface to the article "Another Fragment of History," *AA Grapevine* by Bill Wilson, February 1954, 2–5.

39. A World Series season for the Cleveland Indians. Thus, Bill's humorous reference to them.

40. See note 37 above.

41. Ibid.

42. Ibid.

43. Anonymous letter written to Sister Ignatia, Mount Augustine Archives, Richfield, Ohio.

44. Personal interview recorded November 9, 1986, Frank M. and the author in Cleveland, Ohio.

Chapter 6: An Unfinished Mission: Alcoholism and Catholicism

1. From a letter dated March 30, 1954, Alcoholics Anonymous Archives, New York, N.Y., and Mount Augustine Archives, Richfield, Ohio.

2. See note 1 above. Wilson's response to Manley's letter.

3. From a letter dated June 5, 1954, Mount Augustine Archives, Richfield, Ohio.

4. Dated June 28, 1954.

5. From Mount Augustine Archives, Richfield, Ohio.

6. Ibid.

7. Ibid.

8. Ibid.

9. Ibid.

10. Ibid.

11. Ibid.

12. Ibid.

13. From a letter written by Richard J. Cushing, S.T.D., then archbishop of Boston, to Edward F. Hoban, archbishop of Cleveland, September 22, 1953. Courtesy of the Diocese of Cleveland Archives.

14. From a letter to Richard J. Cushing, archbishop of Boston, November 1, 1953. Courtesy of the Diocese of Cleveland Archives.

15. The Blue Book, vol. 5, 171.

16. Ibid., 167.

17. From a telephone interview with the Rev. Raymond Atkins, Tiffin, Ohio, April 1, 1986.

18. The Blue Book, vol. 1, foreword.

19. Ibid., 100.

20. Ibid., 144–45.

21. The Blue Book, vol. 5, 94–95.

22. *Alcoholism: A Source Book for the Priest,* 126.

23. Ibid., 127.

24. Ibid., 131–32.

25. Personal interview recorded March 9, 1987, the Rev. James O'Donnell, the Rev. Msgr. R. C. Wolff, and the author in Cleveland, Ohio.

26. From an interview recorded June 14, 1985, Robert S. and John F. Finnegan in Cleveland, Ohio.

27. Ibid.

28. Inscription on Dr. Bob Smith's desk plaque, Rosary Hall Archives, St. Vincent Charity Hospital, Cleveland, Ohio, July 1985.

29. See note 21 above, 107–8.

30. Personal interview May 19, 1984, the Rev. Msgr. R. C. Wolff and the author, Cleveland, Ohio.

31. Ibid.

32. From "The Duet of Jesus Christ and Sister Ignatia," written and delivered by the Rev. Samuel R. Ciccolini, Interval Brotherhood Home, Akron, Ohio, on the occasion of the Twentieth Anniversary Memorial Mass for Sister Ignatia, the Cathedral of St. John, Cleveland, Ohio, April 4, 1986.

33. Personal interview recorded July 15, 1985, anonymous recovering alcoholic priest and the author in Cleveland, Ohio.

34. Ibid.

35. Ibid.

36. Ibid.

37. Ibid., tape no. 2.

38. Ibid.

39. Sister Maurice Doody, "A Religious Looks at AA." *About AA: A Newsletter for Professional Men and Women* (Winter 1985).

40. This was the statement of James A. Cullen, S.J., founder of the Pioneers Total Abstinence Association of the Sacred Heart.

41. From an anonymous letter to Sister Ignatia, Mount Augustine Archives, Richfield, Ohio.

Chapter 7: "Take Hope All Ye Who Leave Here"

1. From a tape-recorded interview: Dorothy Fuldheim interviews Sister Ignatia on WEWS radio, circa 1957, Cleveland. Courtesy of Vic M. and John F.

2. Ibid.

3. Ibid.

4. Personal interview recorded August 11, 1985, P. W. and the author in Cleveland, Ohio.

5. Remarks of Les S., recorded at the Rosary Hall Twenty-fifth Anniversary Dinner, October 7, 1977, Cleveland, Ohio. Courtesy of Sister M. Victorine, C.S.A.

6. Ibid., remarks of Dick P.

7. From the Rosary Hall Solarium Association Report, May 10, 1955, Rosary Hall Archives, St. Vincent Charity Hospital, Cleveland, Ohio. (Submitted to Mother Clementine by Sister Ignatia.)

8. Personal interview recorded May 23, 1985, Margaret H. and the author in Cleveland, Ohio.

9. Adalyn B. Ross, "Al-Anon Helps Alcoholics' Wives." *Hospital Progress* (April 1959).

10. Ibid.

11. Ibid.

12. Ibid.

13. Personal interview recorded May 9, 1985, Edna C., John Finnegan, Margaret H., and the author in Cleveland, Ohio.

14. Ibid., courtesy of Edna C.

15. Ibid.

16. *Webster's Tenth New Collegiate Dictionary,* 1984.

17. Personal interview recorded May 9, 1985, Ed C., Edna C., and John Finnegan, and the author in Cleveland, Ohio.

18. Ibid., Edna's remarks.

19. Ibid., Ed's remarks.

20. Ibid., Edna's remarks.

21. See note 8 above.

22. Ibid.

23. Ibid.

24. From a letter of Sackville O. to Sister Ignatia, November 15, 1959, Mount Augustine Archives, Richfield, Ohio.

25. From a letter of Remarcelito R. Butiomg, Luliom Sanitarium, Philippines, to Sister Ignatia, 1964, Mount Augustine Archives, Richfield, Ohio.

26. From the letter of Dr. Douglas McD. to the author, April 30, 1986.

27. From the letter of Richard D. O'Hallaron to the author, September 17, 1985.

28. Ibid.

29. Ibid.

30. Sister Ignatia, being of Irish heritage, instinctively put the practices of the Pioneers to good use in her work with Alcoholics Anonymous; though she did not encourage alcoholics to take the pledge, she did seem to practice the Pioneers' principles of prayer, abstinence, and good works as a natural part of recovery and prevention.

31. Courtesy of Thornton and Penny McDonough, Cleveland, Ohio.

32. From a letter dated January 17, 1955. Correspondence courtesy of Thornton and Penny McDonough, Cleveland, Ohio.

33. Ibid., February 14, 1955.

34. See note 32 above, February 19, 1955.

35. Ibid., March 3, 1955.

36. See note 32 above, March 8, 1955.

37. From the letter of Frederick L. Holborn, Administrative Assistant to President John F. Kennedy, March 1, 1961; Mount Augustine Archives, Richfield, Ohio.

38. From the letter of Sister Ignatia to President John F. Kennedy, March 14, 1961; Mount Augustine Archives, Richfield, Ohio.

39. From the letter of Sister Ignatia to Bill Wilson, December 11, 1957; Alcoholics Anonymous Archives, New York, N.Y.

40. From a letter of Tom K. to the author, November 5, 1986, Cleveland, Ohio.

41. From the letter of Sister Ignatia to Bill Wilson, May 23, 1963, Alcoholics Anonymous Archives, New York, N.Y.

42. From the letter of Ralph A. Dungan, Special Assistant to President John F. Kennedy, to Sister Ignatia, August 6, 1963, Mount Augustine Archives, Richfield, Ohio.

43. From "Recommendations to the Secretary of the Department of Health, Education, and Welfare on Methods of Combating the Rising Alcoholism Problem," written by Sister Ignatia, August 12, 1963, Mount Augustine Archives, Richfield, Ohio.

44. From a letter of Arthur S. to the author, January 23, 1988.

45. Personal interview recorded August 9, 1983, the Rev. John B. McCarthy, S.T., and the author in Cleveland, Ohio.

46. Ibid.

47. Ibid.

48. Ibid.

49. Personal interview recorded February 1987, John B. and the author in Cleveland, Ohio.

50. From a letter copy written by Bill W. to a Cleveland-area AA member, March 1964, Mount Augustine Archives, Richfield, Ohio.

51. See note 45 above.

52. From the letter of Sister Ignatia to Bill Wilson, May 18, 1965, Alcoholics Anonymous Archives, New York, N.Y.

53. Ibid.

54. Ibid.

55. From the letter of Arthur O'H., Vermillion, Ohio, to Sister Ignatia, March 31, 1966, Mount Augustine Archives, Richfield, Ohio.

Bibliography

Adams, George, and William Pepperell Montague, eds. *Contemporary American Authors: Personal Statements.* Vol. 1. New York: Macmillan Company, 1930.

Alcoholics Anonymous. New York: Alcoholics Anonymous World Services, 1955.

Alcoholics Anonymous Comes of Age, 2d ed. New York: Alcoholics Anonymous World Services, 1955.

Alcoholism: A Source Book for the Priest, an Anthology. Indianapolis: National Clergy Conference on Alcoholism, 1960.

Alexander, Jack. "Alcoholics Anonymous: Freed Slaves of Drink, Now They Free Others." *Saturday Evening Post* (March 1, 1941): 9–11.

———. "The Drunkard's Best Friend." *Saturday Evening Post* (April 1, 1950): 17–18, 74–76, 78–79.

Barrachina, Ignatius M., O.C.D. *Spiritual Doctrine of St. Augustine.* St. Louis: B. Herder, 1963.

Birmingham, William, and Joseph E. Cunneen, eds. *Cross Currents of Psychiatry and Catholic Morality.* New York: Pantheon, 1964.

Bishop, Charles, Jr., and Bill Pittman. *The Annotated Bibliography of Alcoholics Anonymous 1939–1989.* Wheeling, W.V.: Bishop of Books, 1989.

Burnham, Sophy. *A Book of Angels.* New York: Ballantine, 1990.

Callahan, Nelson J., and William F. Hickey. *Irish Americans and Their Communities of Cleveland.* Cleveland: Cleveland Ethnic Heritage Studies, Cleveland State University, 1978.

Ciccolini, Samuel R. *God, A.A. and Akron: A Golden Anniversary Tribute.* Akron, Ohio: Interval Brotherhood Home, 1985.

———. *The Silence Behind the Music from Akron.* New York: Vantage Press, 1978.

City of Cleveland Directories, 1896–1930.

The Co-Founders of Alcoholics Anonymous. New York: Alcoholics Anonymous World Services, 1972.

Coonan, Thomas, S.J. *Eulogy of Sister M. Ignatia.* Cleveland: n.pub., April 5, 1966.

Cotel, Peter, S.J. *A Catechism of the Vows: For the Use of Persons Consecrated to God in the Religious State.* Trans. from the 6th French ed. Philadelphia: H. L. Kilner, 1868.

Cunningham, Lawrence S. *The Meaning of Saints.* San Francisco: Harper & Row, 1980.

Diner, Hasia R. *Erin's Daughters in America.* Baltimore: Johns Hopkins University Press, 1983.

Dolores, Sister Marian, S.M.J.M. *Creative Personality in Religious Life.* New York: Sheed & Ward, 1963.

Dr. Bob and the Good Oldtimers. New York: Alcoholics Anonymous World Services, 1980.

"Dr. Bob: A Tribute from Bill." *AA Grapevine* (January 1951): 1–47.

The Drug War in America: Crisis in Alcoholism Treatment. A Hearing before the Subcommittee on Health and Long-Term Care of the Select Committee on Aging, U.S. Congress. 102d Congr., 1st sess. Hon. Mary Rose Oakar, Chairwoman. Washington, D.C.: U.S. Government Printing Office, 1991.

Drummond, H. Gordon. *Seven Steps in the Making of a Man.* London: James Spiers, 1901.

Elwell, Walter A., ed. *Evangelical Dictionary of Theology.* Grand Rapids, Mich.: Baker Book House, 1984.

Ford, John C., S.J. *Depth Psychology, Morality and Alcoholism.* Weston, Mass.: Weston College, 1951.

———. *What about Your Drinking?* Glen Rock, N.J.: Deus Books/Paulist Press, 1961. (Reprint of the original work, *Man Takes a Drink.* New York: P. J. Kenedy & Sons, 1955.)

———. "The General Practitioner's Role in Alcoholism." Distributed by the National Council on Alcoholism, New York. Reprinted from *The Linacre Quarterly* (November 1956).

———. "The Priest's Role in Alcohol Problems." *The Furrow.* An address delivered to the First Pastoral Institute on Alcohol Problems,

University of Notre Dame. Published with permission of the National Clergy Conference on Alcoholism and of the author, April 1959.

———. "Moral Re-armament and Alcoholics Anonymous." *Alcoholism: A Source Book for the Priest.* Indianapolis: NCCA, 1960, 394–401.

"For Sister Ignatia: Our Everlasting Gratitude." *AA Grapevine* (August 1966): 2–9.

Fosdick, Harry Emerson. *On Being a Real Person.* New York: Harper & Bros., 1943.

Fracchia, Charles A. *Living Together Alone: The New American Monasticism.* San Francisco: Harper & Row, 1979.

Garvey, John, ed. *Modern Spirituality: An Anthology.* Springfield, Ill.: Templegate, 1985.

Garvey, John. *Saints for Confused Times.* Chicago: Thomas More Press, 1976.

Gavin, Donald P. *In All Things Charity.* Milwaukee: Catholic Life Publications/Bruce Press, 1955.

Goldenson, Robert M., Ph.D. *The Encyclopedia of Human Behavior: Psychology, Psychiatry, and Mental Health.* Vol. 1. New York: Doubleday, 1970.

Gorman, Margaret, R.S.C.J., ed. *Psychology and Religion: A Reader.* New York: Paulist Press, 1985.

Hamilton, Albert. *The Catholic Journey through Ohio.* Catholic Conference of Ohio. St. Meinrad, Ind.: Abbey Press, 1976.

Hough, Theodore, and William J. Sedgwick. *The Human Mechanism.* Boston: Ginn, 1929.

Hynes, Michael J., Ph.D., D.S.C. *The History of the Diocese of Cleveland: Origin and Growth (1847–1952).* Cleveland: World Publishing, 1953.

Ignatia, Sister Mary, C.S.A. "The Care of Alcoholics: St. Thomas Hospital and A.A. Started a Movement Which Swept the Country." *Hospital Progress* (October 1951): 293–96.

Kennedy, Raymond J. H., and John C. Ford, S.J., eds. *The Blue Books: Proceedings of the National Clergy Conference on Alcoholism. Indianapolis.* 1949 (Vol. 1), 1950 (Vol. 2), 1951 (Vol. 3), 1952 (Vol. 4), 1953 (Vol. 5), 1956 (Vol. 8), 1957 (Vol. 9), 1958 (Vol. 10), 1959 (Vol. 11), 1963 (Vol. 15), 1964 (Vol. 16), 1965 (Vol. 17), 1966 (Vol. 18).

Kurtz, Ernest. *Not-God: A History of Alcoholics Anonymous.* Center City,
    Minn.: Hazelden Educational Services, 1979.
*A Manual for Nuns Containing Prayers and Considerations from Approved
    Sources.* Written by a mother superior. 5th ed. New York: P. J. Kenedy
    & Sons, 1912.
Neal, Marie Augusta, S.N.D. de Namur. *Catholic Sisters in Transition
    from the 1960s to the 1980s.* Consecrated Life Studies 2. Wilmington:
    Michael Galzier, 1984.
Pass It On: Bill Wilson and the A.A. Message. New York: Alcoholics
    Anonymous World Services, 1984.
Peck, M. Scott. *People of the Lie.* New York: Simon & Schuster, 1985.
Pioneers We Have Known in the Field of Alcoholism. Mill Neck, N.Y.:
    Christopher D. Smithers Foundation, 1979.
Prevallet, Elaine M. "Personality Types in Spiritual Development."
    Human Development 5 (Fall 1984).
Puhl, Louis J., S.J. *The Spiritual Exercises of St. Ignatius: A New Trans-
    lation.* Westminster, Md.: Newman Press, 1962.
Reese, John D. *But for the Grace of God: The story of an Alcoholic.* New
    York: Vantage Press, 1957.
Reilly, Robert T. *Irish Saints.* New York: Avenel, 1964.
Robertson, Alec. *Christian Music.* New York: Hawthorn, 1961.
Royce, James E. *Alcohol Problems and Alcoholism,* rev. ed. New York:
    Free Press, 1989.
*The Rule of Saint Augustine and Constitutions for the Congregations of the
    Sisters of Charity of Saint Augustine.* Cleveland: Sisters of Charity of
    Saint Augustine, 1909–1926.
*The Rule of Saint Augustine and the Constitutions of the Congregation of
    the Sisters of Charity of Saint Augustine.* Cleveland: Sisters of Charity
    of Saint Augustine, 1926.
Seiberling, John F. "Origins of Alcoholics Anonymous." *Employee Assis-
    tance Quarterly* 1 (1985): 33–39.
Shoemaker, S. M., Jr. *Twice-Born Ministers.* New York: Fleming H.
    Revell, 1929.
Sinetar, Marsha. *Ordinary People as Monks and Mystics.* New York:
    Paulist Press, 1986.

Smart, Ninian. *Worldviews: Crosscultural Explorations of Human Beliefs.* New York: Charles Scribner's Sons, 1983.

Somers, Herman M., and Anne R. Somers. *Doctors, Patients and Health Insurance.* Washington, D.C.: Brookings Institution, 1961.

A Thought from Saint Ignatius for Each Day of the Year. Trans. from the French by Margaret A. Colton. New York: Benziger Bros., 1987.

Thomsen, Robert. *Bill W.* New York: Harper & Row, 1975.

Tiebout, Harry M., M.D. "Why Psychiatrists Fail with Alcoholics." *AA Grapevine* (September 1956): 5–10.

Understanding Anonymity. New York: Alcoholics Anonymous World Services, 1972.

The Way of a Pilgrim. Trans. from the Russian by R. M. French. 3d ed. New York: Seabury Press, 1970.

Wilson, Bill. "Another Fragment of History." *AA Grapevine* (February 1954): 2–5.

Zumkeller, P. Adolar, O.E.S.A. *The Rule of Saint Augustine.* Trans. from the Latin by Lawrence Meyer, S.J. Cleveland: St. Stanislaus Novitiate, 1960.

Index

About the Author

Mary C. Darrah was born and raised in Cleveland, Ohio. Both a job change and keen interest in Alcoholics Anonymous's history prompted her to relocate to Akron, Ohio, in 1989.

Darrah has worked in the alcoholism field since 1976. Her employment history includes that of alcoholism counselor and coordinator of counseling services at Merrick Hall in Cleveland. Housed within Womans General Hospital, Merrick Hall was the first all-women treatment center in the northeastern United States.

Darrah also worked as the Women's Planning Project coordinator at Cleveland's Regional Council on Alcoholism. Part of her duties there included assisting the Ohio Department of Health: evaluating government-funded alcohol and drug programs and writing new grants for upcoming projects.

She served as the state chairperson for the Ohio Task Force on Women and Alcohol and served on the board of directors of the Ohio chapter of the National Council on Alcoholism.

She then researched for ten years and wrote her first book, *Sister Ignatia.*

Darrah was appointed a congressional aide to former Congresswoman Mary Rose Oakar of Cleveland. Her expertise as an employee of the U.S. House of Representatives was in legislation and national policy analysis regarding alcohol, drugs, and health care. She remains involved in advocacy issues today.

Darrah also conducts workshops and retreat days, and she has lectured extensively throughout the United States about Sister Ignatia's life, work, and the early history of Akron AA.

Darrah hopes to continue historical research and writing while also working toward hospital chaplaincy certification through an exceptional program at the Akron General Medical Center. She has a strong belief that, like alcoholism, all illnesses are partly spiritual in nature. Spiritual assistance is indeed part of wholistic care. Those who receive spiritual and physical care achieve far better results in healing and recovery.

The author welcomes comments and inquiries sent in care of Hazelden, P. O. Box 176, Center City, Minnesota 55012-0176.

About Hazelden Publishing

As part of the Hazelden Betty Ford Foundation, Hazelden Publishing offers both cutting-edge educational resources and inspirational books. Our print and digital works help guide individuals in treatment and recovery, and their loved ones. Professionals who work to prevent and treat addiction also turn to Hazelden Publishing for evidence-based curricula, digital content solutions, and videos for use in schools, treatment programs, correctional programs, and electronic health records systems. We also offer training for implementation of our curricula.

Through published and digital works, Hazelden Publishing extends the reach of healing and hope to individuals, families, and communities affected by addiction and related issues.

For more information about Hazelden publications,
please call **800-328-9000**
or visit us online at **hazelden.org/bookstore.**